HOW TO BE A CAPITALIST WITHOUT ANY CAPITAL

HOW TO BE A CAPITALIST WITHOUT ANY CAPITAL

The Four Rules
You Must Break
to Get Rich

NATHAN LATKA

PORTFOLIO / PENGUIN

PORTFOLIO/PENGUIN
An imprint of Penguin Random House LLC
penguinrandomhouse.com

Copyright © 2019 by Nathan Latka

Most Portfolio books are available at a discount when purchased in quantity for sales promotions or corporate use. Special editions, which include personalized covers, excerpts, and corporate imprints, can be created when purchased in large quantities. For more information, please call (212) 572–2232 or e-mail specialmarkets@penguinrandomhouse.com. Your local bookstore can also assist with discounted bulk purchases using the Penguin Random House corporate Business-to-Business program. For assistance in locating a participating retailer, e-mail B2B@penguinrandomhouse.com.

ISBN 9780525534440 (hardcover)
ISBN 9780525534457 (ebook)

Printed in the United States of America
10 9 8 7 6 5 4 3 2 1

Book design by Pauline Neuwirth

CONTENTS

To my mom who taught me the value of money, the power of a decision, and the upside of hard work; and to my dad who helped me build my competitive muscle and a truly remarkable hunger for winning big.

INTRODUCTION

"Wealth is the ability to fully experience life."

    —Unknown

"Many folks think they aren't good at earning money, when what they don't know is how to use it."

    —Frank A. Clark

A s I began writing this book, my mom called. "You're making so much money," she said. "It's going to cause havoc if you happen to die, God forbid, and you don't have a plan for your assets." It's funny. Three years ago she was skeptical when I chose to drop out of school. Her message changed from "Stay in school!" to "Get a will!" More on me later. . . . Let's talk about you first.

You know those people whose lives you just can't figure out? They travel the world whenever they want. They barely work. They're always with their family, or conquering the kind of grand life adventure you've reserved for . . . *someday*. Somehow, they're happy with their life as it is—not just hiding behind a "perfect life" façade on social media.

There's the kid from your college dorm who dropped out and has since raised $1M in start-up funding. The dad you see at your son's soccer games, or at your gym, who drives a Range Rover and is always around in the middle of the week when most parents are working. Your neighbor who quit her corporate job and now has her own business that you hear is making her $10K or $20K a month.

You know these people are average at best. They're not supertalented or smart, but they're living like kings and queens and you're dumbfounded.

What they know that you don't is how to be a capitalist without any capital. There are four golden rules that the business world has sold us to keep us from being successful. Those rules must be broken. And the people you're thinking about have mastered breaking those rules.

It's easy to dismiss the superrich as trust-fund babies, or to assume their spouse is the breadwinner. Or we think maybe they're not rich at all and just racking up credit card debt. These scenarios will be true for some people, but I'm not talking about them.

I'm talking about the people who are wealthy by their own doing. Their families have nothing to do with their fat bank accounts. You can't stand their weekday Instagram posts from their sailboat, or the sight of them on another overseas vacation, but as much as they annoy you, you're also dying to know how they do it. How are these people so successful—and free—while you're withering away underneath fluorescent lights at your desk job 50+ hours a week?

It's because they're part of the "New Rich," as Tim Ferriss calls the segment of the population who have figured out how to maximize everything in their life—even if it's not much—so it becomes an asset that works for them. The New Rich are resourceful with their time, their money, and their energy. They get what they want when they want it. They travel however much they want. They have blank calendars. And they have very, very few expenses.

Tim Ferriss introduced us to the New Rich over a decade ago in his book *The 4-Hour Workweek*, but a lot has changed since then. Today, my peers and I are getting rich not just by starting companies from scratch, but by leveraging gold mines like Instagram and Airbnb that didn't exist in the early 2000s. We drive wealth by taking advantage of new tools quickly and figuring out how to get those tools to work for us so we can work less.

When an average person sees a New Rich person, they assume that new rich person has some magical quality. It's not magic. The average person just doesn't understand how the rich person got so rich, so they explain it away as "magical." A magician practices a series of "moves" or "tactics" behind a curtain so that when the trick is put together, the average viewer misses the sleight of hand. If you saw the magician practicing behind the curtain, you'd think, "I can pull that trick off, too!" Building wealth is the same.

These magicians practice behind the curtain, but I'm holding back nothing in this book. I've been a wealth magician for the past decade, and despite my lawyer's recommendations, I'm sharing everything in this book so you can pull off your own "wealth magic." You'll see my tax returns, my profit and loss statements, my email negotiations when buying and selling companies. I'm sharing it all so you can study and get a very real sense of how I've built my empire. I'll take you behind the curtain of the New Rich so you can become part of the inner sanctum.

The lifestyle you want is not out of your reach—you just don't know the moves yet. This book will lead you through those moves, starting with some I began making at the age of nineteen. You'll learn how to replicate the inner workings of more than twenty revenue streams I now have at twenty-eight years old.

If you're ready to join the New Rich, read on, my new wealth magicians!

MY STORY AND WHY YOU NEED THIS BOOK

There are a few things you should know about me:

- ▶ I'm a college dropout.
- ▶ I started my first company in my Virginia Tech dorm room when I was twenty. Within four years I hired forty people and grew the company to $5M in sales and a $10.5M valuation.
- ▶ I walked away from a $6.5M acquisition offer for that company when I was twenty-two.
- ▶ I don't have a résumé.
- ▶ I bought my first piece of real estate on my own when I was twenty-four.
- ▶ I bought my first company when I was twenty-six.
- ▶ Today, at twenty-nine years old, I run my own private equity firm, buying and selling companies.
- ▶ I use patterns and data to drive my decisions.

That last detail is probably the reason I've gotten this far, and it's how I'm going to help you get here, too. I'm not going to waste your time with small talk and rah-rah positivity. If you're familiar with my podcast, *The Top Entrepreneurs*, you already know this about me. I have interviewed more than five hundred of the world's top thinkers, disrupters, and CEOs in search of patterns that anyone can apply to gain wealth, work less, and get what they want out of life. I get to the data and I get to the numbers so you and I can learn from the real stuff. In fact, I pressure these CEOs so hard, they share secret strategies they wish they didn't share, and threaten to sue after their episode goes live. Their fault! (Your gain!) An unfortunate side effect is that I'm the most sued podcaster—you should see my wall of cease and desist letters (a beautiful thing! I always win these contests!).

This book is a natural extension of my podcast. I will present the secrets of the New Rich and feature real stories from twenty-year-old dorm-room CEOs, Airbnb millionaires, filthy rich software founders, and financial technology billionaires—all of whom are building their wealth every day, right now. We'll get their stories, but just as important, we'll look at the real numbers behind their businesses so we can understand how they make it work.

Then there are the patterns. In all my time talking to top entrepreneurs, I've noticed that their execution plans follow similar patterns that counter conventional business wisdom. These patterns directly correlate to wealth, freedom, and a lot of winning—and they'll surprise the hell out of you. Once you learn about them in the chapters ahead, you'll realize building wealth is so easy it's unbelievable, and you'll join those rich friends whose success baffled you just a few months earlier.

My obsession with numbers is so fierce that it's the reason I dropped out of college. That, and the money-smart mindset my mom has instilled in me since before my memories kicked in. She swears that during a car ride when I was five years old I asked her why we never went out to dinner anymore. She explained that she and my dad had to make choices. They'd recently decided to move our family into a new, big house in the country. Since making that choice, they had to choose not to spend money on other things, like eating out.

I sat quietly in the back seat for a long time. Then I said, "So, Mom, can I choose to get into my piggy bank and take us out to Pizza Hut tonight?" She didn't take me up on it. Instead, she and Dad chose to take us out to dinner that evening, but the lesson was clear.

I have no memory of this conversation, but when I hear the story it says so much about how my parents raised me to think like an entrepreneur. Mom wasn't talking about the family budget that day—not exactly. Her bigger point was that you have to make choices based on the life you want to live now—and the life you want to live in the future. It's all about opportunity cost. Sometimes that means less pizza in exchange for the big country house (except when your five-year-old breaks your resolve in a two-minute conversation). Other times it means following your gut when you see a big opportunity in front of you, even if it goes against everything you're told you're "supposed to be doing" with your life.

That's where I found myself when I decided to drop out of college. I stayed until my junior year, but I'll never forget the moment I realized school wasn't for me. It was during a statistics course very early on in my time at Virginia Tech. I should have loved this class, but the teacher was so boring and I had other things on my mind.

The midterm that semester was my wake-up call. I'd stayed up the night before preselling a Facebook fan page product I'd just launched. I was very tired, but I'd sent out $1,400 in sales proposals that night, so I had no regrets. I had set up a ping on my phone so it would make a sound every time a new PayPal sale came in. My phone was across the room during the test, but I heard it ping twice in the two-hour exam period. I was selling my product at $700 a pop, so I made $1,400 before the exam was done. I failed it, but that failure turned into unstoppable momentum to keep growing my business.

I realized I was a capitalist the moment I got those failed test scores. I thought, If I can fail this exam and make $1,400 while doing it, school is just not my thing. I stuck with it a couple more years but I knew I had to get out and build my company. If you're a student reading this, keep going. It gets even better . . .

When I finally did decide to leave school, one of the first things I did was call Mom. I thought she'd be livid with me for wanting to quit—especially after she'd worked three jobs to pay her own way through college. Now my parents were paying my tuition, and there I was, throwing it away. But she wasn't angry at all. She just told me it was my choice, but I should think about my options. It was the only time in my life when my parents would pay for me to go to college (I was fortunate and thankful), so she suggested I finish my degree in case one of my business ventures failed down the line.

She had a point, but I knew I'd never push myself to be successful if I had that safety net under me. I told her I just had to go. Mom said she knew she'd raised three stubborn, ambitious kids, so she wasn't going to stand in the way of what we wanted to do. She just pushed me to consider my choices before jumping.

All I could think about were the numbers. I knew I could go way bigger than $1,400 in an afternoon if I put more time and energy into my business. Forget the rules, or what anyone said I should be doing with my life at twenty years old (thanks, Mom, for not being one of those people). I saw my opportunity and I was going for it.

MY INCOME STATEMENT AND WHY YOU SHOULD LISTEN TO ME

When I was twenty-three, in 2013, that company I started in my dorm room (called Lujure, later renamed Heyo) passed $939K in annual sales. Politicians love tax returns so I figured I'd share mine:

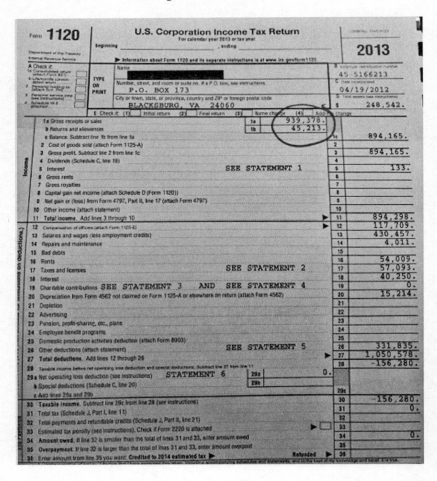

Two years later, in 2015, my company passed $5M in total sales, and I've now bought four companies over two years to drive more revenue, faster and cheaper. I now make $100K in passive income every month, and I work about fifteen hours a week.

My point isn't that dropping out of college pays (although it did for me). It's that you, or I, or anyone can join the New Rich if we just decide we want to.

So, do you want to?

WEALTHY PEOPLE SOLD YOU THESE FOUR LIES

There's a secret many of the New Rich don't want me to share: You don't need to be Ivy League educated, have money, be creative, or even *have an idea* to reach their level of financial success. You just need to be willing to break the rules and start looking in the right places.

To start, forget most of the business or money "rules" you've learned because they're dead. It amazes me that a book like *Rich Dad Poor Dad*, which has sold twenty million copies, is no longer relevant. That book was my bible growing up, but it simply doesn't work today because it gives old business advice that's rooted in the old economy. One example: a big message in *Rich Dad Poor Dad* is that your home is a liability, whether you rent or own. Today, the New Rich would categorize their home as an asset because the few days they're traveling each month, they can put it up on Airbnb and generate cash flow. When I was in college, I rented the most expensive apartment in town and lived there for free while *earning* $1,300 a month off the rental. Liability? My bank account didn't think so.

The New Rich baffle so many people because they don't play by the old rules of business that the masses follow. You've been sold these rules by "mentors," but you must forget them to join the New Rich:

- ▶ Focus on becoming an expert at one thing.
- ▶ Come up with a remarkable idea.
- ▶ Set goals and work toward them.
- ▶ Give customers what they want.

I'll unpack each of these in the chapters ahead and arm you with this new set of rules for joining the New Rich:

RULE 1: Don't Focus on One Thing. Your parents always told you, you've got to do one thing and do it well. College encourages us to do the same by picking a major. But this is a terrible strategy if you're looking to build wealth in the new economy. Focusing on one thing gives you a single point of failure—whether it's a job, an investment opportunity, or an entrepreneurial venture. When engineers design a bridge, they never want to have a single point of failure. If the wind picks up to two hundred miles per hour and a cable fails, the bridge still has seven other cables to back it up. Likewise, you'd never want to build your wealth around one endeavor. If that one thing fails, you're destroyed, and you have to start again from scratch. Ignore the conventional wisdom that says it's impossible to multitask. I'll walk you through my Three-Focus Rule, showing you how you can always have at least three new ideas launched and brewing without spreading yourself too thin. (Most say "You're doing too much!" because they're jealous!)

RULE 2: Copy Your Competitors. Every. Single. Detail. Have you ever thought, "Ugh, I would be rich if I'd only come up with XYZ idea that is making that other guy millions"? Are you kidding? Copy him. You don't need your own idea. Launching a new idea is actually a terrible approach to gaining wealth—you have to pay for all the mistakes yourself. Why?! The way to get filthy rich is by aggressively copying others and then adding your own twist. Facebook very publicly copied Snapchat. When Snapchat released Snapchat Stories, Facebook rolled out Facebook Stories and Instagram Stories. When Snapchat released disappearing messages, Facebook added that to its messaging app. Facebook was ruthless—it went feature by feature and copied every one. Copying competitors isn't revolutionary. It just *seems* outrageous because most people are scared to do it. In the late 1800s, newspaper tycoons Joseph Pulitzer and William Randolph Hearst were in a raging circulation war to win over New York City readers. Pulitzer published his paper, the *New York World,* with zero competition for more than a decade until Hearst entered the market with the *New York Journal* and copied every single one of Pulitzer's strategies. Hearst copied Pulitzer's newspaper layout. He stole Pulitzer's top cartoonist. Hearst copied, and then he pushed each strategy a few notches beyond what Pulitzer was doing. When Pulitzer charged $.02 for an eight-page paper, Hearst charged $.01 for sixteen pages. By the early twentieth century, Hearst had solidified his spot as the top newspaper publisher in New York City. The best (or worst?) part: Pulitzer was actually Hearst's mentor before they became rivals. Hearst clearly wasn't sentimental about that. You have to copy to win, but I get that it's hard to know what to do, whom to copy, or where to start. The key is to analyze a business and pinpoint a need it's not meeting for its customers—and then meet that need yourself. I'll show you how. Let go of the excuse that somebody is already on an idea. Unless you're Elon Musk, Jeff Bezos, or already a billionaire, every idea that you can launch quickly and commercialize has already been thought of. You're going to build yourself rich by copying one, making it better, and creating momentum. You can go invent brand-new ideas after you have a billion dollars. But it's not efficient to try doing that from the start.

RULE 3: Quit Setting Goals—They're Keeping You Broke. Setting a goal is like saying, "I want that golden egg." It can be a Rolex watch, Beverly Hills mansion, $500M private jet, $2K dinner at your favorite restaurant. Whatever. If you build your life around a goal, the second you achieve it, it seems like there's nothing left to achieve. And you end up bored. You'll have to remotivate yourself to come up with another golden egg to chase. It's much better to invest your energy into creating, feeding, and nursing a system that pumps out golden eggs every day. That way, no matter where you are in the world, whether you're working or not, whether you have twenty kids or no kids, you'll have a golden goose that keeps making golden eggs for you. Systems make the rich richer, and goals make the poor poorer. Those are the culprits behind the saying you hear often: "The rich get richer, and the poor get poorer."

RULE 4: Sell Pickaxes to Gold Miners. The essence of this rule is to let others cut a trail through the thick jungle so you can then peacefully walk in and capitalize on their hard work. That's what people did during the gold rush. The gold miners went west, hunting, searching, sweating, bleeding, killing, and dying just to make it out there. After they arrived they realized they needed pickaxes to mine more efficiently. Well, then others just traveled over on the paths already created to sell those pickaxes to the gold miners. They got rich without any of the risk, sweat, or bloodshed. In today's world this translates to siphoning revenue from a hot market that others put the effort into building. So if you're creating a tool for people to use on top of Facebook, you're essentially capitalizing on the money Facebook has already spent by selling into the market they created. Pay attention to what's blowing up today. If weekly food delivery is big, don't try to compete with HelloFresh and Blue Apron. Rather, figure out the infrastructure that those businesses rely on and offer it to them. Food delivery companies need last-mile delivery from warehouse to consumers' homes. I'll help you discover your own pickax to sell to your local gold miners—the people going after the hot thing in your space, geography, or niche. When you do that, your business is much more likely to succeed because you're piggybacking off of a giant.

FAQ: WHO THIS BOOK IS FOR, AND NOT FOR

This book is for you—you with the debt, the four kids, the $1K to your name, and without any business ideas. Don't worry if you've never launched a business, or if you don't know the first thing about running a company. I'll walk you through every step and system with real-life screenshots, tax returns, and email exchanges that landed six-figure business deals. By the end of this book, you'll know how to:

- ▶ Build a business that runs itself, with no start-up capital.
- ▶ Get that business to tap into an established customer base that you put no effort into creating.
- ▶ Buy real estate at below-market value that is cash flow positive from day one.
- ▶ Make off-the-beaten-path investments with instant returns that are double what you'd wait 10+ years to get out of the stock market.
- ▶ Work up enough momentum to consistently build (or buy) and sell companies every two years at a seven-figure profit.

But don't worry about any of this yet. You'll just start by turning every one of your liabilities into assets using the sharing economy, which will erase most of your expenses. This probably sounds impossible, but the New Rich found a way to do it, and I'm going to let you in on their secrets. Once the cash starts to flow, you'll use that money to build, buy, invest, and sell your way to wealth.

Joining the New Rich has only two requirements: a desire for more free time to do what you want while making money on your terms, and ambition. I can't teach ambition, so you'll need to bring your own.

If you have these two things, you're probably the type who does not want to cement your life to the "hustle 24/7, get no sleep, and work your ass off for the empty promise of retirement" mentality. Good. That will get you far. The motivation to design your own life—whether it's a life traveling the world or building a log cabin in the woods—is all you need.

I also want to be clear about whom this book is *not* for. This book is not for you if you love getting advice like "follow your passion"—because that's the most reliable way to stay poor. If you're looking for someone to give you permission to follow your dreams, even if it means being too broke to afford health insurance, you're not going to get that from me. Yes, you'll be living your dream life if you follow my advice, but your dreams won't make you money. Passive income first. Then you can dream bigger than you ever thought.

This book is also not for the person who is intimidated by those who love to compete. You'll have to copy, negotiate, undercut, and outperform others at every turn. If the thought of doing these things doesn't give you a thrill, you won't last long.

Finally, this book is not for anyone who dislikes the 1 percent—because after you're done following the advice here, you're going to *be part of* the 1 percent, with an eye toward joining the .01 percent.

If all this sounds improbable, remember that the New Rich are people you hang out with every day. They're the cube mate you sat next to for years who finally said, "I'm sick of working so much and only making $90K a year. I'm quitting." Maybe your private reaction at the time was, "Oh my God, I could never quit my job. I have health benefits and security, and I have two kids to take care of. I'm never quitting." Well, your coworker has three kids and was her family's breadwinner when she quit. Fast-forward five months and you see her taking her family on vacation. You run into her at the coffee shop with friends and you overhear her saying she'll pay for the whole order. She hangs out with whomever she wants and does what she wants more often. The next time you meet up, she's telling you that her business is doing $30K a month. Guess what? She doesn't have any more intellect, talent, or hustle than you do. Stop asking how she does it and start now, with the tactics on the next few pages.

YOUR NEW RICH PLAN AT TEN THOUSAND FEET

Here's an aerial view of what your journey to wealth might look like if you follow the advice in this book:

1. Start at zero. No start-up capital. No trust fund check from Grandma. No high-earning spouse contributing the cash to get your ventures off the ground.
2. Leverage the four tactics I used to generate over $10K in cash and start funding my own ventures by the time I was twenty-one years old.
3. As money comes in, you will:

   - Spend it however you want to make sure you're living a happy, healthy life. Go on vacation. Get a mocha every morning. Buy that Anthropologie dress even if it's not on sale.
   - Invest it back into your current ventures in unique ways.
   - Invest it in real estate using very little capital.
   - Outright buy other companies for pennies on the dollar using the negotiation tactics I teach.
   - Build a war chest to fund any next business venture you want as you see fit.

I will show you how to do all of these things.

Is it simple? Yes.

Is it easy? No.

In music, there are only seven notes. Anyone can know them. So why do some people create hit songs while others can barely sing? The answer is in the combination of those seven notes.

Business is even simpler—it only has four notes. This book will teach you the unique ways to combine those four notes, or principles, to create masterpieces that put money in your

(continued)

bank account. You'll also see how I've combined these four principles, which are the four rules I recommend breaking, to create incredible wealth. The journey starts now.

Flip to the next chapter to learn how I made my first $6,400 from my podcasting company.

RULES TO BREAK, RULES TO EMBRACE

RULE 1: DON'T FOCUS ON ONE THING

A single point of failure (SPOF) is a system that, "contains only one component to do a job . . . if that single component fails, there is no alternate one to take its place."

—PC Magazine

Our parents and professors were wrong. Most of them pushed us to focus on one thing and get really good at it. Pick a major. Become an expert. Be the go-to person everyone calls when they need whatever skill you've mastered.

That's fine if you aspire to become, say, the world's top neurosurgeon. But it's terrible advice if you actually want to get rich and work less.

I already mentioned one problem with this approach: it gives you a single point of failure. If you put all your trust and resources into one thing, and that one thing fails, you're screwed. This is true whether you're talking about a day job, a new business, or anything in which you invest your time and money. You're forever vulnerable to the competition. Even if you *do* become the world's—or your region's—top neurosurgeon, or marketer, or software engineer, someone can always replace you. It's just too easy these days for people to move around and get new jobs. Employers can find better talent quicker than ever; customers are constantly trying new ideas and canceling on businesses. Your *one thing* is always under attack—and so is your livelihood.

I'm sure this sounds familiar. We've all been told at some point that we shouldn't "put all our eggs in one basket." But what's the counterstrategy? The cliché fails to tell us that part. If you want to get rich, you need a strategy beyond just *keeping your options open*. Yes, focus on more than one thing. But you also need to know what projects are worth chasing, how to split up your time, and how to make the ventures you do pursue work for you.

Let's put strategy aside for a second, though. It helps, but strategy plays a small role in success. The two biggest factors in success are actually timing and luck. (Don't believe anyone who tries to tell you their success has nothing to do with luck.) You can't control either of these things outside of setting yourself up to get lucky and positioning yourself at the right time. And the only way to do both is by taking more chances. You may have heard this expressed as "fail more."

HOW A COLLEGE SIDE PROJECT MADE ME $6,400

There's also a more subtle reason you won't win big by focusing on one thing, and it's potentially the most powerful: it keeps you from ever being able to multiply your income. I'm not talking here about just adding up income streams. *Multiplying* is when you find the patterns that link different projects and then leverage those connections so each venture makes way more than it could have on its own. Multiplying is the epitome of working smarter, not harder. And it's what separates the round-the-clock hustlers from the umbrella drink sippers.

Luck and multiplying are the reasons my podcast, *The Top Entrepreneurs*, has ten million downloads and earns me $50K a month.

When I started the podcast in 2016 all my revenue came from sponsorships. My first sponsor actually reached out to me a few months after the podcast launched:

From: Justine Smith ███████████████████
Date: Wed, Feb 24, 2016 at 10:47 AM
Subject: Podcast sponsorship?
To: ███████████████████

Hi Nathan,

My name is Justine and I represent ████████ the cloud accounting solution for small, service-based business owners with over 5 million users worldwide.

As a full-time business owner, I'm a big fan of your podcast and was wondering if you'd be open to exploring a sponsorship from ████████ We think it would be a great fit on both sides and are eager to learn more about partnering with you.

If yes, I'd love to know:

- What sponsorship rate you charge per episode?
- How many downloads each episode gets?

Thank you,
Justine

This turned into a $6,400 deal to run a software company's ad on the podcast for two months:

Primary Contact							Notes
Podcast Name: The Top							
Contacts: Nathan Latka							
Address:							
Telephone:							
E-mail: ████████████							

Month	Flight Dates	Placement	# of Spots Per Show	Gross Cost Per Episode	Estimated Downloads Per Episode	# of Episodes in Month	Total Cost
Mar-16	TBD between March 15-31	:15 Pre, :60 Mid	2	$400	8,000	8	$3,200
Apr-16	TBD between Apr 1-15	:15 Pre, :60 Mid	2	$400	8,000	8	$3,200
						Subtotal:	$6,400
						TOTAL COST:	$6,400

Terms and Conditions:
(1) All ads voiced by host.
(2) The Top will provide makegood spot for any ads that run incorrect copy or does not highlight the proper call to action and offer.
(3) Featured mention in the show notes and on sponsor page, including textual link(s) to the Advertiser.
(4) Audio advertisement shall remain on archived versions of sponsored episodes.

Accepted By : _~signature~_   Date: 03/08/2016
on behalf of ███████

Accepted By : /s/ Nathan Latka 3/8/2016   Date: _____
on behalf of The Top

Three months later I signed on my second sponsor, who paid me $5K to feature them on the podcast for thirty-five consecutive episodes.

All of my podcast revenue still comes from sponsors, only now I've figured out how to leverage one of my other companies, The Top Inbox, to grow sponsorship income way beyond what the podcast earned on its own. How the magic happens:

The Top Inbox is a Gmail tool that lets you schedule emails to be sent later, set inbox reminders, track opens, and schedule auto follow-ups. When I bought The Top Inbox I had no idea I could put a pop-up on the software's interface. It's just something I stumbled on. So I decided to experiment with using pop-ups to drive traffic to my podcast sponsors.

Most of my podcast sponsors are software companies selling productivity, sales, and marketing tools to small and midsize businesses. Turns out, a lot of small business owners use The Top Inbox to stay productive, and they've proved to be a prime audience for whatever my podcast sponsors are offering.

THE $180K "POP-UP" ACCIDENT

I started experimenting by using psychological leverage in those pop-up boxes to make The Top Inbox users feel like they've won a prize—that is, a free trial of the sponsor's product. This lets me drive thousands of high-quality clicks very quickly to any sponsor I want. The outcome: my sponsor gets bigger returns and stays onboard as a happy, long-term partner. I ran this pop-up for an email marketing company:

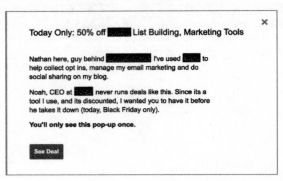

Sumo got 941 clicks to its page in the two days this promo ran. Happy Sumo. Happy Nathan.

Today, podcast sponsors each pay me $150K to $180K a year, and my Top Inbox pop-ups are driving a lot of that success—something I literally stumbled onto. The opportunity just wouldn't exist if my podcast, or The Top Inbox, were my only projects. I got totally lucky. Now the ability to cross-promote is a staple I look for when I'm acquiring companies.

Overlap like this exists everywhere. Elon Musk capitalizes on the patterns that link his projects at every turn. At the moment he has ventures in artificial intelligence and neuroscience through his company Neuralink, solar roof tiles via SolarCity, high-speed transportation with Hyperloop, electric cars through Tesla, and rockets with SpaceX.

Each company works independently, but Musk links them whenever he can. His electric car and solar tiles both tie into green energy. Both products use lithium batteries to efficiently store energy. Since he's generating such huge demand for the batteries, he's building Gigafactory, a massive plant to service that demand. He's created multiple products that touch the same resource—lithium ion power—and he's leveraging economies of scale to bring his costs down.

Multiplying is going to play a huge role in whatever strategies you embrace from the chapters ahead. It's also the reason that most successful people in the new economy have just an OK understanding of many different things. They get multiple ventures going and then pull out the patterns that link them. If you pigeonhole yourself into one thing, you'll lose the chance to recognize patterns and capitalize on them to multiply your income streams. I don't care whether you're running a business or renting out a room in your apartment. Always have more than one thing brewing, and always look for the patterns that can help your ideas feed off one another.

MY THREE-FOCUS RULE

OK, so you're not Elon Musk. You're on chapter 1, so it's likely you haven't even launched anything yet. That's good. You're much better off because this book will teach you how to maximize your efforts before wasting any time or money.

Don't let the idea of juggling multiple ventures scare you off just because you're not working on Musk's level. It's even *more* important for you to focus on a few things when you're just starting out, regardless of what popular advice tells us.

Often when founders have meetings with investors and advisers, they're told to "pick an idea and go all in." This advice goes way back—there's even a proverb that says, "If you chase two rabbits, both will escape." The problem with that guidance, at least from a business standpoint, is that it's only relevant if you're going for a huge, billion-dollar hit. And you're not going to do that when you're just starting out.

The chances of you building a billion-dollar business on your first try are essentially zero. You'd have better luck playing the lottery. You're much more likely to succeed by taking over or building a $4M or $5M business in a predictable way. And I'm still talking to you if the idea of launching a multimillion-dollar *anything* sounds out of reach. Everything I'm saying here applies even if you're running an Etsy store or working an office job.

However you start out, my only rule is that you're always pursuing three new opportunities at the same time. Once a venture is up and running, you're going to set it on autopilot so it only takes an hour or two of your time per month. I'll show you how to do that later. At that point it's no longer one of your three new projects. It's just happily humming in the background, calling attention to itself only when you notice the passive income that it pours into your bank account.

It's fine if whatever you're doing doesn't bring in huge money to start. The most important thing for now is that you're learning to maximize your time, your effort, and your output. If you don't, you'll never hit the next level. You'll never get the win.

The strategy here is similar to what makes a great batter in baseball. The batter who repeatedly gets the win takes multiple swings, hits many balls, and understands how to hit doubles over and over again. He doesn't step up to the plate planning to hit one grand slam that will win the game. That's the same person who has the idea they're working on now, plus two others on the side. Businessperson or batter, they'd never bank on one big hit.

These people know there are good balls flying at them all the time and it's a given that they're going to miss some. That's why the rules of baseball allow three chances to swing at a good pitch. The same goes for your business ventures. Sometimes you'll miss those good balls because you're not looking; or you'll have other life emergencies that keep you from calculating that perfect swing.

It's OK to miss, but it's important that you *actually swing* at those good balls. You get three, and if you fail to swing at them, it does a lot of bad things. The first and obvious one is that it decreases your chance of having three different income streams. As in baseball, an umpire is going to call a strike if you sit there and watch a good opportunity fly by. That's like letting a $5K check per month pass you by. Reach out. Capture it. Make it big or shut it down a few months after you've tried and learn from it.

Another big reason it's so important to swing at those good balls is that when you swing and miss, you get to diagnose *why* you missed. Any venture you attempt and then shut down accelerates your learning. Swinging at each good opportunity sets you up to learn three times faster than if you'd never tried.

It's also easy to forget that some of the biggest success stories involve a lot of luck. The luck may have been random, but the people behind those successes set themselves up to capture that luck—and *that* was intentional. It's well documented that Thomas Edison ran thousands of experiments not knowing which would work. When some things did work, he wouldn't always know *why* they worked. I consider that luck. From there, he had to figure out why he got lucky. If atom one hit atom two in a certain way that made the lightbulb work, he would reverse engineer the process to figure out why it succeeded and then replicate it. We see only the working light-bulb at the end, but that success was the result of literally thousands of chances to win that Edison set up for himself.

Many people don't want to admit that their wealth was a result of luck. They like to say they saw the big win coming from the start. But in a lot of cases, that's just not true. Luck played a major role. Chasing three opportunities at once is a big way to set yourself up to get lucky.

MY CALENDAR PATTERNS:
THREE PROJECTS AT ONCE DOESN'T = THREE TIMES THE WORK

On page 88 I talk about batching time, a strategy many successful people use to tackle huge projects. My three biggest projects at the time of this writing are my *Top Entrepreneurs* podcast, The Top Inbox, and GetLatka .com. Looking at my schedule this week you can see how I batch: 10 percent is The Top Inbox related, 20 percent are podcast interviews, 40 percent are GetLatka.com sales calls, and 50 percent are miscellaneous. These projects are all well established now, but as I worked on launching each one I focused most of my time on building the infrastructure that would make each project print money. I'll show you how I did that for each one in the chapters ahead. My schedule varies each week depending on where I need to drive revenue.

Remember, I said the most important thing to focus on right now is learning to maximize your time, your effort, and your output. So my Three-Focus Rule is not meant to send you on a crazy multitasking stint that will burn you out. That's exactly what I want to help you avoid. To make the Three-Focus Rule work, you're going to leverage the 80/20 rule when pursuing new opportunities.

You won't have time to work on three huge, time-consuming projects at once. So focus 80 percent of your time on one project—the one that brings in the most money or that has the potential to be your biggest earner. Split the other 20 percent of your time between the two remaining ventures. That may mean launching them on a smaller scale or putting them on a slower schedule. Or choose ventures that are inherently more passive for the 20 percent of time you have left: invest in another business rather than starting your own, build a new income stream off one of your projects already on autopilot, etc.

When you break up a five-day workweek, this means you want to spend about three days a week on the 80 percent idea. That could be a software start-up, consulting, hunting for real estate (see chapter 8)—whatever you want. It could even be your full-time job while you're building up savings so you can quit to focus on growing one of your other two ventures. Just don't try to launch three huge new projects from scratch. You'll likely fail at all of them and kill your spirit in the process.

THREE-FOCUS: TEST, MULTIPLY, GROW

The last reason I'm obsessed with the Three-Focus Rule touches on everything I've said so far: it lets you test ideas (swing, miss, learn), multiply them (find and capitalize on the patterns), and then *use that knowledge to launch brand-new ventures.*

Your current businesses are loaded with potential for new income. Sometimes it's built into what you're already doing, like realizing you can use scrap leather from your handbag business to make keychains and bracelets. Other times new money comes from just talking to your customers and figuring out what else they might want that you can offer.

I own rental units in Blacksburg, Virginia, that generate cash flow for me. I constantly talk to my renters to understand why they're paying rent and how they think about rent.

At the same time, I'm an investor in a hostel where I live in Austin, Texas. One thing I'm betting on is that as we move into the next four or five years, people are going to hate the idea of paying rent. They'll much rather pay a monthly subscription fee to live anywhere they want in the world. If I want to tap into that demand, I'll have to own hostels in multiple cities around the world. People will pay me one fee of, say, $1K per month and they can choose to stay in whichever one of my properties they want, whenever they want. They'll have location freedom.

I can test out that concept on my tenants who are paying a fixed rent. All I have to do is ask them, "Hey, if I allowed you to live anywhere you wanted, you'd pay the same rent, you'd have total location freedom, would you do it?" If it works out, I'll be leveraging two separate ideas—investing in hostels versus investing in real estate—to launch an entirely new venture.

Then the multiplying can continue. Let's say I launch a book after my hostel idea is off the ground. What if I worked with the hostels to put a book on every bed? That could be a great distribution channel.

Elon Musk used this exact strategy to launch Gigafactory. The plant exists only because his other businesses generated the demand for lithium ion batteries. Ideas beget ideas like money leads to more money. None of us have gotten rich by sticking to one thing.

So forget the old advice.

Test your luck.

Open your odds to good timing.

Ditch what's not working and learn from it.

Or stick to one thing and risk losing everything.

2

RULE 2: COPY YOUR COMPETITORS

"Good artists copy, great artists steal."

—attributed to Pablo Picasso

You're wasting your time reading this book if you don't embrace this one idea:

You have to copy your competitors.

Do it now. Do it aggressively. Do it quickly. And do it by spending the least amount of money you possibly can.

I constantly talk to people who won't give themselves permission to copy. They think it's unethical and that they have to invent something new if they're going to launch anything. That's where they're completely wrong.

Every successful entrepreneur has copied, even if they won't admit it. You usually just don't notice it because they've taken someone else's idea and tweaked it for an entirely different industry. Wealthfront CEO Andy Rachleff did exactly that to drive his customer base.

Wealthfront uses software, not people, to manage its customers' investment portfolios. New investors get their first $10K managed for free. For every friend they invite who accepts, they get another $10K managed for free.

They're the first company to bring this invite-a-friend model to the financial sector. As Andy and I spoke over a spotty Skype connection, I asked how he came up with his growth model. His answer surprised me:

"WE JUST COPIED DROPBOX"

Dropbox gives users a certain amount of storage for free. Invite a friend who joins, and your free storage limit goes up. Sound familiar?

Fifteen percent of the invites that get sent out by Wealthfront's customers lead to a new user who puts at least $500 into a new portfolio.

Blatant copying. No harm to Dropbox. Big win for Wealthfront.

Sometimes copying will be brutally cutthroat, like the Hearst versus Pulitzer circulation war (page 8). When Facebook is on Snapchat's tail copying every new feature, they're clearly out to slay them. But it doesn't have to be that way. Sometimes copying is just research. You're seeing what works and what doesn't so you can be hyperefficient with your resources. By the time you're done with your product—or whatever you're launching—it may look nothing like the competition you've shadowed. Or maybe it will. It's your call.

In chapter 11, I'll show you exactly how to pull data on a company that will help you launch your own. I'll also show you some copying tactics I used when launching my first software company, Heyo.com.

For now, just focus on killing any resistance you have toward copying. It's the best way to bring in big money fast—and you can be as ruthless as you want to.

HOW TO DECODE A WINNING PATTERN TO COPY

I told you I'm obsessed with patterns. Finding the patterns that link successful businesses is like decoding the secrets behind a win. That's essentially what you're doing when you're copying—you're looking for the patterns that got your competitors to the top. Then you're using that information to match or beat them. When you do this, you're essentially getting a free business lesson. If you don't copy these free lessons, you'll have to do what those with less knowledge do: pay to learn the lessons yourself.

If you're just starting out with a side hustle, the opportunities for copying are huge. Let's look at Airbnb rentals, or, really, any product or service you'd offer through an online marketplace. All of your competitors' strategies are laid out right in front of you. Scroll through the top-rated listings in your area and find the patterns they share.

If you're doing Airbnb, start with the headline. How are the rentals with loads of ratings described? As I'm writing this, the top search results in Denver, each with more than two hundred five-star ratings, have these headlines:

1880s CARRIAGE HOUSE IN CURTIS PARK

COLORFUL & LOVING DENVER CONDO

LIVE LIKE A LOCAL IN TRENDY RINO

FIVE STAR—2 MILES TO DOWNTOWN—FREE PARKING—NEAR ZOO

These clearly tell you what draws people in: fun or convenient location, historic charm, lively living space, etc. Think of your property in these terms and highlight the qualities that people will want.

Also look at the pictures. How can you make the first picture in your listing stand out against a competitor's? Sometimes you'll want to copy, sometimes you'll want to do the exact opposite of what others are doing to make your listing pop.

Then the description: How do they describe the Wi-Fi? Do they say: "Wi-Fi perfect for business professional," or "Wi-Fi perfect for streaming YouTube videos while you party with your friends"? Are properties that are obviously old being pitched as "rustic" or as having "farmhouse charm"? Zero in on the lexicon these top listings use so you can cater to the same market they're reaching.

Any online marketplace is a gold mine for free business lessons. Another popular one for side hustlers: Etsy shops. Let's say you want to launch a new women's tank top. Go to Etsy.com → Clothing & Shoes → Women's → Tops & Tees → Tanks and see what patterns the most popular sellers share.

You can quickly see that tanks with cheeky sayings are huge sellers. As I'm writing this, a tank that says FEED ME TACOS AND TELL ME I'M PRETTY has 2,941 reviews. If you search for just that phrase, you'll see the copying on this one is fierce. At least five different sellers offer a shirt with the same saying, all with more than five hundred reviews. Anything referencing coffee, wine, cats, or yoga is huge.

Also look at style. As I scroll through, a lot of the bestsellers are white text on a black shirt.

Keep digging as you think up strategies for your own product. If you don't already have a shirt idea, you can join the pretty taco party and do it better: lower prices, more color offerings, custom lettering, etc., depending on your capabilities. Or pull details from several of the most popular items and launch a version with your own twist: A cat sipping wine while doing a yoga pose? Find an artist on Fiverr or Upwork to create the design for you (if you can't do it yourself), crunch numbers to find an affordable vendor to print your shirts (if you don't do it yourself), and you're on your way.

I don't want to underestimate the work that goes into creating a successful Etsy (or any other online) shop because it *does* take a ton of effort to get your products noticed and turn a profit. You likely won't become a millionaire doing it. But you can make the long road to a steady income stream much shorter through strategic copying.

SECRETS TO COPYING USING FREELANCE SITES

If you're setting up shop as a consultant, look at sites where people list their services. On the low end (price-wise) are Fiverr.com and Upwork.com. You'll find higher-priced services on hubs like Toptal.com. Look at what some of the top-rated consultants are selling. Pick up the patterns in terms of how they present their services, pricing, or what guarantees they make. Scour their bios, portfolios, and photos for clues on how to best set up your profile if you want a consulting empire.

I take a deep dive into copying tactics for physical products in chapter 11. The best places to look for physical product inspiration if you're just starting out are crowdfunding sites like Kickstarter and Indiegogo. Look at the products that are doing really well and focus on understanding why they're succeeding. Is it in a product niche? Are the creator's story and video so moving that the product just naturally sells? That happens a lot. The product is crap but the story is unbelievable. People love to buy the story.

If you're launching a digital product like a podcast or YouTube channel, you have to troll Patreon.com. It shows you how much creators are earning through monthly pledges and exactly what they're offering to attract those paying customers. I go there all the time to see what podcasters are doing.

Some are making up to $80K a month off their podcast alone. I try to understand what content they're giving exclusively to paying members, and what they give for free, and it gives me ideas of what to make exclusive on my podcast. Patreon also lets me see how the top-grossing podcasters communicate with their fans, how they set up their payment tiers, and how many people have picked each different tier. All of the information is right there. I get to see what's working and I copy it.

3

RULE 3: QUIT SETTING GOALS—THEY'RE KEEPING YOU BROKE

"I've always thought that each person invented himself . . .
that we are each a figment of our own imagination. The
problem is, most people have no imagination."

—David Geffen

Most people love setting goals. They live for the rush of pushing themselves out of their comfort zone to achieve something new. And the reward feels so worth it: the promotion you deserved, that vacation to Mexico you've saved up for, finally buying your dream car . . .

Sound familiar? If this describes you, the "goal set" trap got you.

The biggest mistake you can make when trying to build wealth is to set goals you think you can meet. Nothing is more limiting. If your goals feel even remotely achievable in your lifetime, they're holding you back.

I'm not saying you need to work harder. You're actually already working too hard—and that's your problem.

NO GOALS? THE RICH DO THIS INSTEAD.

Remember the story of the goose that laid the golden eggs? Well, there's more to learn from this goose. There are two kinds of people in the world:

people who obsess over the golden eggs, and people who obsess over optimizing the golden goose's health so the golden eggs become bigger, better, and more plentiful over time. The goose is the system. The golden egg is a goal.

Systems can pump out goals at a higher and higher speed the more you refine them, with minimal input from you. It's why smart people build systems to join the New Rich, and it's why broke people stay broke as they obsess over goals—even with their brand-new luxury car (probably with a lease payment that will ensure they stay broke longer). See page 118 to see how I got my $350K white Rolls Royce Ghost for free.

Advertising's number one purpose is to get you to want something, a golden egg. Luxury goods companies spend trillions convincing you that their hot new golden egg should be on your goals list. Roger Federer wearing the Rolex watch at Wimbledon is meant to make you want a Rolex. Designer brand Versace hiring Kim Kardashian for its next product launch photo shoot is meant to make you want that Versace gown. It distracts you from thinking about building the goose that could pump out a new Rolex or designer gown for you every month.

Imagine how your life would change if you didn't buy these items unless you could actually afford to buy one every day. This is a good rule to use, and it's also why most goals are so dangerous. When a goal is small enough to seem doable, even if it's hard, you focus on the win and never put effort into mastering the process that will get you that result plus more (over and over again).

So set big, audacious goals, then forget the goals and focus on creating a system to produce the outcome you want not just once, but over and over again. That's how we improve our performance, productivity, and results. Once the system is in place it will free you up to achieve *even more* audacious and imaginative things that seemed impossible.

TO GO BIG, FIRST GET MICROSCOPIC

So how do you master systems? Get laser focused on the minutiae for a brief time. They are what create the systems that make the audacious goals possible.

This may sound dull—the exact opposite of imaginative, even—but obsessing over the details is the only way you can forget about them. Knowing the minutiae that go into a process lets you create systems that automate the details. It gives you flow and routines. It frees up your brain space so you can keep scaling up with minimal input. That's when the wealth kicks in. This is what the New Rich are doing that others are not. And it's the reason why billionaires like Warren Buffett tend to have blank calendars.

Today I do fifteen to twenty podcast interviews over the course of three to four days each month. That's the only time I put into the podcast. But in August 2015 I started building the system that would keep it running with no revenue, no team, and no media experience. Today, the podcast does six million downloads and $50K in monthly revenue with one freelancer helping drive the podcast system. This frees up my time—the definition of scaling with minimum input.

Systems thinking requires you to give up making money today in exchange for taking the time, energy, and sweat equity to set up systems that will do the work for you in the future. It's a lot of up-front work, and that's the problem for most people. They prefer the short-term win. They need the instant gratification. They want to have sex right now. They can't put off current consumption. They can't give up rewards over the next week even if it means getting a better return as soon as the week after. It's why most people are too shortsighted to invest time in creating systems, and I'm glad. Let them be wooed by the flashy golden egg. They'll stay broke while you join me in creating amounts of money you never thought possible.

Once your system is set up it should work like a machine: put less into the machine and get more out than when you were doing something yourself. Inputs and outputs. More on those in a minute.

THE FIRST $700 I MADE

When I was building my first company, Heyo, it was an agency. I sold custom Facebook fan pages at $700 apiece under the name "Fan Page Factory."

Audra was one of my first clients back in 2010:

After she paid me, I then did the work to build each page: the design, the coding, writing the Facebook Markup Language (FBML—that's what it was called in 2010). Eventually I realized it would be way more powerful and fun for me not to focus on actually coding new customers' pages every month. If, instead, I spent some time and money developing software that's a system, I can sell that system to other people, and they can drag and drop elements to build their own fan pages without my doing custom work. *That* would scale, save me time, and print me money. I'll tell you how much in a minute.

I had to give up selling for a few weeks to focus on finding my technical cofounders on TopTal and start coding a system that would automate the work. I had to make a system for my system. It took a long time to build up that recurring revenue, but eventually I had thousands of people paying me $30 to $300 a month to use the system I'd built. It was an epic jump from having about one hundred clients pay me $700 one time for a professional service.

SEE THE BIG MISTAKE IN MY BOARD DECK?

The graphic on the next page is from our October 9, 2012, board meeting, which was about five months after we raised our initial $500K in capital (the line spikes up in April).

If you look at the January, February, and March columns, you'll see how getting users to pay you $30 to $300 per month creates a revenue stream that "stacks." As long as they don't cancel, you keep stacking on revenue and it becomes a very efficient system.

I was twenty-one years old at the time, and we went from nothing in late 2011 to $99K in monthly recurring revenue in April 2012:

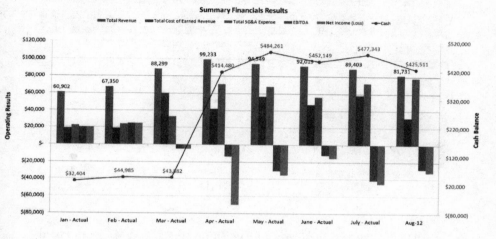

One of my biggest mistakes at this point in building the system was hiring too fast. You can see we scaled up to about eighteen full-time folks, in the process of hiring four more at the time of our October 9, 2012, board meeting:

Organizational Build-Out

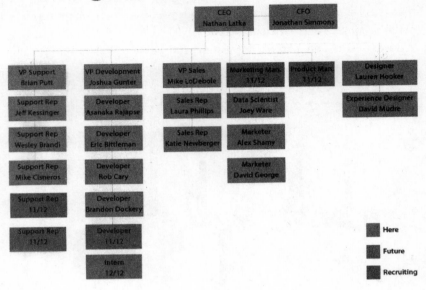

All that being said, we'd have an acquisition offer of $6.5M+ go to a final board meeting and a valuation of $10.5M just one year later when I was twenty-two. More on that later (including a scan of the actual deal so you can read it yourself on page 243).

SYSTEMATIZE THESE THINGS ONLY

Build systems around the things that take up most of your time. Sadly, most people don't even know what those things are. How many of us are constantly busy but can't look back on our day and say what we did? It's all a blur. If that's you (and even if it's not), spend a week documenting what you're doing. This kind of awareness forces you to be reflective and intentional, not reactive to whatever thing is in front of you.

When I'm first coming up with a system, I use Apple Notes and my BestSelf notebook:

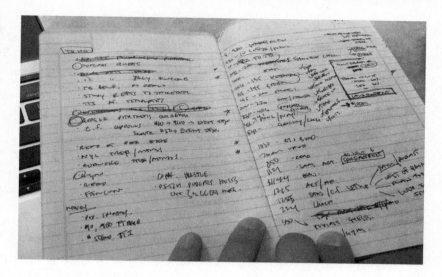

Drill down to the little things you have to do daily or weekly to produce what you want, whether it's saving for a house, launching an e-commerce store, getting fit—whatever. Go as small as you possibly can: how you respond to a customer when an order comes through, how you print your mailing labels, what you eat for breakfast.

OUTSOURCING: MY "STARBUCKS PROCESS FOR SYSTEM TESTING"

If you find yourself doing the same related tasks every day or every week, create a Google doc and document what that task looks like. Don't get lazy when trying to document what you're doing. You want to be so detailed that someone else should be able to read your document and execute the task completely, without your help. Don't take details for granted, such as:

1. The login info needed for a tool you use. When you pass this task to someone else, they'll need login info.
2. The personal details of your relationship with another person who is part of the process. This sort of thing is very difficult to pass off.
3. Any subconscious steps.

After you think you have a process documented accurately, print it off and take a trip to your local coffee shop. Then go test your system:

1. Buy five $5 gift cards.
2. Walk up to strangers who have a computer and say: "Your coffee looks low; I'll buy you another one if you take my three-minute challenge. It just requires your brain and computer. You up for it?"
3. Hand them the steps you'd printed.
4. Ask them to follow the steps by reading them out loud so you can hear where they get confused.

In the steps above, I'm assuming this task is something virtual, or done on a computer, like sending an email template to fifty potential podcast guests. If your task is not done on a computer, apply these same steps but in a different setting.

Your goal is to find someone who knows nothing about what you do and watch to see if they can follow the steps for executing your process. You are testing your ability to fully document a system.

After several rounds of this you should have a much fuller picture of what steps need to happen each day to get something done without taking any steps for granted.

Try giving your process to a high school freshman in your neighborhood. If they can do it, good news for you: they are probably looking for a $10/hour job that will beat what they are making at their fast food restaurant gig.

This is the essence of systems leverage. If you have a clear system, it can be done faster and cheaper by somebody (or even some*thing*) other than you.

UNCOVERING THE BLIND SPOTS
THAT MAKE YOUR MONEY MACHINE WORK

The up-front effort of uncovering every detail of your process will be worth it. Once your system is humming, you can step back and forget all about it—except when it comes to counting your money. You'll probably want to do that yourself. There is nothing I enjoy more than counting money—it's a beautiful big stack and way too much fun to pass off to someone else.

The coffee shop test may be enough to get you all the info you need. But if your project has many layers it will help to also think ahead to anticipate the blind spots you're likely to miss.

You'd be surprised at how much you can easily miss. We take most parts of our day for granted because aspects are hidden or unknown. You're reading this book right now to get smarter and improve your business. I bet you didn't think about:

1. Were the trees sourced to make this book from Central America or the eastern United States?
2. Are the words you're reading right now printed using pigment-based ink or solvent-based ink?
3. Were the microthreads that hold the binding together made from linen thread or from its substitute, mercerized cotton thread?

Who cares, right? Well, if you were setting up a printing and binding business you'd care a ton. These questions showcase one type of system blindness: **Material Blindness**, and it's important to anyone who is developing a physical product.

Time Blindness is another common oversight. We always project that things can be done faster than they actually can be done. Time savings typically kick in after a system has been operational for a period of weeks or months and you can begin to make system tweaks to juice time savings. Henry Ford created the assembly line where cars moved and people stayed stationary after observing the time inefficiencies of having the *cars stationary* and the *people moving* to build each car. He realized it was more efficient to have the cars move and people stay still.

Start/End Blindness also trips people up. A multilayered project can have several systems, but it can be hard to articulate where a system starts or stops—or where another begins. Newer businesses tend to have a CEO who does everything. On the streets, this sounds like: "I'm wearing so many hats!" Compare this to a well-defined system printing $50M+ a year, where the problem sounds more like: "I'm sick of doing the same thing every day!" This is because the business has been broken down into clearly defined systems and people have been plugged in to operate parts of the system that are harder or more costly to automate.

You can break the start/end haze by identifying one activity that triggers a system or a procedure, such as an interview invitation going out to a CEO (the start of my podcast booking system). This is your start. Next, think of the last action performed, such as submitting a completed, edited podcast episode to iTunes. Your system is everything that happens in between.

Clearly defining where systems start and end lets you piece them together in a perfect puzzle that will reveal your overall business makeup.

ANATOMY OF A NEW RICH SYSTEM

Once you've uncovered your blind spots, it's time to line up your parts and build your system. New Rich Systems are made up of the following elements:

Inputs: What do you have to feed the system to make it work? Your golden goose needs water and food every day to survive—among many other things.

Outputs: What does your system produce for you once it's set up? Keep your golden goose alive, keep getting golden eggs.

Feedback loops: Can an output of your system get you better, cheaper, or faster inputs to create a snowball effect? What if you could use your golden goose's golden eggs to buy Goose Protein Enhancers to add as a system input that helps your goose produce two golden eggs per week instead of one?

Stocks: Stocks are whatever assets pile up inside the system that then get used to generate an output. The input is food your golden goose eats for energy. The output is golden eggs. The "stock" is the energy in your golden goose. If it goes down, no more golden eggs. If stock stays low long enough, goose dies. No one likes a dead goose. A stock is a measure of change. It's controlled by how fast or slow different inputs or outputs are interacting with a system.

Getting your system set up is more important than deciding you want to make $1M per year. That's because once you have the bones of your system set up, the way you crank up production is by changing your inputs and outputs, better managing your stocks, and creating feedback loops that give you a true unfair advantage against your competitors.

The New Rich go to extensive lengths to clearly define inputs, procedures, and outputs, then always study their stocks and look for feedback loops that can save them time and make them more money.

HOW I PAY $29 TO GET BACK NINE HOURS OF MY TIME

Here's how these ideas play out in my *Top Entrepreneurs* podcast system:

INPUTS
- Guests
- Traffic
- Editors
- Me (Limit your "me" inputs to crank up your free time while still growing your income. I'll show you how.)

OUTPUTS
- *The Top Entrepreneurs* podcast episode published successfully on my blog, iTunes, and SoundCloud every morning at 6 a.m. EST.
- Sponsor revenue
- Influence

STOCKS
- Downloads (Shrink and grow based on how I dial up or down inputs and outputs. If I want to dial up sponsor revenue on the output side, without changing inputs, my audience [stock] probably will decrease because more ads will annoy them.)

FEEDBACK LOOP OPPORTUNITIES
- A guest (input) shares their episode on my podcast with their audience (input), which increases the number of downloads (stock) and enables me to charge more for sponsorship (output).

Here's how everything works together to create a system for producing and publishing a podcast episode:

PROCESS:

1. Nathan uses NathanLatka.com/acuity to schedule podcast guests in a batch format. (Red are interviews—I interview about fifty software CEOs every week.) I pay Aaron on my booking team $12 per booked guest.

2. When it's time to do the interview Nathan records it via Skype using Ecamm.
3. Nathan puts Ecamm files into Audacity, then exports audio files to Google Drive, where Sam takes over.
4. Sam finalizes each audio file by adding the pre- and post-roll open loop, intro, and sponsor mentions, then uploads the final version onto Google Drive, YouTube, Libsyn. I pay Sam $7 per episode for this step.

5. The release schedule is managed in a massive Google spreadsheet. When the episode goes live on Libsyn, I pay a virtual as-

sistant to publish the guest's bio, headshot, and SoundCloud embed on my blog. This costs about $5 per episode.

y of Week	Release Dat	Episode	Who	Title (Nathan Writes Titles)	Gues	Guest Bio
ursday	7/26/2018	1097	Brandon Kelly	CMS CEO: How to Move 1 Time License Model doing $	brand	Brandon is the head honcho at Craft CMS, the wo
ednesday	7/25/2018	1096	Babak Hedayati	How TapClicks is Managing 60% yoy Growth in Marke	baba	With over 20 years as a senior executive at Fortur
esday	7/24/2018	1095	Dominic Edmunds	Why He Gave Up $5m Agency for Customer Data Saa	domi	As the founder & CEO of SaleCycle, I am focused o
onday	7/23/2018	1094	Brian Reale	How he bought 15 people off cap table, hit $9m in ARR	brian	Brian Reale is a serial entrepreneur. Prior to foun
nday	7/22/2018	1093	Jeremy Adams	If you're under 30, is agency/coaching a good way to m	jerem	Being one of Forbes' & Influencive.com's Top 30 E
turday	7/21/2018	1092	Jordan Mitchell	Why Chef Creator Raised $30m to Replace Walkie Talk	jorda	Jesse Robbins is CEO and founder of Orion Labs. P
day	7/20/2018	1091	Daniel Nissan	Founded in 1999, How He's Managed a 20+ Year "Ove	Dani	See https://www.linkedin.com/in/danielnissan/
ursday	7/19/2018	1090	Chris Ingham Brooke	CEO Eating Own Dog Food for $25m Revenue, $5.5m	chris	Chris Ingham Brooke is the founder and CEO of Pu
ednesday	7/18/2018	1089	Vijay Tella	Workato CEO: "We're Enterprise Version" of Zapier, Se	vijay	Vijay has led the creation of market leading integr
esday	7/17/2018	1088	Sati Hillyer	How Ex-Salesforce Leader Launched Video for Salespe	sati@	Sati is a seasoned entrepreneur who loves building pro
onday	7/16/2018	1087	James Kappen	Yeah I'd sell (Live negotiation)	james	Designer and entrepreneur who loves solving problem
nday	7/15/2018	1086	Jake Atwood	Sales outreach tool hits $1.2m ARR, would you sell for	jake@	Jake Atwood is the Founder & CEO of BuzzBuilder. He
turday	7/14/2018	1085	Joshua Tillman	We're #1 in Salesforce for Call Routing, Tech with $10m	joshu	Joshua Tillman began building DialSource in 2005, whi
day	7/13/2018	1084	Murry Ivanoff	Bulgarian company spends $45k of $65k MRR on paid	murry	Murry founded Metrilo in 2014 to help eCommerce stor
ursday	7/12/2018	1083	nancy hua	How she 2x ARR yoy in mobile testing space to $6m in	nancy	I'm the CEO of Apptimize! We're probably installed on
ednesday	7/11/2018	1082	Mark Grether	Why Public Sizmek Went Private to Fuel Growth via Ma	Sizm	Mark Grether is CEO of Sizmek. He focuses on guiding
esday	7/10/2018	1081	Eric Frankel	With $2m in ARR and $16m Valuation for 7+ Years, Do	eric@	Eric Frankel is an innovative business leader with a pro
onday	7/9/2018	1080	Danny Wajcman	15,000 Customers at $35 ARPU is $500k+ in MRR righ	danny	
nday	7/8/2018	1079	Soeren Stamer	How He's Pivoted 3 Times Since 1996, Moving to Clou	soere	CEO & Co-Founder of CoreMedia. Recipient of the Ge
turday	7/7/2018	1078	Nick Mason	How agile content marketing solution Turtl hit $125k/mo	nick@	Please can you use the one from my previous submiss
day	7/6/2018	1077	Collin Holmes	We Bootstrapped Our Way to $2m in ARR, Now $10m	collin	Collin Holmes, founder and CEO, started chatmeter in
ursday	7/5/2018	1076	Chris Kenton	We pivoted to pure play SaaS, now $1m in ARR growir	ckent	I'm CEO of SocialRep, providing social sales enableme
ednesday	7/4/2018	1075	John Panaccione	LogicBay CEO: Love Venture Debt! Helped us pass $1	jpana	As CEO of LogicBay, John works with leading compan

6. The same virtual assistant then posts the episode on LinkedIn and emails the guest that the interview went live. This costs another $5 per episode. Steps 5 and 6 come out to $10 per episode. You can see the invoice below for thirteen episodes is about $130:

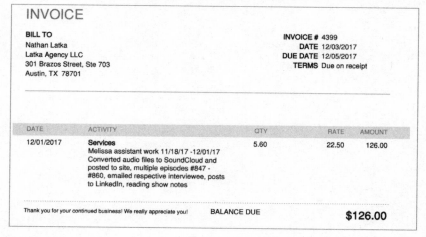

INVOICE

BILL TO
Nathan Latka
Latka Agency LLC
301 Brazos Street, Ste 703
Austin, TX 78701

INVOICE # 4399
DATE 12/03/2017
DUE DATE 12/05/2017
TERMS Due on receipt

DATE	ACTIVITY	QTY	RATE	AMOUNT
12/01/2017	**Services** Melissa assistant work 11/18/17 -12/01/17 Converted audio files to SoundCloud and posted to site, multiple episodes #847 - #860, emailed respective interviewee, posts to LinkedIn, reading show notes	5.60	22.50	126.00

Thank you for your continued business! We really appreciate you!   **BALANCE DUE**   **$126.00**

USING MY TIME:

Per episode time it takes me without help: ten hours
Per episode money cost without help: $0

USING OTHERS' TIME:

Per episode time it takes me with help: twenty minutes (just me re-
cording the fifteen-minute interview)

Per episode money cost with help: $29

Aaron: $12 per guest booked

Sam: $7 for editing each episode, uploading, scheduling

WMM Virtual Assistants: $10 for posting to my blog, emailing guest that
they're live

Using this system, I went from spending 300 hours of my own time each
month (not possible if you do the math) to spending just 10 hours (30 episodes × 20 minutes) of my time and paying out $870 ($29/episode × 30
episodes).

I saved 290 hours of my time by paying $870. Absolutely worth it. Look
for time arbitrage systems like this to set up in your business.

I'll talk more about income strategies later, but on this cost of $870 per
month, I sell multiple sponsors at $10K+/month in sponsor fees.

Here's one of many annual deals I signed for 2017 sponsor placements:

TOP **The Top Entrepreneurs in**
1   **Money, Marketing, and Life**
Nathan Latka brings you entrepreneurs who...

The Latka Agency LLC– The Top Podcast

SPONSORSHIP AGREEMENT

DATE: ▮▮▮▮▮▮▮▮

1.   Project objectives
This is a sponsorship agreement between ▮▮▮▮▮ & The Latka Agency LLC (dba The Top Podcast). This will be a 12 month long promotion from Jan 1 2018 to Dec 31 2018.

2.   The Top Podcast Pricing and Industry Metrics

- Syndicated on ▮▮▮▮▮▮▮▮ podcast feature

- INC #1 rated show with ▮▮▮▮▮▮▮

- Podcast launched August 1st, 2015 by Software as a Service CEO Nathan Latka, hit #1 in New and Noteworthy August 23rd, #1 Management and Marketing Podcast October 2nd, #34 Overall Business Podcast October 3rd, 2015.

- According to 2014 statistics, 90% of podcasts receive less than 100 plays per month. As of October 2015 the Top Podcast with host Nathan Latka is on track for 3.8 million listens in 2016.

3.   Sponsorship Options
The deliverable(s) for this project are as follows:

a.   Mid-Roll
   This runs between minute 10 and minute 15 of the podcast.
   - 30 Second Mid-Roll
     ▮▮▮▮▮▮▮▮▮

b.   Post-Roll
   This runs at the end of each show.
   - 30 Second Post-Roll
     ▮▮▮▮▮▮▮▮▮

4.   Estimated fees and expenses
The sponsorship package is a 12 month contract for a mid, and post-roll in 15 episodes per month with different CTA layouts. Ex: Mid is "Here's how I use ▮▮▮▮▮ Post is "Go get started on ▮▮▮▮▮ now". For this particular project, ▮▮▮▮▮ will be given the rates presented in Fig 1.1 below bringing total cost for ▮▮▮▮▮

▮▮▮▮▮

Title	Cost per month	# Months	Bi-Annually
Mid	$15000	12	$180,000
Total			$180,000

The Top Entrepreneurs in Money, Marketing, and Life
Nathan Latka brings you entrepreneurs who...

The Latka Agency LLC– The Top Podcast

5.   Payment schedule
All invoices are due and payable within 30 days of receipt by The Latka Agency LLC. ▉▉▉▉ will receive an invoice for this sponsorship contract with terms that stipulate 100% of the sponsorship agreement price payable within 30 days of sponsorship agreement signing.

6.   Authorization
Work cannot begin until authorization has been received from ▉▉▉▉▉

Authorization – ▉▉▉▉	Authorization – The Latka Agency LLC
By: ▉▉▉▉▉	By: *Nathan Latka*
Name: ▉▉▉	Name: Nathan Latka,
Title: ▉▉	Title: President
Address: ▉▉▉▉▉	Address: ▉▉▉▉▉
PHONE: ▉▉▉▉	PHONE: ▉▉▉
Date: ▉▉▉	Date: ▉▉▉

GETTING YOUR SYSTEM HYPEREFFICIENT (AND GETTING YOURSELF SUPERRICH FROM THAT SYSTEM)

The sweet spot is a balance: start by drilling down to every possible detail of what needs to be done, then look for ways to minimize steps. You don't want to be doing all the work yourself, but keep your team small by reducing the number of steps humans have to take.

Look for opportunities to automate tasks as soon as you can afford to. Kitchen is an Asian-inspired, fast-casual restaurant that serves wok-fried rice and noodle bowls fresh, fast, and for under $10. They were paying $9K+/month for bookkeeping services. To drive down costs, they switched to an automated bookkeeping provider botkeeper, saving them $4K/month. They now get faster data processing, more reporting, and greater accuracy than they had ever experienced when they had someone on staff doing their books. They had to spend to save, but it was absolutely worth it.

After you write out a process, you can generate job descriptions by identifying the steps that one person can cover. In my podcast, I have one person, Aaron (Piper Creative if you want to hire him), doing everything involving guest bookings and Sam on all tasks audio-related.

Your system has zero chance of getting more efficient if it relies on only one resource. This is even harder if that single resource is your time. Leverage and efficiencies always come from combining one resource with another and making $1 + 1 = 3$.

To get there, make sure some of your output is "saved money" that you can use to add inputs and increase feedback loop potential. So the iterations of your system over time would look something like this:

Stage 1: Input = You + Fiverr freelancer

Stage 2: Input = You + Fiverr freelancer + Automation software

Stage 3: Input = Two Fiverr freelancers + Automation software (Your time is now free, so you use it to start building another system.)

Stage 4: Your system is creating cash flow as an output, which lets you go invest in new systems or invest in making your inputs and current systems more efficient.

Stacking systems like this is like making a layer cake. The more sweetness you stack, the richer it tastes!

Until you reach Stage 4 you'll always be looking for ways to decrease inputs and maximize cash flow. A smart way to do this is by negotiating down expenses that you can't avoid (versus a sole focus on driving revenue).

Amazon and Walmart do so much volume, they have leverage to demand that the providers of their inputs (goods Amazon and Walmart sell) charge them less. They then pass on most of these savings to the consumer, which gives them more market share. Classic feedback loop.

Think about all of your expenses right now. Now go negotiate all of them down using hard and soft power (hard: "I'm canceling my account unless you give me a $100/month discount"; soft: "I'm trying to save money and it would mean a lot if you could decrease monthly payments for two months until the business regains its footing"). Here are some expenses I bet you have that you can significantly decrease:

Software: If you spend a lot on software, point out that you have choices for whom to buy that software from and ask for a lower rate from your current vendors.

Material Expenses: If you spend loads in China on gray form 390x plastic for the widget you produce, ask for a volume discount. Put in the work to research what you could get from alternative plastic providers so you know what your true bottom line is should you have to switch from whomever you currently purchase from.

People Expenses: Head count is usually a company's largest expense. It's hard to negotiate this cost down. However, sites like Fiverr, Toptal (for developers), Upwork, and others are making it very easy to replace high-dollar talent with lower-dollar talent. Freelance talent is also variable (you can turn it off and on) compared with full-time employees, which are fixed expenses (way more difficult to turn off and on). Investing in tech when you can is another smart way to drive down people expenses. Panera realized spending $1K one time to install a virtual terminal to order your food is cheaper than paying a cashier a $15 minimum wage.

Also, look at your outputs as potential sources of cash flow. Are there ways your bad outputs can be someone else's good inputs? If a software company is losing customers every month—a big negative output—they can turn this into a positive cash-generating output by selling their churned leads' contact info to a lower-priced competitor (this helps everyone!).

THE SEVEN-FIGURE PODCAST SYSTEM

Once your system is producing golden eggs, you can shift your attention to bigger things and print more money. For me that golden egg is an episode a day, because an episode is worth several thousand dollars based on sponsorship revenue (in February 2018, I made $4K per daily episode on expenses of $29—good margin!).

If I hadn't set up podcast production to run itself, I never would have had the brain space, energy, or time to reel in that kind of money. And how do I get new sponsors? Another system.

Each podcast episode is a new interview with a CEO. I use a tool called Acuity that lets the CEOs pick a time from my calendar. No need for a middle person to deal with scheduling. Immediately after the interview happens Acuity sends the CEO an email to thank them and let them know when the interview will go live. The email also mentions that we have one or two sponsorship spots open and asks if they're interested in sponsorship.

This is the email that goes out from our system in Acuity Scheduling. William was our guest CEO for the day:

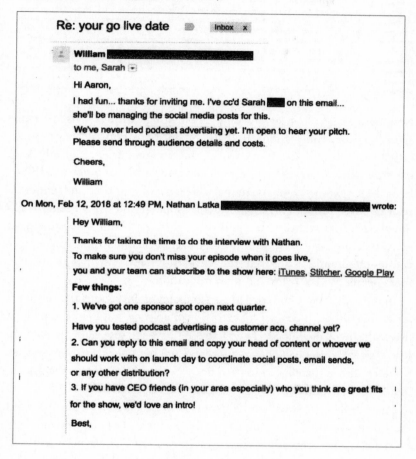

The reply rate on this follow-up email is over 90 percent:

Jared Schrieber (2)	Inbox	Re: your go live date - for your podcast. > > I'm writing because my wife (and I) got quite a shock yesterday when she > Googled my n			Mar 16
Bernardo Letayf	Inbox	Re: your go live date - 1) We don't have budget for ads yet... I'll get back to you if we get some :) 2) You can coordinate all things with me			Mar 14
Peter Lamson	Inbox	RE: your go live date - make sure you don't miss your episode when it goes live, you and your team can subscribe to the show here: iTur			Mar 13
Petr .. Monica, Charlie (26)	Inbox	RE: your go live date - > Hope you had a great holiday season. Wanted to circle back to see if you > had this interview scheduled yet?			Mar 13
Collin Holmes	Inbox	Re: your go live date - me and you didn't receive permissions for any of this. On Fri, Mar 2, 2018 at 8:47 AM Collin Holmes wrote: > Na			Mar 12
Darshen, Emily (2)	Inbox	Re: your go live date - Aaron, 1) We haven't, but we'd be open to it provided that you can prove that your audience is our target audien			Mar 12
Iba Masood	Inbox	Re: your go live date - Here you go! Tam will help co-ordinate social posts on launch day. Thanks Aaron. "Iba Masood"	Co-founder & (			Mar 9
Jai, me, Jai (3)	Inbox	Re: your go live date - right away 1. Swym : https://swym.it/ 2. Kwanzoo: http://www.kwanzoo.com/ 3. Reflektive: https://www.reflektive.			Mar 9
Allen Bonde	Inbox	Re: your go live date - 2018 at 1:04 PM, Nathan Latka < scheduling@acuityscheduling.com> wrote: > Hey Allen, > > Thanks for taking			Mar 9
William, Sarah, Aaron (3)	Inbox	Re: your go live date - on the Podcast that William at EasyRedir did with you, and check on timing. We have signed up to the channel			Mar 8
Jessie Yarrow (3)	Inbox	Re: your go live date - When can we expect to access it on iTunes? > > Also copying Natalie, who heads up social media for Ping Ident			Mar 6
Eric Berry (2)	Inbox	Re: your go live date - recording the podcast with you a few weeks ago. What's the normal lead time to go-live? Definitely wanna make			Mar 6
Robert Jacobi	Inbox	Re: your go live date - , Thank you for the opportunity to talk about Joomla with you on your podcast. Sandra Decoux is Joomla's Director			Feb 28
Stephen CEO LoopMe	Inbox	Re: your go live date - - did you have Elle and my skype I am available in the next few days - please can you suggest new times we lo			Feb 28
Howard, Max, Neil (4)	Inbox	Re: your go live date - make sure you don't miss your episode when it goes live, you and your team can subscribe to the show here: iT			Feb 27
Kistie Adams	Inbox	Re: your go live date - ! Do you know the date when this interview will go up? Regards, Kistie Adams Senior Publicist Pitch Public Rela			Feb 27

Now, because I do an interview a day, I'm inviting wealthy CEOs to become sponsors thirty times a month. If 10 percent reply and say they're interested, that's three leads. If one closes, that's a great deal, especially since one deal will start at $30K minimum and can grow to as much as $180K.

Make sure the systems you're spending most of your time and money on scaling have a direct correlation to additional cash flow, whether that's downloads that translate to sponsor dollars, website impressions that convert to an increase in your average cart checkout size, if you're an e-commerce brand, or a system for marketing the newspaper that drives more people to your brick-and-mortar location.

In my podcast system I used to post graphics on Instagram and Facebook for every episode. It cost me an extra $3 per episode, but I noticed it didn't drive additional downloads. I know that if I have ten thousand more downloads per episode I can charge another $500 per episode to sponsors, so there's a direct correlation to cash flow. Because that step in the system didn't work in terms of driving more downloads, I deleted it.

People often get stuck working on systems that suck up their time but don't bring in cash. It's so tempting to lie to yourself because a system feels good when it isn't actually accomplishing anything. So be hyperintentional about where you're spending your time and ruthlessly kill any systems that don't have a direct correlation to growing your bank account.

SHOULD YOU HIRE PEOPLE WHO ARE ONLY 60 PERCENT AS GOOD AS YOU?

If you're resisting replacing yourself it's probably because you keep telling yourself one of two things:

1. No one can do this as well as I can.
2. If I replace myself, my team won't need me anymore!

The likelihood that you are actually the best in the world at something is very small. It's more likely your ego telling you this so you feel important. Even if it were true that no one could do something as well as you, two people who are only 60 percent as good as you will lead to 120 percent of your output, and it requires none of your time.

I always try to find, influence, and persuade the person who is the best in the world at something I need done to do my work for me. That's a skill set that can be applied to getting anything done—a generalist approach—versus specializing in one thing and being pigeonholed.

"But, Nathan, if I replace myself, my team won't need me anymore!"

It's only a matter of time before this sort of thinking kills your team entirely. Look at the US political system. There's a reason presidential terms are four years each. In other countries, without term limits, leaders who get power tend to add complexity below them on the ladder they climbed up to make it harder for other political challengers to climb up and challenge them. (By the way, that's a great business strategy after you find a system that makes you loads of cash. Just look at the US taxi system and the complexity taxi lobbies added. Uber is now challenging that complexity head-on and is on its way to a $100B+ IPO.)

If you complicate the business version of your ladder, you're isolating yourself as an input to a system that will never grow output. The only ways to grow output are to:

1. Make the machine more efficient with the same inputs.
2. Put less costly inputs into the system so ratio of output to input increases.
3. Do #1 and #2 at the same time.

To position your overall success for the long term, you want to become a master at producing more. That means updating inputs and machines, your own time and energy (as an input) included.

When looking for human talent to replace yourself in a system, try many mini-projects as tests. Projects judged on performance are much more effective than scanning résumés all day. Nobody loves creative students who got Fs in school like Nathan Latka! Email me, I'll hire you: nathan@nathanlatka.com

To find potential talent, use sites like:

1. **Fiverr:** A freelance marketplace where all projects start at $5. Once you have a process defined, upload it as a task to Fiverr, find a talent, and watch how they execute. If they perform well, reach out and see if you can persuade them to join your system as an input however you see fit (hourly, contract, etc.).

2. **Toptal:** If the input you need requires coding or development, use Toptal. Toptal is a site that has already vetted and curated the top 3 percent of developers across the world. Work starts at $50/hour. I put a $1K project through Toptal for the first version of GetLatka.com. The developer performed well and I've since put more money through Toptal to continue using him.

3. **Upwork:** A nice mix of Fiverr and Toptal both price- and talent-wise. Contractors on Upwork will work for as little as $2/hour depending on the task. For my first iteration of TheTopInbox .com, I put a $2K project through Upwork, liked the developer very much, and ended up paying him $20K over six months.

Sometimes a human is not the best way to replace yourself in a system. You might feel the work you're doing is very repetitive. If that's the case, you might find it cheaper and more efficient to pay a site like Zapier to write code that links your application processes together.

HOW I GO TO THE OSCARS USING "DECISION SYSTEMS"

How do you decide whether a big purchase is worth it? The other day I was considering splurging on staying at the Beverly Hills Hotel in LA instead of my usual spot. At $600/night, it's a splurge that's tough for most people. I came up with a very simple "Decision System" I filter these kinds of purchases through. It saves me energy every time this sort of purchase comes up, and its simplicity gives it a very high utility value.

If, with my current monthly income stream, I couldn't afford to purchase one of these things every day, I don't buy it.

Simple as that. That's the rule. For cars, houses, vacations, dinners, everything.

Let's say I'm making only $3K/month and only $1K after expenses. If I'm considering spending $600 on a hotel for one night, I'd ask myself, well, can I spend this every day? $600 per night for a month is $18K. I bring in only $1K per month, so I say no to this hotel.

As an aside, I go to the Oscars every year to support Elton John's AIDS foundation and have no problem doing what most consider "splurging" on staying at the nicest hotel in Beverly Hills—the London at $800/night. My systems generate passive income that exceeds $24K/month ($800/night). Because I could actually pay this and live at the London full time, I have no problem "splurging" on a night or two.

When I splurge like this I tend to let myself really splurge before going back to my very-easy-to-manage wardrobe of black T-shirt and black jeans from Banana Republic.

Here I am in two outfits for the 2018 Oscars in Versace jacket, Ferragamo shoes with Swarovski crystals, and Ralph Lauren accessories, totaling over $20K (plus stylist).

Wearing Versace on Rodeo Drive in Hollywood in one of only two Tiffany's penthouses in the world:

(continued)

At the 2018 Elton John Oscar party:

This sort of thought process is how the New Rich think about buying versus renting. Rent a jet for a day for $5K or buy a jet for $5M? Only do the latter if you could afford to buy a new jet every month.

This Decision System lets you preserve your energy on a daily basis. Simple rules. Quick decisions.

TOP SEVEN BOOKS ON SYSTEMS

1. *Thinking in Systems* by Donella Meadows simplifies what makes any system work and how to build your own.
2. *Mastering the Rockefeller Habits* by Verne Harnish is the easiest blueprint to follow to clearly define what outputs you want in your business—the first step to figuring out the process and inputs.
3. *Business Adventures* by John Brooks highlights CEOs and companies that created the most shareholder value over their tenure.

You'll start to notice business models and their underlying systems that will set you up for success.

4. *The Outsiders* by William N. Thorndike Jr. is a collection of eight stories from eight CEOs who set up systems that provided the highest capital returns in history.

5. *Thing Explainer* by Randall Munroe visually diagrams how things work using only one thousand of the most commonly used words in the English language (forces simplification and makes pattern recognition easier).

6. *McDonald's: Behind the Arches* by John F. Love helps dissect one of the most replicated, valuable systems ever built: the burger stand. No matter what industry you're in, you're guaranteed to learn systems tidbits.

7. *The 4-Hour Workweek* by Timothy Ferriss will help you find ways to systematize your business and your life to save time, energy, and money.

4

RULE 4:
SELL PICKAXES
TO GOLD MINERS

"'You can mine for gold or you can sell pickaxes.' This is of course an allusion to the California Gold Rush where some of the most successful business people such as Levi Strauss and Samuel Brannan didn't mine for gold themselves but instead sold supplies to miners—wheelbarrows, tents, jeans, pickaxes etc. Mining for gold was the more glamorous path but actually turned out, in aggregate, to be a worse return on capital and labor than selling supplies."

—Business Insider

You already know that trying to come up with a brand-new business idea is stupid if you want to get rich. There are too many opportunities for failure, but beyond that, it's the kind of road-most-traveled thinking that rarely gets you ahead.

If you want to defy the odds, you need a counterintuitive approach. Forget trying to appeal to the masses. Look at what the masses are going after, and then sell into the market that others have built around it.

That's the beauty of what I call "selling pickaxes to gold miners." You let the gold miners do all the work and then siphon profits off the market they've created. This works in B2B selling and on the consumer side, too. So while everyone's spending money on fidget spinners, you might sell the "Fidget Spinner Sticker Kit." While Amazon pulls a profit from third-party sellers, you might create an inventory-tracking program for those sellers.

Pickaxes are hiding behind every popular marketplace. They can be hard to spot at first, but the more you start thinking this way, the more they'll show themselves to you.

Most people love this idea when they hear it, but it takes a lot of self-restraint to choose pickax production over gold mining. The temptation to jump into a promising industry after seeing others' success is just too alluring. It happened to me recently when I was talking to an investor friend about venture capital. He told me that in 2014 the total amount of venture capital raised by start-ups was $48.3B. In 2016, that number hit $69.1B. Curious about the data, I started talking to other start-up founders to see what they thought of VC. Many of them privately shared that after their start-up, it was their dream to join a VC firm. The industry was doing a great job selling the sexiness of VC. My money-loving heart tried to tell me I should go into VC, too, but my brain found the smarter pickax option.

VC is the gold mine everyone wants to go after. The pickax to the VC industry is data. VCs rely on great data to make sound investments. I realized that while there are many hundreds of VC firms, they actually have limited access to company data. So I decided I'd get rich off selling data to them by launching GetLatka.com.

Some companies were already doing this, so I set out to learn + copy + do it better. Michael Bloomberg got rich off selling his Bloomberg Terminal to financial communities. He owned the data. Other companies competing in the VC firm data space included PitchBook, HG Data, Mattermark (dead), CB Insights, Crunchbase, Zirra, and Owler. I needed to find out if they were actually doing well to know whether this was a pickax I should build.

WHY DO THOUSANDS OF PRIVATE CEOS TELL ME THEIR REVENUE?

I couldn't just call the CEOs and ask, "How much money did you make last month?" So instead, I cold-emailed them asking if I could feature them on my podcast. On the podcast, I'd ask them how much money they were making and other business metrics so I could reverse engineer their business and then fight like hell to beat them. Mattermark did $2.4M in 2015 revenue, had forty-seven employees, $18M in funding, and was doing about $275K per month as of April 2016 (dead now in flash sale to FullContact for $500K). Owler was pre-revenue but had raised $19M. CB Insights did about $8M in 2015 revenue and $14.4M in 2016 revenue. This pickax was hotter than a mouthful of wasabi if I could avoid Mattermark's mistakes. They were selling only to VC firms at a price point of a few hundred dollars per month. Eventually they ran out of VCs to sell to and had already anchored to a price that was way too cheap. By the time they realized this, they tried to pivot to selling to sales teams but it was too late.

GetLatka.com needed to stand out if I was going to aim for a higher price point. I didn't want it to be a data dump wrestling for attention among the established competition. That's where my podcast came in. It was like my golden goose gave birth to another golden goose—only this one was even bigger and more fertile.

My podcast system creates two assets for me. I monetize golden goose #1, my podcast, by selling sponsor spots. These are big, six-figure deals, and I have several running throughout the year. (See page 45 for contract.)

Then there's goose #1's golden child: GetLatka.com. Once I interview a CEO on my podcast, I put the numbers he or she shares into a database. The output is a bunch of private software companies' revenue data, growth data, etc., which I sell back to VC firms that want to connect with those CEOs so they can invest in their companies. If VCs aren't constantly making deals, their big $500M fund dies. They have to find the top entrepreneurs, and that's why the biggest VC firms and private equity firms are paying me between $5K and $15K a month to access this data set. I increase prices every month, so more today as you read this.

In addition, I'm doing fifteen to twenty-five new calls every week with new B2B software CEOs. Most analysts at these VC firms scrape by trying to get four to six calls a week.

Here's what an example week might look like.

	8am Austin eye pre surgery 8 – 9am	Ry Walker: The Top Er. 8am
		Yannis Psarras:
		David Hart: The To, 8:40am
		[INTERVIEW] The T. 9:20am
	Sami Linnanvuo: Tl 9:40am	Vaibhav Kakkar:
	Pieterjan Bouter	Chad Rubin: The Top. 10am
	Robin Mellstrand 10:20am	Loren Wilson: Tl
	Giles Palmer: Th	Thomas Beattie: 10:40am
Drew D'Agostino: The 11am	Mark Kornfilt: The Ic. 11am	Zack Rosen: The
Hank Leber: The	Brad Siff: The To	
Stacy Chapman: 1 11:40am		Manny Medina: Tl 11:40am
Joe Griffin: The	Amit BenDov: The Te 12pm	Ashwin Jacob: 1
Aaron Fessler: Th, 12:20pm	Ajeet Singh: The	Elizabeth Osder: 1 12:20pm
	Andy Beal: The Tc 12:40pm	Scott Brandley:
	Chris Lynde: The	Jay Habegger: The To. 1pm
	Allen Gannett: The. 1:20pm	Adam Peterson:
	Zach Goldstein:	Airbnb checkin! 1:30 – 2:30pm
Oren Harnevo: The To. 2pm		Hair cut with all 2 – 3pm
Todd Olson: The		
Mike Donnelly: The To. 3pm	Neal Patel: Latka B2B SaaS, 3pm	
Arun Sivashanka	Bennett Carroccio: Latk, 3:30pm	Berger and Latka meet up 3:30pm, Seventh
Darshan Kaler: The To. 4pm	Bao-Y Van Cong: Latka B2E, 4pm	Drive to Pats 4 – 5:30pm
Michael Jensen:		
Mark Sylvester: Th. 4:40pm		
Tyler Anderson:		
Omar Zenhom: Tne, 5:20pm		

What makes my data so valuable, and worth the expense, is that it's straight from the CEO's mouth. Nobody has more accurate revenue data, customer count data, team size data, average revenue per user (ARPU) data, or churn data, with a source that is as reliable as the CEO him- or herself. My competitors get their data by scraping websites and blog posts for relevant metrics and customer counts and they're never accurate. Many of them don't even have revenue numbers. They just can't find them.

Technically the VC firms could get this same information by listening to every episode of my podcast. But they don't have time for that, so they pay for the database. I'm ultimately making it easier for them to consume the content that my podcast publically puts out for free.

Here's how that works.

1. Go to GetLatka.com to see 5 percent of the full database for free:

NAME	ARR	MRR	RAISED	2016 REVENUE	TEAM SIZE	REVENUE/EMPLOYEE
CloudCherry	$1M-$1.2M	$88K-$100K	$9.5M	$333.3K	74	$4.5K
LeanData	$5.0M-$7.5M	$416.5K-$625K	$18M	$5.0M	50	$100.0K
Cirrus Insig...	$12M-$14.4M	$1M-$1.2M	$1.1M	$7.7M	58	$132.4K
Chatmatic	$300K-$540K	$25K-$45K	$0	$1.4M	8	$175K
Buzzbuilder	$1.2M	$100K	$0	$600K	10	$60K

2. Click a company you want to know more about:

3. Click a data point you want to know more about (underlined). In this case, I want to hear when the Cirrus Insight CEO says, "We are doing $1M a month or about a $12M run rate right now":

4. At timestamp 0:40 Brandon Bruce, the CEO, shares that data point. All data points in the database tie directly back to the CEO's voice when I interviewed them for my podcast.

Short of looking at these companies' bookkeeping, no information on them is more reliable. And it's *exactly* what VC firms need to hit their investment goals. So while my friends dream of joining a VC firm to strike gold, I'm selling the firms the tools they need to be able to look for gold at all. My database made $100K in the first three months of being live, and has made multiples of that figure to date—output that I invest into other business ideas. It's a glorious cycle of profits and investing.

LOOK IN THESE SEVEN PLACES TO FIND YOUR NEXT $5K

Some top experts will tell you to mine for lucrative business ideas by interviewing consumers on what they want. Terrible advice. Ask customers what they want and they'll tell you about some big, sexy idea that *maybe* could get you rich. Anyone can ask questions like this, which means most big, sexy ideas are already being worked on. Why would you jump in and compete, all in the name of "listening to your customers"? It's bad advice and a great way to go bankrupt.

Talk to customers but don't actually do what they say. If customers tell you they want food delivered to their door weekly, don't go compete with Thrive Market, HelloFresh, and Blue Apron. Rather, go figure out what those business models rely on and build that. Last-mile delivery from warehouse to consumer's home is one of them. Onfleet.com is doing this and has just passed three hundred customers, $2.1M in 2016 revenue, and $4.5M raised. It's a B2B software product that helps delivery companies manage and analyze their local delivery operations. HelloFresh is a customer.

This is like the part of the iceberg that floats above water—it's big, it's shiny, and everyone talks about it. You know the rest of this story. The bigger part of the iceberg is the part people can't see, underwater. *That's* the part you can win, the part that will bring you cold hard cash. It's also the part that's completely off consumers' radar, so you'll never hear about it from them.

This strategy has worked for generations. Remember—the wealthiest people during the gold rush were not the gold miners. They were the people *who sold pickaxes* to the gold miners.

If you don't have access to a customer base, or just don't want to go that route, there's still plenty of opportunity to uncover pickax ideas:

▶ **Sell add-ons for massively popular items.** Any top-selling item offers an audience that you can sell to. It's why Amazon shows more than fifty thousand search results for the term "iPhone case." It works. Ride a whale (Apple) and sell into it (iPhone cases).

▶ **Read news headlines each morning in a new way.** As I write this businesses are talking about hacking; consumers are obsessed with drones, ride sharing, and on-demand food delivery; and nearly everyone is talking about cryptocurrencies. So instead of buying into cryptocurrencies, or doing your own ICO (initial coin offering), maybe you can create a dashboard for people to track ICOs. That's taking advantage of a hot market—the crypto token gold rush. Your pickax is basically a data set that tracks ICOs, kind of like what the New York Stock Exchange does for companies when they go public.

Coinbase was built so people could manage their cryptocurrency and convert it to dollars to use in the real world while the company takes a transaction fee. Coinbase was founded in 2012 and its growth is directly tied to the media's current obsession with cryptocurrency buzzing valuations. Coinbase raised $100M in 2017 at a $1.6B valuation.

▶ **Look at other marketplaces.** If you offer consulting services to salespeople you might go into the Salesforce AppExchange or HubSpot—big software companies that service salespeople—and look at what's trending in those communities. As I write this, GetFeedback, Dropbox, and HelloSign are apps trending in Salesforce. GetFeedback is software that lets companies survey their customers and then sends the data to the company's sales team. It's a top-ranked app, so it's clearly making a lot of money. Well, you might launch a consulting service focused on helping salespeople understand survey results. Perfect for salespeople training. So you're not joining the gold miners by competing directly with the software; you're piggybacking off the market they created by offering professional services that help people use the product more effectively.

Your hack for finding clients: click on GetFeedback in the Sales-force app, see who's left a review, and reach out to those people as the first potential customers for your new consulting service.

▶ **Leverage online learning platforms.** See what courses are hot on e-learning platforms like Udemy. You can launch similar courses with a twist (if you have the skills people want to learn) or start a stand-alone company that serves a similar need. Mark Price did a little of both with his company Devslopes. Price started out teaching people how to code through his Udemy course. After teaching more than 40,000 students, Price launched his own learn-to-code SaaS company in 2017, Devslopes, and got 130 students paying him $20/month in the first month, for a total new recurring revenue of $2,600. Within three months that had scaled to $10K in monthly recurring revenue.

▶ **Eavesdrop on the influencers.** What are celebrities and people with 1M+ social media influencers talking about? You'll often see them posting from their private jets and exotic Airbnb locations. Guesty feeds off the back of the whale that is Airbnb by offering property management software for your rental property. AirDNA does the same by giving you rental data on Airbnb listings. JetSmarter tapped into the private jet community by creating a hub where people can rent out their jet or ride in someone else's. Both companies service high-net-worth clients in an already-established marketplace. Brilliant.

Also study blogs in a space you want to go after. Which companies are they writing about?

▶ **Look at what's trending on Kickstarter campaigns and other crowdfunding sites.** If something gets overfunded you know that's a hot space and things are trending generally in that direction. Consumers gave Liberty+ Soundbuds more than $1.7M via Kickstarter. Combine that with Apple AirPods, and all the other companies playing in the sound/voice space like Google Home and Amazon Echo. The upward numbers are a strong signal that sound/audio is a thriving market. All of these agencies help you build Alexa Skills to deliver your audio content to consumers with Alexa devices in your home. Their consulting agency is the pickax to the voice/audio gold mine.

IPG MEDIA LAB	ISL	isobar	MATCHBOX
IPG Media Lab	**ISL (iStrategyLabs)**	**Isobar**	**Matchbox**
The IPG Media Lab is a creative technology agency that builds conversational experiences for leading brands.	ISL invents digital & physical experiences for the world's biggest brands. Our designers, developers, marketers and makers build everything from apps, to connected devices, to wildly creative campaigns that reach audiences globally.	Isobar is a global full-service digital agency driven to solve complex client challenges with ideas that transform businesses and brands.	Matchbox is an experienced voice interaction design and development studio, with several published Alexa skills and tools on developing for Alexa.
Learn more »	Learn more »	Learn more »	Learn more »

▶ **Scan Patreon.com to see which digital products are hot.** Creators in everything from comics to podcasts publish how much they're making each month. This will give you a sense of what's working and what's not. At the time of this writing, I could see in Patreon's podcasting section that *Chapo Trap House* is making more than $100K per month. Go to their creator page and study why their patrons are donating to them. Listen to their content and figure out why it's so popular. This will help give you ideas about things you might build to help them serve their audiences. If you want to do something in the tech space, watch which ProductHunt.com products get the most up votes.

EXPLORE CREATORS		Top 20 creators in Podcasts
Video & Film		
Comics		
Podcasts	**S&S** is creating The Sword and Scale Podcast	12705 patrons
Comedy		
Crafts & DIY		
Music	**Chapo Trap House** is creating Chapo Trap House Podcast	21863 patrons $97,560 / month
Drawing & Painting		
Games		
Science	**Ralph Garman** is creating a daily audio show!	6904 patrons
Dance & Theater		
Writing		
Animation		
Photography	**Mike Ward Sous Écoute** is creating a Podcast	2929 patrons
Education		
All		

Ask yourself: What are these business models dependent on? All artists on Patreon have to deal with patrons who churn every month. So what if you built a Patreon add-on that helps them manage churn? You can say,

"Hey, podcaster, each month one hundred of your patrons paying $50 a month churn, so you lose $5K a month. If you use our little tool it will help you save 20 percent or 10 percent of that lost revenue. Do you want to try it?" That's a potential pickax to content creators on Patreon because they're all selling to digital subscribers who churn. It's a universal problem.

When you look at industries through this lens the ideas will start flying. Your task is to validate the ideas that others say they want—that tip of the iceberg. Once you know it's legit, start building the hidden part that will keep the whole operation running. Or sell add-ons that ride the whale. You want to grab a market that's already proven and sell into it. It should be dead obvious—gold miners need pickaxes; iPhone users need cases; Keurig owners need coffee cups. Here are some ways you can suss out whether an idea or industry is generating solid revenue:

- ▶ Use Siftery.com to see what tools companies are paying to use inside their own businesses. You can spot winners before everyone else knows about them.
- ▶ Use app store "top gross sales" lists to see if consumers are paying for apps.
- ▶ Use liquor license sites to get revenue data for the bars around you (liquor, wine, beer).
- ▶ Use investor relations links on websites to see sales of public companies.

The beautiful thing about this business approach is that once you've validated your idea, you don't have to jump through hoops to convince people it's worthwhile. Others have already done the hard work of building up the market. Now you're just building on that whale and enjoying all the upside.

Look at video. Facebook's newsfeed algorithm alone shows how much video's prominence has grown in the past year. Video marketing is the future, especially if you want to reach people on social media. Well, creating videos is hard. That's why companies like Vidyard and Videoblocks are so successful. Vidyard has raised $70M in funding, has 132 employees, and passed $8M in 2016 revenues, all from making it easy to buy and use stock videos. Videoblocks is in the same space, with $20M raised, $16M in 2016 revenue, and more than 150,000 customers.

COPY PATTERNS FROM THE PAST

Another powerful way to find your pickax idea is to apply successful business patterns from the past to today's hot markets.

DroneDeploy did this when they started selling drone software. Since launching in 2013 they've raised $30M, passing one thousand customers and $1M in annual revenues. Although they're in a new market, they're essentially doing what app developers started doing a decade ago: printing money off software that runs on the hottest new gadgets.

Study the greats to find history's lucrative patterns. Read biographies of successful businesspeople and identify the behaviors and strategies that got them to the top. You can also turn to documentaries—like *American Genius* and *The Men Who Built America*—to learn how pioneers built businesses.

The Acquisition + Pickax Double Punch

Ted Turner built a brilliant pickax empire by making money off the TV gold mine. Turner knew advertisers—the gold miners—were eager to reach consumers through TV. But he also recognized that TV wouldn't be valuable to them unless people's eyeballs were glued to it. So he set out to build amazing content.

Turner was obsessed with keeping people watching: he covered the Iraq War behind enemy lines; he bought sports teams partly so he could own their telecasting rights; he acquired World Championship Wrestling (WCW) and revived the audience for wrestling; he even made bank off of sitcom reruns and classic movies. Every one of Turner's assets worked as a pickax that he'd then sell through to advertisers. He even gave advertisers a way to spend more money with him through branded content inside of his shows.

Turner started with a local Atlanta TV station in 1970 and went on to create a huge portfolio of networks by acquiring local stations. Then he used that leverage to keep growing. When he fought his way into the Satcom 2 launch it gave him a satellite connection that let him turn CNN into a worldwide distribution network. Now he could reach every consumer's home.

Anyone today can copy the patterns that Turner leveraged to build his empire. He did two things on repeat:

▶ He grew his business through acquisitions. Turner understood
that it's much easier to buy up companies than it is to build one
from scratch.

▶ He figured out what pickaxes he could sell (advertising) to the
gold miners (advertisers) who were eager to profit from a hot,
growing advertising space (TV).

Whatever your business or industry, remember that the gold mine is the
hot trend. That's the part of the iceberg above the water that everyone sees
and wants. The pickax is the part of the iceberg below the water—the part
nobody can see but that the hot trend relies on to function.

ROCKEFELLER AND HIS SULFUR PROBLEM: WORK A LIABILITY INTO YOUR GROWTH PLAN

John D. Rockefeller is another business icon who made his fortune through
acquisitions. He took some major risks by taking on liabilities as he bought
up assets, but his plan worked.

Most people remember, and fixate on, the 1911 Supreme Court order for
Rockefeller to dissolve his Standard Oil Company for being in violation of
antitrust laws. That's one part of the story. What most don't realize is that
amid the accusations of price discrimination, spying on competitors, and
the like, Rockefeller was revolutionizing the oil industry.

In the late nineteenth and early twentieth centuries, the hot market was
light. Everyone wanted light in their house via flame—this was before
Edison—and they needed kerosene to get it. So kerosene was the pickax
that the gold miners (anyone who wanted to "sell light") were after.

Part of Rockefeller's strategy was to buy up mines full of oil that could
not be processed into usable kerosene because of its high sulfur content.
He took a risk, hoping he could find a chemist to get the sulfur out of the
oil. It worked. To solve his problem Rockefeller hired Hermann Frasch, a
chemist who had invented a desulfurization method to process oil in his
own mines. He incentivized Frasch by paying him in shares of Standard Oil
stock. The net result was enormous wealth for Frasch, as his method un-
locked more and more usable oil for Rockefeller and his company.*

---

* https://dash.harvard.edu/bitstream/handle/1/4686409/RWP11–008_Scherer.pdf.

When building a business today, think about how you can work a liability into your growth plan. If you can buy an asset or a group of assets that have one common liability like sulfur, and you're confident in your ability to solve that liability, you can unlock loads of value. That's the essence of private equity today. And it's the essence of a pattern from history that you should copy. The Top Inbox had a $100K liability on its books when I bought the company. I knew I could solve that liability by renegotiating it. I did and unlocked free money. More on that later.

Shrink the Time Gap

If you're in the fast food business, or food or processing in general, read *McDonald's: Behind the Golden Arches* or watch the movie *The Founder*. It's incredible to see how Ray Kroc and the McDonald brothers got McDonald's laid out so they could deliver a hamburger every few seconds with the smallest possible footprint.

They would actually map out their restaurant layout on a basketball court with chalk to perfect their process of getting a burger from the point where the consumer orders it at the front counter to delivering it to them, as fast as possible. Their obsession with setting up this system and being so maniacal about saving consumers time was a pattern that they went all in on.

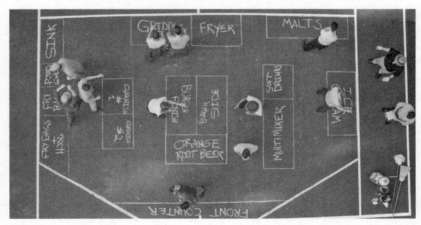

The pickax to the restaurant industry is systems. Every fast food restaurant's biggest expense outside of humans and food is typically renting the space. So you have to figure out how to do the most in the smallest amount of space. Today there are armies of software, tools, and consultants that sell restaurant layout plans, restaurant systems, and machines that consolidate the griddle and the fryer with the malt machine and the soft-drink machine to make it more efficient and take up one tenth of the space.

2018 GOLD RUSH? SELL TO AMAZON AND EBAY SELLERS?

Today Amazon is bringing that same level of obsession to saving people time. It's building innovations in truck delivery systems, putting robots in warehouses, dispatching drones to pick up items from warehouses and deliver them to houses—all with Jeff Bezos's singular focus of getting products to consumers faster so that they'll buy more. And that's why he's the richest man alive.

Feed off that whale if you're in this space, which is essentially supply chain management. Also think about saving sellers time. Many people are doing this by selling software to Amazon and eBay sellers. Victor Levitin created CrazyLister in 2013 in response to sellers' frustration over the complicated process of posting items on eBay. CrazyLister lets sellers drag and drop photos, text, and design elements to customize their item listings. When they're done they just copy and paste the code that CrazyLister generates into eBay's back end. Within five years Levitin grew the company to $25K in monthly recurring revenue, two thousand customers, eight employees, and $600K in venture capital funding. His drag-and-drop software also works for Amazon now. There is also a whole breed of consultants that support this industry. However you approach it, if you can figure out how to shrink the time gap for people on either side of the sales process—for sellers getting their products up or customers who want those products in hand—you're going to win.

There's something to learn—and copy—for every successful business in history, no matter how antiquated they seem. Just look for the patterns that kept getting them the wins. They're always lurking in plain sight.

Become an Expert, or Find One

Scouting for pickax ideas can get addictive. There's so much opportunity everywhere you look, but you're likely to have the most success in an industry you know, at least a little. So start by identifying hot markets in your world.

Tucker Max decoded a pickax to book publishing when he became an author. He realized there's a huge market of people (gold miners) who want to establish themselves as thought leaders so they can charge higher consulting and speaking fees (gold mine). Publishing a book is a silver bullet to accomplishing that. The problem: most people don't have the time or expertise required to become an author. Max immediately spotted his pickax cash cow and got to work launching Book in a Box (now Scribe Writing) in 2015. Since then the company has worked with more than five hundred authors and passed $11.3M in revenue as of September 2017. They charge clients a minimum of $25K to write their book for them, in their voice. All the client has to do is answer a few interview questions. Max realized that Book in a Box had the potential to be more lucrative than his own best-selling books, which is why he spends more time on the business these days than on his own writing.

If you're in media, look at trends on Facebook, BuzzFeed, Google, and other big media companies. If you're in the engineering space, look at what Boeing is doing, or what Rolls-Royce is creating. Play on your playing field and make sure you have at least some expertise there.

Then again—there's always room to learn new things. A great way to develop expertise that you don't already have exposure to is by interviewing people in the space. It's one of the reasons I created my podcast. It allows me to quickly tap into the brains of people who are very smart in spaces I may not know much about, understand what they think is trending and what will be hot a year from now, and dive in. I'm doing this right now with cryptocurrencies. I've had many of the top cryptocurrency experts on my podcast, asking them where they see the industry going, where they're spending their time, what they're investing in. Their feedback gives me ideas on what the bottom part of the iceberg might be.

If podcasting appeals to you, it really is a great gateway to meeting top thinkers. Don't worry about starting from scratch. Before I had more than six million downloads, I had zero. The trick when you're launching is not to tell your prospective guests that they'll be on your first episode. If you do they'll just fixate on the fact that you have no audience. Instead, say, "My show will have a million downloads by X date." Experts and people you want to connect with will love that kind of confidence. And it will pull them in. Once you get them live they actually help create a self-fulfilling prophecy for building your audience since they're big names themselves.

There's rarely a magic bullet for immersing yourself in a new industry—but Toptal is pretty close. You can know nothing about a particular business area, but post your project on Toptal and they will recommend experts for you to work with. So let's say you want to develop an app that helps salons book appointments more efficiently. You can post that exact sentence on Toptal and they'll help you find mobile developers. It's that simple.

If you have absolutely zero experience in something, you'll have to put in extra time and energy to find a Toptal freelancer because you'll need to learn along with them. But the beautiful thing about doing this is that the person you hire ends up teaching you more and more about the space—a space you knew nothing about. So the next time you work on a project, you'll do it more efficiently. Your work will get easier the more you do it, and your returns will compound over time.

5

THE NEW RICH ARSENAL

"Fear is free to create, which is what makes it so profitable."

—Nathan Latka

My advice in this book boils down to helping you do one core thing: set yourself up to have an unfair advantage against others.

That's what will get you membership into the New Rich.

By "unfair" I don't mean dishonest. You'll just have such a major lead on your peers and competitors that they won't possibly be able to catch up with you. It will be like they're trying to wrestle someone two weight classes above them. They'll have no chance at a win.

But you don't get that advantage overnight. Aside from taking up the strategies in the surrounding chapters, there are skills you'll need to master that will get you into that higher weight class.

Don't worry—I'm not about to bore you with Business 101 crap. You already know most of that stuff, and if you don't, there are plenty of books that will teach you. The key tactics that the New Rich leverage do involve universal business skills, but they use them in very specific ways to get what they want.

It starts with masterful persuasion. Most people use their persuasion skills, or muscle, in the wrong ways every day. They try to persuade people to do stupid stuff, like getting their boss to give them a better office or their Facebook friends to like a post.

The trick is to use your persuasion muscle for things that directly correlate to freeing up your time. Think about it: freedom is what most of us want. We want control over our own lives. The quickest and easiest way to get that freedom is by persuading others to do things that free up your time.

Once you hit the sweet spot of having others doing the time-consuming stuff, you can focus on generating more cash flow for yourself. There you'll need the art of **negotiation**.

Then things really get fun and lucrative. Calendar free, big wins negotiated, you'll start valuing your time more because it's all yours. That's when **productivity** kicks in. Once you've put a higher value on your time, you'll realize you're worth $X per hour, or $Y per week. You'll know what amount of money gets you out of bed. This clarity will help you see what you should focus on today, and why it's where you should be spending your time.

SHOULD YOU USE FEAR TO SELL?

This is not a crash course on persuasion. But I will share the specific persuasion techniques I used to build incredible wealth at a very young age. I target one thing: fear.

I do this because our emotions drive most of our purchases, and fear is the strongest among them. When we fear something, we'll do anything to fix the worry. The most profitable salespeople know this and they feed off our fear by selling the fix. Think about it: the reason you bought renter's insurance, car insurance, and even insurance for your laptop is because you're afraid of what *could*, in theory, go wrong.

A lot of people still try to persuade using reason, and it puts them at a major disadvantage. Look at Hillary Clinton. She tried to use rational facts— real facts—to win an election, and lost to someone who used and said what appealed to people's emotions. You have to go where the emotions go.

This may sound slimy, but it doesn't have to be. People today are less rational and more emotional than ever, but it's your decision whether to use that opportunity for good or for bad. Sell a great product and you can profit off fear without the moral dilemma.

The key is to tell a story that taps into fear—one that says, "This could happen to you." Then sell businesses or consumers the vitamin.

We all take this bait every day. We buy fish oil supplements in case we ever get cancer, a jump starter in case our car ever breaks down, AppleCare in case we break our iPhones, fire extinguishers in case there's a fire. Look around you right now. You can probably spot at least one item you bought and haven't touched in the last year because someone made you think, "I need this in case of XYZ."

I've found seven fear principles that are most directly tied to driving sales and cash flow. This is not a definitive list of persuasion tactics. There are plenty of other things you can do to, say, convince your partner to stay with you, or your kid to do his homework. The focus here is on getting people to buy from you, or getting them to do what you want as it relates to cash in and out of your pocket.

When thinking about how your business ties into these, it's not so much about how you can blatantly use one of these fears to sell your product. Rather, if you understand which fear you're catering to, you can make sure your messaging reflects that. So if you were selling into Fear of the Unknown, you'd use words and phrases like "hidden," "clever," "never before seen" versus selling into Fear of Missing Out with words like "too late," "few left," "regret it later," etc.

Fear of Missing Out: I mentioned earlier that the quickest way to free up your calendar is to get others to do the time-consuming stuff for you. When I'm recruiting someone to join my team I'm subtly using fear-based persuasion—in this case the fear of missing out—to persuade them to work with me. The pitch sounds something like this: "Hey, the company is growing really fast. We launched three months ago, we're now doing $100K, and we're going to do a million by the end of the year. I want you in on the ground floor, but in exchange for getting in early we don't have a huge budget. Can you do this for a little bit cheaper? Can you take this part of my system and handle it so I don't have to handle it anymore (e.g., podcast editing or data entry on GetLatka.com)?" The message is, "Don't miss out on this big company I'm building. Get in early."

It's the same concept when you're using fear-based persuasion to drive sales. You see this a ton with conference organizers who say, "There are only ten tickets left, buy today before they're all out. . . . Buy today before prices go up." Many digital products will use the "open cart" technique, saying, "Hey, we have an open cart, it closes

Friday. Make sure you buy before we close the cart. We don't know if we're ever going to open it again." You can use this tactic on anything that won't be around forever—an event, an online course happening on specific days, or services you may be offering for a limited time.

Fear of the Unknown: There is huge earning potential when you tap into people's fear of the unknown. Look at everything from insurance to Band-Aids. Let's even ignore health insurance for now. Billion-dollar industries have been built around selling insurance for things like your car, home, and phone. Businesses pay for general liability insurance, board insurance, workers' compensation insurance. Stores offer add-on insurance for everything from toys to refrigerators. Insurance aside, we buy flashlights and batteries in case of blackouts. We stock our bathrooms and glove compartments with first aid kits.

We spend tons of money triggered by what-if thinking. And companies love to heighten those what-if scenarios, those fears. The best advertisers are masters at planting "what if" questions in our heads that we never would have thought of. Once we hear their message, it feels urgent. A Tylenol ad might say, "Heading out on that beach vacation? Don't forget Tylenol in your pocket to make sure headaches don't ruin your trip."

Current events are fodder for new what-if fears, too. Look at security software alone. Vladimir Putin and Russia have been the number one reason that KnowBe4.com has grown revenues of its hacker prevention software. Before Russian hacks took center stage in the 2016 election cycle, KnowBe4 did $20M in sales. They broke $60M in 2017 and saw direct correlations between their revenue growth and any widespread hacks like Target credit card breaches, Chipotle chip reader intrusions, or Russians hacking the US government.

Fear for Your Life: Think every life insurance policy ever sold. Every lawyer offering services around writing wills. Companies today are getting more creative about tapping into this fear, too. Forever Labs sells the ability to store your stem cells for $2K up front and $250 a month. They'd just launched when I interviewed them and had already made $400K in sales. They're alleviating customers' fear for their lives by saying, "Hey, if you ever get cancer, we can use your stored stem cells to grow new, clean cells outside of your body and then use them to help you heal."

Tons of products also tap into our fear for our life: Tracking devices that skiers and snowboarders carry so searchers can find them in a life-threatening situation. Fold-out window ladders in case of fire. Second parachutes designed into skydiving backpacks. Oxygen masks in airplanes.

What's the first thing you do when you find a spot on your skin and think, "Oh my God, it's cancer"? You Google it, and sites like WebMD .com pop up. They're swimming in cash by preying on people's worry that something is wrong with their body. They also overlap with the next fear. . . .

Fear for Your Health: Many Fear for Your Life ideas also tie into Fear for Your Health. Health insurance speaks for itself. Why am I paying $800 a month for a plan that covers only catastrophic events when the deductible is $1,500 and the out-of-pocket cap is $5K? Because: *What if I get cancer? What if I get in a car crash that leaves me debilitated?* Millions of us pay to alleviate that what-if fear. That's why health care is a trillion-dollar industry.

Vitamins and supplements, gym memberships, gym trainers, and protein bars—all tap into our fear for our health, and our life.

You'll probably find these last three fears most relevant to your work:

Fear of Losing Freedom: The entire market of productivity tools feeds off this fear. Best-selling books like Tim Ferriss's *4-Hour Workweek* and David Allen's *Getting Things Done* also tap into it. We're afraid of somebody else controlling us—controlling our time, making us work eighty-hour weeks, putting a cap on our earning potential. We want our time back, and we want our freedom back. That's why you're reading this book.

Fear of Loneliness: This is why social networks have taken off. They prey on your fear of being lonely by arbitrarily making you feel important with those little red notifications. They make you feel other humans are thinking about you, and it's been widely argued that those little dopamine hits are not helpful at all.

Selling off the fear of loneliness goes beyond social media, too. Think of all the dating apps. Every one of them taps into our fear as we think, "I'm never going to find a friend," "I'm never going to find a partner," or "I'm never going to go on another date." Then we fire up our apps, hoping to meet someone.

Looking at physical products, one can even argue that makeup companies prey on people's fear of loneliness. Most people wear makeup to look their best and feel confident. What if you walk out the door *not* feeling that way? Would you worry that people won't be as attracted to you or your energy? Makeup companies rely on that fear when they market to you.

Pfizer absolutely makes bank on men's fear of loneliness by selling Viagra. The same goes for any product that promises to help us physically connect with others, or feel confident and create sexual energy—colognes and perfumes, hair products, lingerie, teeth whitening kits. . . .

Fear of Failure: This is such a universal feeling that everything from software to shoes can tap into our fear of failure. Say you decide to run a triathlon with your friends. You want to make sure you have the right shoes so you don't get blisters or twist your ankle while running for eighteen miles. So you just do it—you buy the best shoes out there. If you're launching a business you might spend thousands to alleviate your fear of failure: coaching services, online courses on how to pitch investors, top lawyers.

Your odds of success spike if whatever you're selling taps into multiple fears: People will pay for gym memberships out of fear for their health, fear of failure, and fear of loneliness if they worry they'll never meet someone unless they get into shape. They'll shell out on an expensive business conference out of fear of missing out, fear of losing freedom, and fear of failure if they believe the conference will help them make connections and take the next step with their business.

Fear is a powerful, powerful persuader. It's obviously not the only persuasion tool out there, but it's the most powerful motivator you can use to drive cash flow, even over the rosey-dosey "make the world a better place" sales points. It's one reason charities that want to change the world might find it hard to raise money from regular consumers, but businesses selling headache medicine, life insurance, stem cell storage, or shoes can charge a premium even though they're not changing the world or curing cancer.

Speaking of fear, one of the reasons you lose negotiations is when you fear you're going to lose the negotiation. That's why it's best to start negotiations when that fear doesn't exist. In other words, negotiate when you don't have to.

NEGOTIATE WHEN YOU DON'T HAVE TO

You'll be negotiating deals all the time as you venture into New Rich territory. I'll get into tactics for handling those scenarios later (chapter 13 shows screenshots on how I sold my first company). As you're starting out, I want to help you use negotiation to create instant cash flow wins today. The more cash you have, the more freedom you have to grow those golden geese.

The most immediate way to free up cash is by driving down your big expenses. I'm going to guess your biggest costs are your rent or mortgage, car payment, and/or student loans. Most people feel trapped into paying these bills, but they're more flexible than you think. I'm not talking about moving to a cheaper place, buying a clunker car, or consolidating your loans. That's all obvious stuff. Assuming you're already living within your means, you can keep your current setup and still negotiate down most of your bills (if you work at Starbucks and lease a BMW you have bigger problems than I can help you with).

Let's say you've got enough money in the bank to cover two or three months' rent. You're not feeling financial pressure, but you'd still prefer to pay less than the full amount. That creates leverage for you. And the best time to use leverage is when you don't have to use it. So if you're reading this right now, I want you to negotiate when you don't have to. Send an email to your landlord that simply says the following:

Subject line: Money Troubles

I'm going to have trouble hitting the rent payment this month. Is there anything you can do to help me?

· · · · ·

That's it. Click SEND.

What you're doing here is forcing the other side to think about their opportunity cost. You're creating doubt. And like fear, doubt is free to create, which is why it's used so profitably.

In this case, your landlord's opportunity costs are huge. Evicting you will be stressful and time-consuming. The apartment might be empty for a couple months while she looks for new tenants, and she'll lose the full rent amount in that time. She'll also have to spend money painting the walls and cleaning up the place before new tenants can come in.

Looking at those turnover costs, your landlord will not want you to stop paying rent and she will not want you to move out. She understands the value in keeping you. So when she gets your email she's likely to give you a break on rent to avoid those big turnover costs. If she doesn't lower your rent you might get an extension on paying it, or a discount in return for paying it back the following month. Any of these outcomes is a win! You get more time to pay, or you pay less. By simply creating that doubt you can gain yourself some leverage and save money.

The email above can also work if you own your home and have a mortgage with a small lender. It's a big deal for your loan officer if you default on your loan. There are processes and procedures. It's stressful. He has to report the issue to his boss and he doesn't want to look bad. You won't have much leverage if your mortgage is through a megacorporation, but if you have a personal contact for your loan that person is likely to work with you on taking money off your payments. Everything I'm saying also applies to your car loan or student loans.

Another option is to do something similar when you're renewing your lease. Your landlord will inevitably want to raise your rent with the new contract (I always do). When he tries, negotiate like hell. I have six tenants living in one of my properties and each pays $375/month. When their leases were up for renewal I tried increasing everyone's rent by $40/month, which is a pretty critical percentage hike. They negotiated and would only go up by $10/month. I went for it because I didn't want to deal with the trouble of finding six new renters. You'll always have this leverage over a landlord. Use it.

The critical detail here is to do these things *when you don't have to.* Don't wait until your bank account is at $0 to tell your landlord you're not going to make rent that month. That gives them all the leverage. Do it when you don't need the help. Then, if you really can't get them to give you a discount you'll still pay like normal. That will actually strengthen your relationship with your landlord because you'll have underpromised and overdelivered. This isn't about lying. It's about creating a perception that you can use to your advantage.

Negotiating when you don't have to also gives you options. Creating options goes beyond haggling over bills, but as you practice freeing up cash you'll start adopting this mindset for everything you do. You'll look for ways to create new options in how you spend your time and money. You'll be more inclined to make unconventional choices so you can get closer to achieving what you want.

I've taken this concept so far that when someone asks me today what I do, I say, "I can't really tell you." That's a good thing, because if they don't know what I do, they can't attack me. It's the difference between being a round ball with no edges versus a square. People know how to hit a square. They know your edges. They know what you're doing. A circle has no corners. It's not defined. It can roll anywhere. You want to be that. You want to be unpredictable. It gives you incredible leverage because you can become the center of your competitors' interest. They'll want to know where you're going, what you're doing. They'll worry if you're going to compete with them. You want all of that leverage and you do that by creating options. You need to be able to go in any direction, or in as many directions as you possibly can, given the number of things that can happen to you in business and in life.

I play with creating options for my podcast all the time. When CEOs reach out to me asking about sponsor opportunities (happens weekly), I usually don't have a spot for them. Sponsors are booked out months in advance so I could easily say I don't have openings. But why would I do that? Same goes for anyone working in an agency model when you get new client inquiries, or any business that chases leads. Even if you don't have room for the client or sponsor, or you don't want them for any reason, let the conversation happen and see where it goes.

My response to anyone who asks about sponsorship is, "Yes, tell me what you're thinking." From there, I work them to some terms that outline what they'd be willing to pay per episode, how many episodes they want, and what return they want on that spend. And because I don't *need* them as a sponsor I can be unforgiving with my pricing.

Once I've taken the conversation to the finish line and know my options, I can decide if I want to make room for that CEO as a sponsor. It's a much better situation to be in than if I'd shut them down right off the bat.

That's a big blind spot for people. They shut down opportunities they're not interested in rather than letting the conversation play out. But remember, your best analysis is done when you have people's best and final offers in hand, whether that's employees you want to recruit, CEOs you're trying to sell your company to, or customers you're trying to sell a product to. You want to be as close to the finish line as possible before you decide on anything so that you have the best and most accurate data possible. Do this even if you don't want the deal. Remember, your best position in a negotiation is when you don't need it to work out. Your upper-hand approach may get you terms so good that you'll change your mind.

HOW THE NEW RICH USE TIME DIFFERENTLY

You're going to have a lot more time on your hands as you start mastering the concepts in this book. Time to dream up your golden goose, obsess over the systems that will keep it going, execute, and then create another one. Every golden goose you set in motion will open up more options for you.

Most people, though, won't accomplish anything. They'll get charged up by a project's potential, obsess over their to-do lists, then feel paralyzed by the enormity of it all. Or at best, they'll get through 10 percent of what needs to be done before they quit.

To-do lists ruin us. We try and fail to cross things off them, then we think: If we can't get through one day's worth of tasks, how can we get that giant life-changing thing done in just a few months? It's because we overestimate what we can do in a day and underestimate what we can do in a year.

Your brain short-circuits in the face of a huge project if you don't organize your thinking. You have to sort your ideas and group them into year-long terms. Then execute them weekly and make sure you live in the day so you don't miss out on life. So you're going to:

Dream in Decades ⟶ Think in Years ⟶ Work in Weeks ⟶ Live in Days

Dream in Decades

This is where you let your mind wander. Find a quiet space and let ideas build up as you dream about all the golden geese—and their golden eggs—that you want in your life. Think long, and think concretely: picture where you want to be in ten years, what your business, life, and home will look like.

Do whatever you need to actually feel that success. In the last chapter, I warned against the dangers of letting rewards motivate you, but if you have to focus on the golden eggs to feel that happiness in this dreaming phase, do it. Just make sure to aim for the ambitious eggs that are way out in your future.

I like winning; it's what motivates me, so I tie my big goals to mini-competitions with other people who are my age. Some of my private mini-competitions right now are:

▶ I want my first book to sell more copies than Ryan Holiday's first book (200,000+).
▶ I want to build a software company bigger than Mathilde Collin's Front ($900K/month).
▶ I want to build a real estate business bigger than Nate Paul's

World Class Holdings (thirty-year-old in Austin with $1B in real estate assets).

Think in Years

Remember when I told you in chapter 3 to take your big, audacious goals and break them down into systems? That's thinking in years. You're planning every part of the twelve-month layer cake that will churn out your golden eggs. This can be either new systems you're going to build or current systems you're going to improve. Also see which systems you can layer on top of each other for maximum output. Building that connective tissue between multiple systems is how you make $1 + 1 = 5$.

I'm doing this now as I make plans to launch a new software company. I plan to build it through mergers and acquisitions, and I'm figuring out the systems I need to set up to get the company off the ground. I've figured out I need:

► A fund-raising system for bringing in investors. I will contribute a significant amount of my own money, but others will want in, too. When my partners and I were raising capital for Heyo in 2011, our fund-raising system involved putting together a one-pager with a quick overview of the business's financials and market (you can see the document at NathanLatka.com/surprise). Then we made an Excel list of thirty or forty prospective investors and emailed the document to each person on that list with a hard closing date. Once one or two people committed I reached out to the others on the list and said, "If you're curious about what it's like to work with me, I can introduce you to two or three others who have already committed to invest. Would you like the intro?" They ended up selling each other and we ended up oversubscribed. We only wanted to raise $500K and we got $550K.

► A system to go prospect and find companies to purchase. Here is a screenshot of the Excel file I use to track all my deals. You can see I rank them by most likely to acquire, company type, whether it's a company I should buy or sell to, their user base, the last action I took with them, next steps, and what I think the acquisition price might be. That's the basic system I use to find companies to purchase.

Likley to acquire?	I	L	Notes/Type		Type	Link	users	Action		Next Step	Acq. Price	F
3			B2B Leads		Buy	https://gainful.io/		Emailed 1/27/2017			$22,000	0
10		In	Dhruv chatting w		Buy			Emailed 10/28/2017		Dhruv chatting w	$100k	$
Done Deal			Direct		Buy		35,094	Emailed 6/20/16			$1,000	
Done Deal			Direct		Buy	https://chrome.go	7000	Emailed 10/28/2016			$100	
Done Deal			Direct		Buy	https://chrome.go	39493	Emailed 7/5/2016			-$15k	F
7			churn saas reduc									
		1	Direct		Buy			Called 1/9/2018				
			B2B leads									
8			Direct		5/5/2016	https://chrome.go	378,000 users 1/	Emailed 10/29/2017		com	1.4 cents per ma	$
8			Direct		5/5/2016		11984	Emailed 8/7/2017			$1,200,000	
7			Direct			https://chrome.go	1700	Emailed 1/27/2017			$10,000	
7		S	Direct		sold scripted to S			Emailed 8/7/2017		He's holding on t	$200k	
7			Direct		Buy	https://chrome.go	2337	Emailed 1/27/2017		Asked Trever Fa	like nothing	
7			Direct					Emailed 8/7/2017			$250k total rever	
7			Direct			https://chrome.go		Emailed 8/7/2017		One of them goir		
6			Direct			https://chrome.go	15,000	Called 1/27/2017		He's thinking for		
5			Direct		Buy	https://chrome.go	98000	Emailed 11/10/2016				
4			Direct		not sure							
4			Direct			https://chrome.go	26109					
4			Direct			https://chrome.go	3439	Meet in SF, 212-729-7551				
1			Direct		5/5/2016	https://chrome.go	1107530 users					1
1			Direct		5/5/2016	https://chrome.go	54300					

► Contract boilerplates on hand to get multiple deals done quickly.
► An execution framework that systematizes what I'll do with a company I've just purchased so it can grow.

Each one of these is a part of my layer cake, and I can get them in motion within the year. Once that happens, I can start to understand what that cake might taste like when it's fully baked. For my software company, that fully baked cake tastes like a new revenue stream to the tune of about $1M per year. And the systems that pump out that cash flow will allow me to invest more into the company and to continue to build that layer cake into an asset that grows for the rest of my life.

Work in Weeks

This is where the huge dreams mesh with reality. You know what you want to do in a decade, and in a year. You know the systems you need to set in motion to make it happen. Now, zoom in on the day-to-day for each system. This is when you obsess over the details. If you're in a project's development stage, what do you have to do from week to week to get it off the ground? If your systems are already running, what needs to happen every week to keep the project going and growing?

I take notes on all of my systems that include the details and time required for each step. When a system starts occupying too much of my time, or I just think we need to double down on a system for it to be most effective, I use those notes to figure out how to automate it and add it to the layer cake. That involves either finding software to help me execute or hiring someone to take over for me.

My system for booking podcast guests used to take up four to five hours of my week. In the time I was doing the work I wrote hyperdetailed process notes that I then passed on to Aaron, the person I hired to take over the job. Aaron is incentivized by $12 per booked episode.

When Aaron first started I showed him my system and asked him to focus on making it better as he used it. He takes notes on his improvements so that the next person can use that process if Aaron ever leaves me. Now I don't spend any time on getting interview guests. It just happens. A beautiful system added to the layer cake. The best part: the more interviews that get booked, the more my wallet and Aaron's wallet win.

Live in Days

This is where the work thrives or dies because of our dysfunctional to-do lists. Most things on our list never get done. We add to them and let tasks roll over to the next day, and the cycle never ends. I used to put my to-do list in Apple Notes. It was in one file and it would get longer and longer as the weeks passed.

The big reason this happens is because we don't set up a mental framework for removing to-do items from our list. I'm not talking about crossing off a task when it's done—I mean killing the items that sit on our list day after day, week after week.

I now evaluate my to-do list the same way I do my closet: the thirty-day rule. If I haven't worn it in the last thirty days, and I don't plan to wear it in the next thirty, it's out. Same goes for my list. If I haven't done it, and don't see myself doing it, within thirty days, it's gone. It's a black-and-white decision. It takes too much energy to decide what to do with those lingering items if you don't have a rule for dealing with them. You have to take a hot knife to that piece of butter and cut through it quickly.

When you live in days you're focusing on the two or three things you can get done in one day that will help you reach what you want to accomplish in weeks. That work will feed up to the systems that you're building over the course of a year. That's it. If something on your to-do list isn't achievable today, and it doesn't feed up to your weekly and yearly targets, cut it before the thirty-day rule even applies.

Making sure your daily work feeds into your systems will also help you avoid that false sense of momentum so many people create when they do a bunch of easy tasks all day. They get the thrill of crossing those things off their list, but by the end of the day they're sapped and never get to the big, tough stuff.

The quick rule I follow for myself here is to always tackle the big stuff first, right in the morning. When your decision tank for the day is full you have plenty of energy and total focus on the bigger picture—what you want to accomplish this week, this year, this decade.

I know someone who is working on launching a career as a voiceover artist. His plan looks like this:

> ▶ In the next **decade**, he will have a full client base and will bring in a high six-figure annual income from his VO work.
> ▶ This **year**, he plans to secure ten regular clients and get an agent. To accomplish the year's goal, he's setting five systems in motion:
>   ■ System 1: Record/produce demos for the genres he plans to work in: audiobooks, radio/TV commercials, corporate videos.
>   ■ System 2: Build a portfolio website to showcase his demos.
>   ■ System 3: Audition for thirty gigs a week through websites like Voices.com and Voices123.com.
>   ■ System 4: Reach out to ten agents a week.
>   ■ System 5: Reach out to five audiobook publishers a week.
> ▶ Each day of the **week** he'll focus on building out one of these systems. If one system has to launch before he can start another (demos before website, website before auditions and agent/publisher outreach), he'll dedicate his week to building each layer of the cake that will ultimately provide him with year after year of voiceover success.

As you hustle all year to hit those big goals you'll eventually want to step back and see how you're doing. But it's cheesy to think about opening up your black Moleskine journal right before New Year's Eve to "analyze" what you've accomplished. No one actually does that. I don't care how many best-selling productivity books you've read.

So here's the secret to recognizing what you've accomplished over the past year without having to measure everything. You just need to measure one thing: money in the bank. If that number has gone up in a year, then double-check that you're living the life you want by asking yourself: *Do I feel good?*

If you answer yes to both, welcome to the New Rich.

HOW THE NEW RICH GET MORE DONE IN LESS TIME

So your golden goose strategy is set. You know what you're doing today, this week, this year, this decade. It's 9 a.m. You fire up your email on Day 1 of your New Rich action plan so you can get your first task going—a custom quote request to a clothing manufacturer in China for T-shirts you want to sell.

You're about to click COMPOSE when you notice new emails. You decide to deal with them quickly: delete ten. Open three, read, mark as unread to revisit later. Shoot a quick reply to a vendor saying you'll send payment on his invoice today.

Real quick: Jump on Venmo, pay vendor as promised. But first, reply to the three texts that came in since you last looked at your phone. Check Twitter *super quickly* because those notifications keep dinging. Reply to the two people who tweeted @ you. OK, back to Venmo. Vendor paid.

This reminds you that two clients haven't paid you. Oh, crap—it's because you haven't invoiced them. Throw together their invoices, send, remember another client's payment is overdue.

You're about to email the delinquent client when your eye catches the time: 10:30 a.m. Your email to China is an empty draft in the bottom corner of your screen—and now you can't even remember what you were going to write. Where did the last ninety minutes go?

You know this scenario sounds way too familiar. And that's just your morning. There are still the impromptu phone calls, chats, and meetings that will kill your focus. It doesn't stop. It won't stop unless you make it.

Every time you switch tasks it takes five to ten minutes to reengage with the thing you were doing beforehand. If you switch tasks ten times during the day, that's one hundred minutes, or almost two hours of productivity you lose every day.

This is why the world's most efficient people batch time. And that alone gives the New Rich a huge advantage over others who let the distractions rule them. While everyone else is bouncing around to a thousand minor tasks a day—and not getting anything meaningful done—they don't put up with it. Never mind those who hire assistants to do the little things for them. You'll get there, but not soon enough if you don't take ownership of your time so you can get the big work done.

The concept of batching time is simple: dedicate blocks of time (at least three hours) to one task or project. No switching to do little things in between. If you have multiple big projects going on, it helps to batch time by days instead of hours. This is how Jack Dorsey runs both Square and Twitter. In an interview with *Techonomy*, he explained how he runs the two companies simultaneously:

> The only way to do this is to be very disciplined and very practiced. The way I found that works for me is I theme my days. Monday at both companies I focus on management and running the company. We have our directional meeting at Square and we have our OpCom meeting at Twitter. Tuesday is focused on product. Wednesday is focused on marketing and communications and growth. Thursday is focused on developers and partnerships. Friday is focused on the company and the culture and recruiting. Saturday I take off, I hike. Sunday is reflections, feedback, strategy and getting ready for the rest of the week. . . . It sets a good cadence for the rest of the company so that we are always delivering, we are always showing where we were last week and where we are going to be the following week.

By batching his time Dorsey is living in days and working in weeks, always looking at the bigger picture with both companies.

I use a tool called Acuity Scheduling to batch my time (you can see it at NathanLatka.com/schedule). It lets others see your availability so they can just pick a time to meet. I set three-hour blocks for podcast interviews, each one for twenty minutes. Guests get a link to my schedule and pick a time in my available window. When my schedule is set, I have three twenty-minute meetings per hour, back-to-back. No switching costs. Hyperefficient.

Batching time sounds simple but it's difficult to start doing from scratch. Our brains have become programmed to constantly react to distractions. So to start, pick a day next week to focus on one task or theme and force yourself to ignore in-the-moment interruptions. You also need to save yourself from yourself. You know that even when someone isn't interrupting you, you sabotage yourself by always checking email, social media, texts, whatever. Put your phone in another room or at the bottom of your bag.

Use an internet-blocking tool like Freedom.to so you can't check whatever your brain swears is so urgent. You're going to feel much better at the end of the day. You'll have more energy because you won't have wasted so much time starting and stopping things. And generally, you'll get significantly more done.

THE NEW RICH TOOLBOX

- Sell Off of Fear
- Negotiate When You Don't Have To
- Ditch To-Do Lists and Build Out Your Systems
- Batch Your Time

MONEY: GET IT, KEEP IT, GROW IT

6

YOUR HIDDEN MONEY

"Rich gets richer with the expenses of the poorest."

—attributed to Pradeepa Pandiyan

"Financial peace isn't the acquisition of stuff. It's learning to live on less than you make, so you can give money back and have money to invest. You can't win until you do this."

—Dave Ramsey

I t takes a ton of work to reach the point of having an empty calendar. Nothing goes on autopilot until you've obsessed over every detail of your project, built your systems, and tweaked the operation to make the cash flow.

But you can make things easier on yourself. The best way to start a new business—or any endeavor—is to keep your expenses really low. I know, common sense, but not common practice. Obviously spending less is smart, but most people completely miss the other side of this equation: turning your liabilities into assets.

Don't tell me you don't have assets. If you really believe that, you've either been drinking stale Kool-Aid or you're just not seeing the earning potential in the things you do have. This especially goes for the items that classic business authors like Robert Kiyosaki (*Rich Dad Poor Dad*) will tell you are a liability because they suck cash from you every month: your home, car, boat, etc. Now, we have to forgive Robert for this. Today's sharing economy just didn't exist back when he was learning the "ways of the rich" in Hawaii.

That's our silver bullet: the sharing economy. Because of it, we have the power to turn nearly everything we own or rent into a cash machine. Robert and his cohorts would have killed to do business in a time when they could make those old "liabilities" they warned us about print cash. If we really work the system, we can use the sharing economy to wipe out our expenses completely.

I know a lot of you reading this think what I'm saying doesn't apply to you. All you see is your debt, your rent, your one car. Just stay with me. Don't underestimate what can be turned into an asset and don't skip this step. It plays a huge role in growing your endeavors as quickly as possible. Getting that extra cash keeps you from having to do things you hate, like taking on clients who you know will be a nightmare, or chasing money in ways you don't want to, just to cover bills. That extra cash also gives you patience. You can spend more time building a great product because you're not relying on it to cover your expenses. The very items that you owe money on are paying for themselves—and in some cases, bringing in extra cash on top of that.

My favorite part: this is so easy. You just need to know how to connect with people who want to use your stuff. You already know about the main-stream tools like Airbnb, but even then, I'll show you some hacks to get the site working in your favor. I'll also clue you in to lesser-known market-places for making passive income off everything from your car and office space to your online content. Believe me, you have way more hidden money than you think.

To be clear, this chapter is not meant to be an exhaustive resource on ways to bring in money or to be frugal. That's a whole other book. Lots of other books. I've kept the focus on things that I do, and that I know work, with minimal effort.

AIRBNB TRICKS YOU HAVEN'T THOUGHT OF

If you've been conscious within the last ten years you've heard of Airbnb. You know it's a site that lets you list your home for rent to people traveling in your area. I'm rarely home, so the majority of the month I rent my house out to Airbnb travelers. As I'm writing this I just bought a house in Austin, and I'm completely covering my mortgage plus making an extra $500 to $600 in rent. Here's the math:

- ▶ The house cost $425K and I made a 3 percent down payment.
- ▶ My monthly mortgage + tax payment is $2,700.

▶ I'm gone about twenty days out of the month and make the house available to renters on those days. On average, I make $3,300 to $3,500 a month through Airbnb. So I'm living free and bringing in extra cash from renters.

I get that this isn't for everyone. Or at best, not everyone will earn enough on Airbnb to cover all their housing costs. It's easiest to attract renters when you live in a city or any kind of destination area (beach, ski mountains, college town, etc.). But don't be so quick to dismiss your home's earning potential if you live somewhere remote. People visit family who want their own space. Businesspeople travel to see clients. Or never mind travelers: locals may need a place to crash while their house is being reno-vated, or their pipes burst, or their visiting mother-in-law is driving them insane.

If there is a functioning hotel within a twenty-mile radius of your house you have a chance at making money on Airbnb. And if not? Maybe your house is *so* remote that people will want to rent it as a retreat space. Think writers, artists, yogis. It's worth trying as long as you're willing to share your space.

If you go for it, here are some tricks I've learned to spike your listing's earning potential:

Decrease your per-night fee, but increase your cleaning fee. Airbnb makes recommendations based on the best value. The listings with the lowest rates, the most rooms, and the best reviews will make the top search results. But cleaning fees don't get factored into this. So you'll rank higher if you bring your price down from, say, $200/night to $100/night and increase your cleaning fee from $25/night to $125/night. You'll make the same amount, or more, but it appears cheaper on a per night basis to those looking at potentially renting. I made $15K in my first three months of renting the house out and it was occupied only 20 percent of the time. Of the $15K, $2K was from cleaning fees alone.

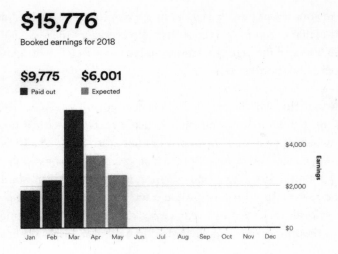

$15,776
Booked earnings for 2018

$9,775   **$6,001**
■ Paid out   ■ Expected

Save on cleaning. I bill my Airbnb renters $150/night for cleaning but my cleaner's bill is only $50/visit—$100 more for me. If you become an Airbnb regular be sure to negotiate a group discount on cleaning. Tell your cleaner, "I can't pay you $75 per cleaning but I can pay you $50 and guarantee you five cleans a month." They'll likely agree to the lower rate knowing they'll have a consistent $250/month coming in from you. Sandy is great—I just Venmo her $50 after each clean.

Pictures are everything. Invest in great pictures. The cheapest way to hire a photographer if you don't have talented friends who will cut you a deal is through Snappr.co, a network of freelance photographers around the world. You can also use Thumbtack.com to find local photographers. Whatever you do, use the best possible photos for your listing.

THREE WEBSITES THAT'LL PAY FOR YOUR CAR WHILE YOU'RE BUSY

If you drive to work your car usage probably looks something like this:

Get to work at 9-ish.
Park your car.
Car sits in parking spot until 5-ish.

Or some variation . . . if you take a train to work, maybe your car sits at the station lot all day. Bottom line, your car goes unused during your work hours. And when you're on vacation it just sits there.

So why not rent it out during the hours you're not using it? Turo.com is one of the best tools for doing this. HyreCar.com and GetAround.com are also reliable platforms for car sharing. You post a rental listing and people in your area pay an hourly or daily fee to use your car. The rental outlets usually cover insurance. If you're willing to share your vehicle you can generate a few hundred bucks per month from what is otherwise seen as a liability.

Reliable online marketplaces also exist for boats (GetMyBoat.com, BoatSetter.com), motorcycles (Riders-Share.com, TwistedRoad.com, Bike Bandit.com), and bikes (Spinlister.com). You can even rent out your parking space (Parklee.com). Books publish too slowly for me to list all the latest sharing marketplaces out there. If you own or rent something that someone else might value, chances are you can hire it out. Google it.

HOW MY BLACK T-SHIRTS MAKE ME MONEY

My clothes aren't exactly printing bills, but my minimalist approach to getting dressed does save me money. I wear the same thing every day: a black T-shirt and black traveler slim cut pants, both from Banana Republic; Patagonia black jacket if it's cold. I just have many copies of these items.

Me at Facebook HQ in the "Small Room" wearing my go-to black wardrobe.

One reason I do this is that when you bring gently used clothes back to Banana Republic they give you a 30 percent discount off your next order. They donate the clothes for you. They often run 50 percent sales off the entire store and that's when I stock up on my two favorite items. So I get my T-shirts, which retail at $35, for about $12 each.

It's not the only way to get money back on clothes, for sure, but it's what I do.

Another easy approach is to donate clothes to a nonprofit like the Salvation Army and then write off the donation on your taxes. It's small, but it adds up. The trick is to do it in bulk. Set a bucket in the corner of your closet and put clothes that you no longer want in it. Then donate its contents once a year, or every six months, and keep your receipt for the tax refund.

If you're willing to put in the time and want to sell your clothes you can set up an account with a local consignment shop and get a cut of the sales on your items. Just remember, again, that the goal here is *minimal input*. You can turn selling used clothes into a full-time job, and hey, maybe that will be your side hustle. But that's a whole other thing. If you're just looking for passive ways to make your clothes work for you, discounts and donations are the easiest ways to do it.

OFFICE SPACE

Those of you who rent or own an office can turn that into an asset, too. Lots of small businesses have spaces that they haven't fully grown into, or that they just don't use every day. Breather.com lets you list your space on a daily or hourly basis. You can list anything from a single desk to a full-fledged office with conference rooms. It's a great option if you don't want to rent out the space full time but hate to see it go unused most days. Make it work for you.

Breather is also great, of course, if you're the renter. You can meet clients, host board meetings, or whatever you need to do, without the commitment of an office if you're not ready for it.

And don't be confused: This is not like a coworking space, which is a dedicated spot for people to rent desks and offices. It's a similar concept, only Breather lets you crash at private offices. It's like the difference between Airbnb and a hotel. You can rent offices in every corner of the world without having to worry about the communal aspect of a coworking space, or whether one even exists where you plan to travel.

HOTEL ROOMS

Most of you reading this book probably don't own a hotel, but maybe some do. . . . If you do, you should know about Recharge.co. It's a site that allows you to rent out hourly blocks of time when your hotel rooms aren't being used. So let's say a guest checks out of a room at the airport Hilton in San Francisco at 11 a.m. The next guest won't arrive until 6 p.m. You have to allocate time for cleaning, but even then, there are five solid hours during which the room goes unused. Meanwhile, someone may be in town just for the day and want to take a quick nap and shower before a meeting. They go to Recharge.co and rent the room from 1 p.m. to 4 p.m. Still time to prep for the 6 p.m. guest. You're getting as much cash as possible out of that room.

I use Recharge.co when I'm traveling and don't need to stay a full night at a hotel. It's so common to be in and out of a city in one day for a meeting. You can wash off the airplane crud and recharge for a few hours for much less money than an overnight would cost.

AUTOMATIC INCOME: PATREON AND OTHER WAYS TO SELL YOUR DIGITAL PRODUCT

I've mentioned Patreon.com in earlier chapters but it deserves another round of attention here. If you create any digital content on a blog, podcast, or other digital platform you should absolutely have a Patreon page that lets your fans make monthly contributions to your project. I recently launched a page for my podcast as a test (you can see it at NathanLatka.com/patreon). After two days we had thirteen patrons pledging to pay $593 a month. Two months in I was at twenty-nine patrons giving $2,300+ a month.

Patreon's model incentivizes backers through a reward system. The more people pledge, the bigger rewards they receive. The key to attracting patrons is to create urgency with your rewards. My profile shows only ten or so rewards available for each tier. The message there is: "If you grab this reward before it runs out you get XYZ valuable thing." Also offer exclusivity—access to content, people, or opportunities that are not available to the public. My top-tier reward is the chance to be interviewed on my podcast for a $500/month pledge. I made only two available and they sold out in the first two days.

Remember, this chapter's goal is to help you monetize your current assets. So leveraging Patreon makes sense here only if you already invest your time in creating digital content. You can use it to build cash flow on a new project, but that's a whole other thing. For now, I'm talking to anyone who is up and running already. Make sure you go get your money.

7

LIVE LIKE A KING WITHOUT OWNING A THING

"Men acquire a particular quality by constantly acting a certain way."

—Aristotle

I f you want to be wealthy, you must act wealthy. "But how do I act wealthy when I have no money today, Nathan?" This is where you must embrace "fake it until you make it." The unique take I'll share with you in this chapter is how to get exactly what you want without paying for it. It'll surprise you how I got my $350K white Rolls-Royce Ghost for free. I explain this in the next few pages. You're going to do this the smart way. Stupid people fake that rich lifestyle by going broke spending all their money. You'd be amazed how many people screw themselves by doing this. That won't be you.

You're going to fake it by getting all the luxurious stuff that the New Rich love, for free. And once you're rolling in cash you'll keep getting it all for free, or for very little. That's another one of the New Rich secrets: They aren't rich because they make (and spend) a lot of money. They're rich because they make a lot of money, keep it, and figure out how to get anything they want without spending much.

I'll also show you how to bring in cash with very little effort. So when you can't get what you want for free you'll at least know how to bring in easy money to either grow your venture or fund your lifestyle.

I want you to jump-start your New Rich lifestyle before you can afford it, for two reasons. First—well, because you can, even if you think you can't. But the more important reason is that once you give off the perception of being successful, more success will find you. It's just how the universe works.

Most of the strategies here just involve knowing which tools to leverage to get what you want. Others, like getting an Airbnb mansion for free, will be more involved, but all you need is audacity and hustle. You'll get as much as you're willing to ask for.

EASY CASH

There is easy money out there for the taking. You just need to know where to get it. These tactics alone won't get you entry into the New Rich, but cash is cash. Get it, keep it, and make it work for you as you build up your empire.

Get Paid $400 Next Time You Fly Using This Trick

I travel year-round and tap into two great tools when things go wrong: ClaimCompass.eu and AirHelp.com. With both sites you just submit your boarding pass and fill out a short form to submit your claim. I usually get a few hundred dollars back for each claim ($400 seems to be average). You get paid for delayed flights even if you still took the flight.

How it works is that airlines legally owe money to millions of consumers for lost bags and flight delays. But you'd have to hire a legal team and dive deep into the airlines' terms of service and end-user license agreements to get what you're owed. No reasonable person would do that. So these companies have lawyers on staff who do it for us. They sue the airlines over and over via class action lawsuits. Then they pay out that money to people who submit a claim to their site. It's so quick to do, and it's an easy way to make $400, which is kind of cool if your flight only cost $300.

Launch a Kickstarter Campaign
Guaranteed to Get $1K in Funding

If crowdfunding is your thing, FundedToday.com can spike your contributions multiple times over. You pay Funded Today a percentage of the money they help you raise, but considering you'd only have made a fraction of that without them, it's worth it. CEO Zach Smith says their success rate is well over 95 percent. It works because they have email lists of millions of people who have already donated to Kickstarter and Indiegogo campaigns. When you work with them, they market your launch to those lists and can essentially guarantee funding.

Turn $100 into $1K Using Smart eBay Trading-Up Strategies

This one's fun, and you can go as far as you want with it. Go on eBay and look for an auction or a first sale that's about to close. Then look up the same item on Amazon. If it's more expensive on eBay than it is on Amazon, buy one or two on Amazon and then list them immediately on eBay.

This isn't totally hassle-free. eBay takes a cut of your earnings, and you have to deal with shipping the item. There's also the risk of your buyer wanting to return the item. But it's worth it if you resell big-ticket items like electronics. You can make an easy $1K or $2K in one weekend if you focus solely on flipping expensive items.

HOW I TRAVELED ASIA FOR FORTY-FIVE DAYS SPENDING ALMOST NO MONEY

Traveling on the cheap, or for free, is the only way to do it. But this doesn't mean roughing it. Far from it.

I recently left Austin, Texas, en route to Bangkok for a forty-five-day trip. I traveled in first class and very much enjoyed the Hello Kitty–themed bed I slept in, dishes I ate off, and TV shows I watched. For normal people who haven't figured out the ways of the New Rich, they'd pay $9K for this sort of first-class ticket. I got it for free. How?

To start, I put all of my business expenses through my Chase Sapphire Reserve card to rack up as many points as possible. This includes Facebook ads, paying for my email marketing provider, literally any expense. I know you're thinking, *Nathan, great tip! I bought this damn book and your recommendation is just to use a card that gives you points?* Hold your horses. . . .

Next, do not try to use the points yourself. Go to Flightfox.com and have their experts figure out the most efficient and most luxurious way to fly you around the world. I paid $50 for the service, and they ended up basically handing me a $4,800 check.

The best offer I found on my own was a business class ticket for $3K. No bed. Limited food. No amazing selfies of me fully laid out being dressed by my flight attendant in the flight's pajama evening wear. My out-of-pocket for this would have been $1K. Points covered the other $2K.

Flightfox.com used the same number of points to knock $8,880 off the price of a ticket, so I only had to pay $120. When I tried hunting for a deal myself, I used the same points but saved only $2K (off an inferior $3K ticket).

I use Flightfox every time I travel. You just tell them what frequent flyer points you have and where you want to go and their travel experts find you the best possible deal. You can also keep it as open-ended as you want to get the best possible deal, just saying something like, "Hey Flightfox, tell me sometime in the next six months when I can fly to China, Japan, or Sydney for under $500 using my points and going on the cheapest dates." They will figure it out for you.

This is all the direction I gave them for this forty-five-day trip across three countries:

Description

Need to land in Bali Feb 10th. Flying out of Austin Texas. Would land back in Austin sometime late Feb.

Have booked these hotels for their respective dates:

Bali:
http://www.samabe.com (Feb 10 and 11)
http://jamahal.net (Feb 12 and 13)
http://www.alilahotels.com/manggis (Feb 14, 15, 16)

Would love to try and figure out how to also get to:
Australia 3-4 days
Bangkok Thailand 3-4 days
Japan 2-3 days

I don't care about order except that Bali is first.

Can you help?

TRADE YOUR WAY TO THAT NEW RICH LIFE

This chapter starts off easy. Anyone can generate cash or save money by using the resources I mentioned. Little or no effort required.

You can stop there and be happy. But if you're willing to do some smart hustling you can get luxury *anything*—mansions, cars, clothes, vacations—for little or no money.

I want to vomit every time I see an Instagram or Facebook "influencer" posing in front of their new car or mansion, or posting selfies from their exotic vacations. You know damn well they don't own—and can't afford—those things, yet they act like they do. (Most of them are broke.) If they'd be up front with you, you'd learn a new way to live like royalty without spending royalty kind of money. They'd never admit to any of this, though, so I'm here to reveal their secrets for them.

Annoying as they are, those influencers are also smart as hell. They've figured out how to maximize the one commodity they have that companies are desperate to tap into: clout.

Companies need to get eyeballs on their products. That's nothing new. And it used to be that advertising was the most effective way to connect with the masses. Remember, it's how Ted Turner built his TV empire in the seventies and eighties. You know that's not the case anymore, though. When is the last time you bought something based on an ad? It's more likely that your buying decision was influenced by an online review, or a recommendation from someone whose taste you admire. Target can spend millions on ads promoting their new home decor line. But they'll get more traction sending free stuff to people with big Instagram followings in exchange for a post tagged #targetstyle. Best part: consumers will see the product plug as an organic recommendation from a friend (even if that "friend" is someone they've never met). Free promo for Target. Free stuff for the influencer. Everyone's head explodes from all the winning.

Anyone with a big following leverages their clout for free stuff. If they say they don't, they're lying. It's how I stayed fifteen nights in luxurious five-star villas in Bali for a grand total of $0.

You can have clout even if you're not hot on social media. The key is to create an inventory of things you can trade that the other person wants. Again, it's usually exposure: I have my podcast, where I can offer to put people on my show in exchange for something; my email list; my Instagram account. These are all things to trade.

If you don't have that kind of reach you can still leverage the *quality* of your connections.

Don't have quality connections? Go out and make some. Just think about the kinds of people a company, or whoever owns the things you want, wants to get in front of. A hotel owner may value a review on a particular travel blog like TripAdvisor. So tell them you'll publish a feature about them on that site if they have room for you to experience their property for a few nights. (Pro tip: Ask for the "media rate." Every hotel has one, and it's usually north of a 30 percent discount.) At the same time, pitch the article to that blog. The blogger will love the free, quality content and you'll make a new friend. Win-win-win.

You can apply this thinking to nearly anything. Introduce yourself to CEOs, Instagram influencers, or the leader of any big community that a company would want to get in front of. Tell the company you'll share your pictures, article, or whatever you can create with that community. You're essentially trading your marketing services for the free thing you want. Jump to page 109 for more on how to broker deals like this.

If you're skeptical that trading can work, maybe my experience at the five-star villa will change your mind. . . .

Hotels

Bisma Eight in Ubud, Bali, lists nightly rates on its website at $325. Tucked into a busy side street where the roads are made of two-foot-by-two-foot lattice concrete pavers with grass sticking up in between, the resort's pool hangs thirty feet above the forest on the back side of the villa where I stayed. I was there for a total of three nights, which would have retailed for $900+. Instead, I traded three Instagram pictures like the ones below, one per night, to stay for free.

YOU HAVE TO READ THIS EMAIL

If you want to copy me, below is the exact email script my partnership manager (Zach) sent Bisma Eight's hotel manager to negotiate the free stay.

Subject line: "Collaboration"

Content:

Hi, I'm NAME,

I would love to take some photos and share my experience on my account which gets engagement from celebrities and successful entrepreneur friends in exchange for complimentary nights at your hotel in your best room for January 22-27th, 2017, two people, plus anything else you would like to offer (airport transfer, food, spa experience etc etc).

We can do the following:

1. Create One (1) positive instagram post per complimentary night (min of 2 nights) 2. Create One (1) positive review (5 star) on Trip Advisor and Facebook.

Our social media channels are @nathanlatka, @mygoodtravel 2

Million+ reach on Instagram with a special concentration on influencers in Hollywood. Demo: 70% female age 18-40 in the United States (85% US followers and 15% European followers).

Our posts will hit the top posts of all of Instagram. So when people search #balihotels #bali, #balispa, etc etc, they will see my post first. They will click on my picture, look at the caption, click on your Instagram page or website which will create more leads and sales for you. I've worked with everyone from the Four Seasons & Sheraton to boutique hotels, villas and resorts like Hotel Villa Carlton in Salzburg, Hotel Muse in Bangkok, Mandala Spa and Villas in Boracay and many more.

Please let me know if you need any references etc, thank you very much!

• • • • •

This is the response Zach got back:

Robbie Woodward
To: Zach Benson
Re: Personal email

January 18, 2017 at 4:32 AM
Inbox - Google

New contact info found in this email: Robbie Woodward ████████████   add... ⊗

Hey Zach

Do you mean us Ohana? or Bisma Eight?? either way that would be awesome.

Also please accept this email as formal confirmation of stay for Nathan Latka

Influencer exchange of:
3 night stay in Canopy suite
17th - 20th February 2017
Inclusive of daily breakfast
1 x evening dinner

In return for:
1 x daily post on IG during stay - @mygoodtravel
1 x post on IG after stay (max. 2 weeks after) #throwback - @mygoodtravel
1 x TripAdvisor Review for Bisma Eight
2 x Snapchats
2 x IG Stories

Can you confirm that Nathan would like to go ahead with this?

Best

--
Robbie Woodward
Managing Director
....
T: +44 (0) 121 408 7496 · M: +44 (0) 773 444 1716

OHANA
COMMUNICATIONS
...part of your travel family

Connect with us on: Instagram | Facebook | Twitter

Use the other negotiation tips I write about in chapter 5 and you'll be sitting on a king's ransom of free luxury experiences before the end of next week.

We did the same deal with the Alila resort in Bali: I posted and tagged them in this picture, and also left a TripAdvisor review. Their rate is $400+/ night. You can see how this starts to add up. Anyone viewing this picture might think: "How does he pay for all of this!?"

The answer is, I don't. I got to stay for free by trading assets.

CLOUT HACK: NO AUDIENCE? BUY ONE.

I'm not talking about buying fake social media followers. It's more effective to buy tiny companies that have a big social media account, then leverage that following to make the trades I talk about in this chapter.

When I look to buy a company, I always check if they have social media accounts attached. I did this with My Good Travel. I bought that company for $3K and it came with an Instagram account that already had 100,000+ followers. Once the company was mine, I started selling sponsored Instagram posts for a few hundred bucks a pop. I earned back my $3K investment after selling ten posts. That's also how I got three free nights at Bisma Eight in Bali.

The beautiful thing about an Instagram account is that it's inventory that never ends. You can sell or trade as many or as few sponsored posts as you want. It's an endless resource once you own it.

A lot of people trying to make money off sites like Instagram or Pinterest make one big mistake—they try to build their own following instead of buying a company for very cheap that already has a built-in audience.

The logistics on this are super simple:

- Find a small business with an Instagram following of 100,000 or more. A lot of times their bio will say, "DM me for questions," or their profile has a link to email them.
- Reach out with the subject line "Potentially Acquiring Your Business." In the text of your email say something like, "Hey, I came across your IG account. I love your business and I'd love to buy it." The legalities on buying and selling social media accounts are murky, so your best bet is to buy the whole company—often that isn't much more than their social media.

(continued)

> ■ Send these emails to a few people. When I did this I got one reply saying, "I'm not selling my company, but I know others who are." Then he offered to add me to a GroupMe Chat with several people who were selling their tiny companies with big IG accounts. That chat is how I bought the My Good Travel business for $3K.
>
> I give you the full how-to on buying and selling companies in chapter 9, but you can keep it as small and as simple as this. Reach out to micro businesses and keep asking around. A "no" can easily lead to a "yes" through a few introductions.

Get Discounts on Airbnb Penthouses

OK, so you don't have a big online following and you're not about to buy a company so you can get a built-in audience overnight. Don't worry. You can still hustle your way to luxury living, especially on Airbnb, by leveraging your quality connections. Even if you don't have them. Seriously. It's called Elephant Hunting—in other words, using one thing to get the other.

Go on Airbnb and find your dream property. Sort from most expensive to least expensive. Then email the owner and say you want to use the space to host a private gathering with top-level people in that city. It can be any group with a high profile—CEOs, artists, VCs, or whoever you think the owner of that property would want to meet. Say you're inviting these people over and name a few, even if you don't know them. Just say you plan to invite them. Once you get the place at a deep discount, use its beautiful pictures when inviting the talent whom you might not even know. They'll feed off each other. When you do this, you're basically becoming a broker between the Airbnb host and the guests you're bringing in. Anyone can leverage this strategy. It just takes balls and courage to go out and actually do the negotiation.

Here's an Airbnb exchange between me and an Airbnb owner that shows exactly how I did this to score a San Francisco penthouse at less than half the $799/night listed price:

ENTIRE APARTMENT
Spectacular Tel Hi 3br Penthouse
San Francisco

The cold outreach and negotiation:

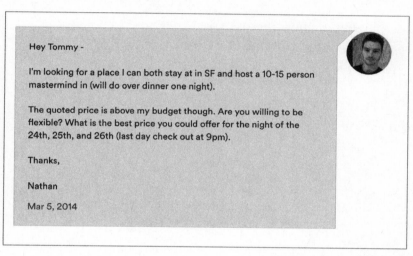

Hey Tommy -

I'm looking for a place I can both stay at in SF and host a 10-15 person mastermind in (will do over dinner one night).

The quoted price is above my budget though. Are you willing to be flexible? What is the best price you could offer for the night of the 24th, 25th, and 26th (last day check out at 9pm).

Thanks,

Nathan

Mar 5, 2014

Nathan:

What you are asking for is 3 nights. We can't let you stay beyond noon on the last day and not pay for it. that night is lost if we do.

the price quoted is already deeply discounted for us for 3 nights. I'm a fellow entrepreneur so i'm sensitive to costs. give me an idea what a "mastermind" is so i have some sort of idea what your use case is for the rental.

cheers!

tommy

Mar 5, 2014

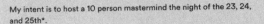

Hey Tommy -

My intent is to host a 10 person mastermind the night of the 23, 24, and 25th*.

24th night: Will be inviting CEO's of San Francisco based Creative Agencies, will have dinner catered via http://www.kitchit.com/bay-area
25th night: Will be inviting CEO's of SF based Tech Companies, will have dinner catered via Kitchit
26th night: Will be inviting thought influencers and speakers I am sharing the stage with at eMA summit, dinner catered by Kitchit

I absolutely don't want to take advantage of the gorgeous property you own. $799/night puts me over my budget though.

Do you have interest in joining in on the masterminds (these will all be movers and shakers, for example Rick Rudman, CEO of Vocus $200MM market cap came to the last one I had - this is the profile of folks I'll get there) in exchange for a discounted rate?

All the folks I'll be inviting are also all potential future renters of your penthouse too - great marketing opportunity.

Let me know. I understand if you don't have flexibility though.

Thanks,

Nathan

Mar 5, 2014

TOMMY SENT A SPECIAL OFFER $560/NIGHT

Nathan:

that sounds like a deal. lets do $1500 for all nights and I'll plan on sitting in. I'm actually running something called Miinsu, which is a hosting and hospitality layer on top of Airbnb-like services for apts like this one, and networking is both a need and a despised activity :)

Let me know if that works. The cost includes cleaning which is normally $180 on top of everything else.

tommy

Mar 5, 2014

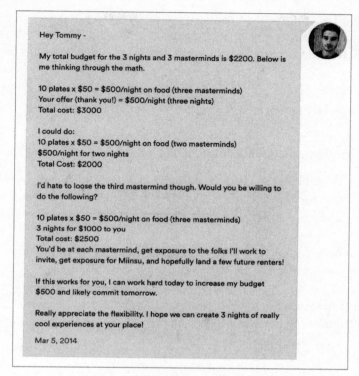

Hey Tommy -

My total budget for the 3 nights and 3 masterminds is $2200. Below is me thinking through the math.

10 plates x $50 = $500/night on food (three masterminds)
Your offer (thank you!) = $500/night (three nights)
Total cost: $3000

I could do:
10 plates x $50 = $500/night on food (two masterminds)
$500/night for two nights
Total Cost: $2000

I'd hate to loose the third mastermind though. Would you be willing to do the following?

10 plates x $50 = $500/night on food (three masterminds)
3 nights for $1000 to you
Total cost: $2500
You'd be at each mastermind, get exposure to the folks I'll work to invite, get exposure for Miinsu, and hopefully land a few future renters!

If this works for you, I can work hard today to increase my budget $500 and likely commit tomorrow.

Really appreciate the flexibility. I hope we can create 3 nights of really cool experiences at your place!

Mar 5, 2014

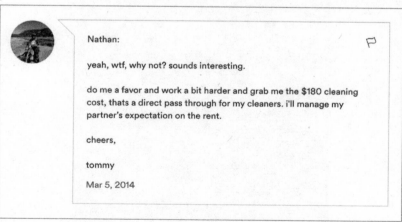

Nathan:

yeah, wtf, why not? sounds interesting.

do me a favor and work a bit harder and grab me the $180 cleaning cost, thats a direct pass through for my cleaners. i'll manage my partner's expectation on the rent.

cheers,

tommy

Mar 5, 2014

So in summary, I got a place for $1K ($333/night) that was listed for $2,400 ($800/night). That's more than a 60 percent discount!

Try this, even if it sounds absurd to you. Anyone can do cold outreach to anyone else. Most people, CEOs included, are willing to meet you if you just ask. They may even come to your party at your swanky Airbnb penthouse. Reach out, give them a good reason to show up (like the chance to meet other like-minded CEOs), and see what happens. Never mind the sick property you'll get to rent in the process. You'll likely make long-term connections with people who become business partners, clients, or mentors in your New Rich journey.

$4,500 Balmain Jacket from Paris

My favorite way to take a bathroom selfie was in the $4,500 Balmain biker jacket that I got to wear for free. Hair coiffed, selfie posted, I hit the streets of Austin in my Rolls-Royce Ghost—a $350K car that I was driving, you know . . . for free.

I got both of these things so easily, it's almost embarrassing. I didn't even ask for the jacket. Someone else encouraged me to take it.

Sure, I had to return both items after a couple days. But who cares? None of my Instagram followers knew the jacket wasn't mine, especially since I'm standing in my bathroom while wearing it. Looks like I just pulled it out of my closet where it sits alongside my Tom Ford suit.

I don't need to fake being rich—I'm already there—but if you're still working on it you can easily fake a rich lifestyle through your clothes. You see this all the time on social media even if you don't know it. If you've ever wondered how someone affords their crazy expensive clothes, the answer is that they don't. The clothes aren't even theirs. And if they can afford them, they probably still don't own them. Why buy when you can borrow for free? I'd rather put that $4,500 into my next business investment.

The next time you need to buy a nice suit or dress do it through a stylist. That's the easiest way to get access to hot clothes. Once you buy one thing from them they'll want you to buy more, so they'll bring you new clothes every month and try to get you to wear them. If there's something you see that you kind of like, tell them you want to think about it. They'll usually tell you to take it home and try it out for a few days.

That's exactly what happened with the Balmain jacket. I'd recently bought a suit through my stylist when he told me about the jacket he'd just gotten in. I said I didn't want to pay that much and I probably wouldn't buy it. His response: "No, no, take it for the weekend and try it." Boom. Bathroom selfie.

That's how you live like a king and feel filthy rich without putting up a penny. It's called leverage, and if you've ever bought a suit or a dress, you have that leverage. Make sure you're maximizing it.

Now, your stylist will be on to you if you try to exploit that leverage too much. But it's a reliable way to get superexpensive clothes on occasion. If you want to flaunt designer clothes more often, you still don't have to buy them. The sharing economy has your back, again. You probably already know about Rent the Runway. If you don't, it's a site (and store in a few major cities) that lets you rent designer clothes. You can also use rental and clothes-sharing outlets like StyleLend.com, DesignerShare.com, LeTote .com, TheMrCollection.com, and TheMsCollection.com. You do have to pay to wear the clothes, but with the perk of being able to cycle through new outfits all the time. You never pay retail. Nobody ever knows the clothes aren't yours.

THE EMAIL THAT GOT ME A $350K WHITE ROLLS-ROYCE GHOST FOR $0

Meanwhile, that $350K Rolls-Royce . . . my secret for getting that is so revolutionary, I may be in line for the next Nobel Prize. You ready for this?

I just asked.

Yup.

Here's how it went:

From: Tobe Nguyen ▌
Date: 12 January 2017 at 2:00:23 AM GMT+9
To: ▌
Subject: Rolls Royce

Hi Zach,
My name is Tobe. I'm the main contact for marketing for Auto Exotic Rental. Thank you for reaching out to us. We can definitely work with you. We have the Rolls Royce Ghost. Is there a particular date that you're looking at? So I can check the availability for you. Please feel free to contact me at any time. Hope to hear from you soon.

Regards,
Tobe

What you're seeing in that email screenshot is Tobe, who works at Auto Exotic Rental in Austin, emailing back to Zach, my administrator. Zach pitched Tobe and said, "Hey, I work with an influencer, he has 15,000 Instagram followers. If he posts a picture inside one of your exotic cars would you be willing to give it to him for free for a day?"

Tobe was happy to accommodate.

Renting that car at the daily rate would be about $2K. So never mind the car's $350K price tag. I didn't even pay for the rental. That's $2K for free for one Instagram post.

This all ties back to finding things to trade that the other person, or company, wants. If you don't have a huge online following, can you connect with someone who does? Or can you host a meet-up with high-net-worth individuals the rental company wants to woo as clients? You can get to anyone you want—you just need to ask.

NATHAN, THIS IS BS! THE AVERAGE PERSON CAN'T GET THIS STUFF FOR FREE

Naysayers, I hear your dissent: "Sure, must be great to be able to flaunt your big Instagram numbers or call up your CEO friends and get what you want. Not everyone has those perks!"

If you're worried the strategies in this chapter won't work for "the average person like you," you need to stop aiming for average. You'll never join the New Rich if you refuse to push out of your comfort zone and build the connections and following that you're frustrated you don't have.

You can't "live like a king without owning a thing" if you don't put in the up-front effort. (That's why this chapter isn't called "Live Like a King Without *Doing* a Thing.") But the connections you make, the audiences and communities you build, will all tie into your New Rich plan when those people also become your business partners, clients, customers, listeners, readers, and followers. Which leads to more free stuff—cue the positive feedback loop.

8

HOW TO INVEST IN REAL ESTATE
(EVEN IF YOU HAVE NO CASH, NO CLUE, AND NO TIME)

"Ninety percent of all millionaires become so through owning real estate. More money has been made in real estate than in all industrial investments combined. The wise young man or wage earner of today invests his money in real estate."

—Andrew Carnegie

I f you found one of those grimy ATMs at the back of a restaurant that was malfunctioning and spitting out $20 every minute, would you tell anyone about it?

Of course not. The same is true for real estate investors. They don't want to tell you how much they make from real estate because then you'd compete with them and take their money.

If you're a student reading this, you're in luck. I'm twenty-eight today and I did my first deal during my last year in college. I had heard that people were making money in real estate but I'd been avoiding it because I thought I didn't have the time to do it myself. Still, I couldn't shake the idea of owning a cash-printing property. When I approached 209 Otey Street, one of the first properties I ever bought, a student answered the door. I was clean-shaven and wearing my Virginia Tech T-shirt. Nobody would have suspected I was on the verge of dropping out of school to build my empire, which was about to include real estate.

"Hey, I'm looking to lease a place for the fall semester," I said. "Do you know if there are any spots open here?" When she said there weren't, I asked if she could give me the landlord's contact info so I could ask about future openings. I got the number and left. My plan was on.

I took the owner out for coffee just to get to know him. His house wasn't for sale, but I wanted to be at the top of his mind when he did think of selling. I learned that he ran a charity and was trying to figure out how to get more cash into the organization. Even better—the charity owned the property.

"Well, when you're ready to sell," I said, "I'm willing to give you $200K."

We reconnected not long after that and struck a deal. Now the house is mine and his charity fixed its cash problem. Keep reading and you'll see that I didn't actually spend $200K—not even close.

This scenario isn't that unusual. The best real estate deals are found by door knocking and it's the number one way I suggest you look for your first properties. I'll show you exactly how to find your first deal even when it's not on the market, how to finance the deal even when you have no money, and how to manage your property even if you have no time for it.

What I love about real estate is that if you do it right, whether you're a college student with no savings or someone else with very little money, you can actually set yourself up to live for free while others pay your rent.

My biggest concern before owning property was how much time it would take me to manage it. I didn't realize then that you could outsource pretty much all of the work and still make passive income. The only time I put into the investment properties I now own is fifteen minutes per month to analyze the income and expense reports my property manager sends to me. Here are my February 2018 reports for two of my properties.

INCOME REPORT FROM MY FIRST REAL ESTATE DEAL

209 Otey monthly report (Feb. 2018): $661 in free cash flow:

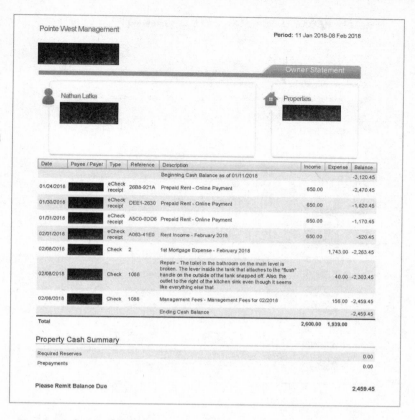

Date	Payee / Payer	Type	Reference	Description	Income	Expense	Balance
				Beginning Cash Balance as of 01/11/2018			-3,120.45
01/24/2018		eCheck receipt	26B8-921A	Prepaid Rent - Online Payment	650.00		-2,470.45
01/30/2018		eCheck receipt	DEE1-2630	Prepaid Rent - Online Payment	650.00		-1,820.45
01/31/2018		eCheck receipt	A5C0-0DD6	Prepaid Rent - Online Payment	650.00		-1,170.45
02/01/2018		eCheck receipt	A083-41E0	Rent Income - February 2018	650.00		-520.45
02/08/2018		Check	2	1st Mortgage Expense - February 2018		1,743.00	-2,263.45
02/08/2018		Check	1086	Repair - The toilet in the bathroom on the main level is broken. The lever inside the tank that attaches to the "flush" handle on the outside of the tank snapped off. Also, the outlet to the right of the kitchen sink even though it seems like everything else that		40.00	-2,303.45
02/08/2018		Check	1086	Management Fees - Management Fees for 02/2018		156.00	-2,459.45
				Ending Cash Balance			-2,459.45
Total					2,600.00	1,939.00	

Property Cash Summary

Required Reserves	0.00
Prepayments	0.00
Please Remit Balance Due	2,459.45

Here's my beautiful cash cow:

710 Roanoke (Feb. 2018): $1K in free cash flow each month:

Beauty #2:

The only other time-consuming task is the ten minutes it takes me to forward these statements to my tax attorney at the end of each year so he can file my taxes. All in all, that's ten or fifteen minutes of my time for about $1,600 in free cash flow each month. And that's just the cash component. It doesn't even count the equity buildup that I'm getting. Have I mentioned it's a thing of beauty?

These charts help me forecast historical versus future cash flows and returns. Here's the breakdown for 209 Otey:

Cash Upfront	$30,000
Annual Appreciation	2%
Loan amount Y1	295,200.00
Annual rent increase	5.00%
NOI relative to rent	30.00%

Time	Year	Start of Year Market Value	Annual Price Appreciation	Year End Appreciated Market Value	Annual Principal Debt Pay Down	Year End Accumulated Equity	Monthly Rent	Fixed Monthly Exp	Prop Man. Fee	Annual Cash Flow	Return on Investment	Return on Equity	Equity Position	Total Annual Return
1	2014													
2	2015													
3	2016	$328,000	$6,560	$334,560	$3,241.41	$32,800	$2,400	$2,200	$144	$672	34.91%	31.93%	10.00%	$10,473
4	2017	$334,560	$6,691	$341,251	$5,125.84	$44,617	$2,800	$1,830	$156	$7,368	63.95%	43.00%	13.34%	$19,185
5	2018	$341,251	$6,825	$348,076	$5,250.00	$56,892	$2,730	$1,830	$164	$8,834	70.80%	37.46%	16.61%	$21,230
6	2019	$348,076	$6,962	$355,038	$5,579.76	$69,233	$2,887	$1,830	$172	$10,374	76.38%	33.10%	19.89%	$22,916
7	2020	$355,038	$7,101	$362,139	$5,788.51	$82,123	$3,010	$1,830	$181	$11,991	82.93%	30.30%	23.13%	$24,860
8	2021	$362,139	$7,243	$369,381	6,072.44	$95,438	$3,160	$1,830	$190	$13,688	90.01%	28.29%	26.35%	$27,004
9	2022	$369,381	$7,388	$376,769	6,072.44	$108,898	$3,318	$1,830	$199	$15,471	98.44%	26.57%	29.48%	$28,931

And 710 Roanoke:

Cash Upfront	$50,000
Annual Appreciation	2%
Remaining Loan EOY2016	97,418.67
Annual rent increase	5.00%
NOI relative to rent	30.00%

Time	Year	Start of Year Market Value	Annual Price Appreciation	Year End Appreciated Market Value	Annual Principal Debt Pay Down	Year End Accumulated Equity	Monthly Rent	Fixed Monthly Exp	Prop Man. Fee	Annual Cash Flow	Return on Investment	Return on Equity	Equity Position	Total Annual Return
1	2014	$216,000	$4,360	$222,360		$52,000	$1,500	$1,261	$90	$6,000	20.72%		23.85%	$10,380
2	2015	$222,360	$4,447	$226,807	20000	$81,000	$1,500	$1,261	$96	$6,000	60.89%	37.18%	36.63%	$30,447
3	2016	$226,807	$4,536	$231,343		$86,436	$1,600	$1,261	$108	$6,177	19.43%	11.24%	38.11%	$9,713
4	2017	$231,343	$4,627	$235,970	2853	$93,918	$2,225	$1,261	$134	$9,971	34.90%	18.56%	40.60%	$17,451
5	2018	$235,970	$4,719	$240,690	2,901.99	$101,820	$2,336	$1,261	$140	$11,226	37.89%	18.63%	43.06%	$18,927
6	2019	$240,690	$4,814	$245,503	3,115.87	$109,549	$2,453	$1,261	$147	$12,544	40.95%	18.69%	45.51%	$20,473
7	2020	$245,503	$4,910	$250,413	3,115.87	$117,575	$2,576	$1,261	$155	$13,927	43.91%	18.67%	47.89%	$21,953
8	2021	$250,413	$5,008	$255,422	3,115.87	$125,899	$2,705	$1,261	$162	$15,380	47.01%	18.70%	50.20%	$23,504
9	2022	$255,422	$5,108	$260,530	3,115.87	$133,924	$2,840	$1,261	$170	$16,905	50.28%	18.76%	52.43%	$25,130

You can totally do this, too, but before I show you how, I want to call out a few common myths about real estate that hold most people back:

1. You need to know a lot about real estate investing to be a real estate investor.
2. You need money to do your first deal.
3. You have to be a handyman so you can fix anything that breaks. (Latka doesn't touch toilets!)
4. It takes a lot of time to manage real estate investments.
5. Now is not a good time.

Keep reading—I'll bust all of these myths in spectacular fashion. The key is finding something you can afford to buy that will generate you enough income even after you pay your monthly expenses. That means getting the right deal with the right financing and with the right management.

HOW TO FIND A PROPERTY THAT COULD BE A GOOD INVESTMENT

Every real estate deal I've done has started with a knock on a door. While most people troll their Zillow and Trulia apps looking for deals, I'm meeting homeowners so I can buy their property before it even makes it to those public listings.

Door knocking gets me better prices, but it also uncovers details that online listings can never capture, and that owners and real estate agents may fight like hell to keep from you. You get to learn a neighborhood (When the listing says "historic," is it a euphemism for "run-down," or are the houses maintained?). You get to see what kind of renters occupy a property (Quiet grad students and families, or unruly frat boys?); whether those renters take care of the place (Is there a herd of pets at their feet when they answer the door? A line of beer cans on the porch railing?); or whether it's a hot spot for renters at all (What answer do you get when you ask if there are openings?).

As far as scouting locations, I only buy within ten miles of a college (I currently own in Austin near the University of Texas and in Blacksburg near Virginia Tech) because students keep those rental markets nearly recession proof. A quick way to confirm this is by researching whether a town's rental rates and property values dipped in 2008. Just Google "property data" + 2008 + the city or county in which you're looking to buy. Browse the results until you find the Property Search Map.

If you can't afford to buy near popular college cities try looking in more rural college towns. Property prices should be lower while rental demand stays high. You'll start developing your own patterns as you do more deals and find locations that work for you. I just know that college towns work best for me.

Family and friends can also be your research across the country. If you're close to someone who lives near a good rental market you can have them be your boots on the ground to help scout locations and later help with property emergencies if you do buy in their area.

Start your search by driving to an area you feel you can afford a deal in and knock on doors. Meet the owners, earmark your ideal neighborhoods, and then start studying the numbers. I'll show you my script for door knocking later. First let's discuss finding a deal you can afford.

HOW TO FIGURE OUT IF PROPERTY CAN MAKE YOU MONEY

As with any investment, you need to figure out how much potential money you could make from something before deciding how much money you'd spend on it. Rental income is how you make money from real estate, but many times it can be tricky to figure out what people are paying for rents on a given unit.

Figure Out How Much Money You Could Make: Ask Local Real Estate Agents for Direct Access to Their MLS

Real estate agents have access to deals via their multiple listing service (MLS). Because agents want to represent you when you buy, their goal is to help you find a deal. So ask your agent: "Can you add my email to your MLS for any multifamily deals that come on the market anywhere in the county?"

When listings come in, you'll automatically see the data, which will include rental information. They'll look like this:

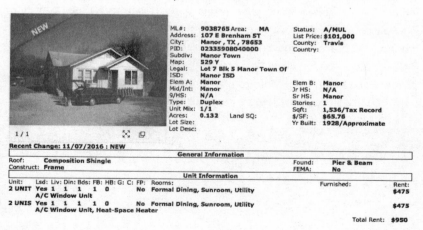

ML#:	9038765	Area:	MA	Status:	A/MUL
Address:	107 E Brenham ST			List Price:	$101,000
City:	Manor , TX , 78653			County:	Travis
PID:	0233590804000			Country:	
Subdiv:	Manor Town				
Map:	529 Y				
Legal:	Lot 7 Blk 5 Manor Town Of				
ISD:	Manor ISD				
Elem A:	Manor			Elem B:	Manor
Mid/Int:	Manor			Jr HS:	N/A
9/HS:	N/A			Sr HS:	Manor
Type:	Duplex			Stories:	1
Unit Mix:	1/1			Sqft:	1,536/Tax Record
Acres:	0.132	Land SQ:		$/SF:	$65.76
Lot Size:				Yr Built:	1928/Approximate
Lot Desc:					

1/1

Recent Change: 11/07/2016 : NEW

General Information				
Roof:	Composition Shingle		Found:	Pier & Beam
Construct:	Frame		FEMA:	No

Unit Information

Unit:	Lsd: Liv: Din: Bds: FB: HB: G: C: FP:	Rooms:	Furnished:	Rent:
2 UNIT	Yes 1 1 1 1 0 No	Formal Dining, Sunroom, Utility		$475
	A/C Window Unit			
2 UNIS	Yes 1 1 1 1 0 No	Formal Dining, Sunroom, Utility		$475
	A/C Window Unit, Heat-Space Heater			

Total Rent: **$950**

MLS listings are great for data and market research, but again, don't count on them for finding a great deal. Any good property listed on the MLS is quick fodder for bidding wars that will jack up the price. So aside from door knocking, target pocket listings. These are properties that a real estate agent knows are for sale, or might soon be for sale, that aren't listed on the MLS. That means the public hasn't had the chance to see them and spoil your chances at a sweet deal.

Build relationships with all your local real estate agents to make sure they think of you first when they get a pocket listing. That way when a friend or client tells them they're thinking of selling, they'll call you and try to close a deal maybe even before they put it up on the MLS. That's where you want to be.

You don't need to rule out MLS listings altogether—just know that they're not where the deals lurk. You can still learn a lot from their data. In the listing on the previous page I see that total rent ($950) is about 1 percent of total list price ($101K), so it's worth exploring (more later on how I did that math). When the numbers look good I'll then use the property tax portal to see when a unit was bought and sold in the past and for how much. Let's dig into that next. . . .

Figure Out What It Will Cost You to Buy

A listing's sale price tells you only what the seller *hopes* to get for the property. You can get a more realistic sense of what a unit is worth, and whether it will make you money after expenses, by searching public records. Every county in the United States posts property records in its online tax portal. The particulars vary from county to county, but you can usually find your county's tax portal by doing a Google search for "Your County Name + Your State + parcel ID." My first deal was in Blacksburg, Virginia (Montgomery County), so I searched "Montgomery County VA parcel ID."

You'll find a page that looks something like this:

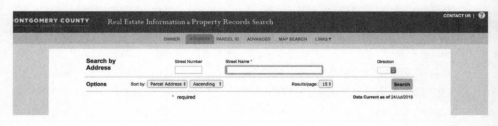

What you'll do next:

▶ **STEP 1: Pull up your county's tax portal.** The page will typically lead you to a map that lets you zoom in and out on individual parcels, or pieces of land, to see their sales history.

▶ **STEP 2: Zoom in to get sales data on the property you're interested in and others nearby.** Similar properties in an area sell for similar prices, so the combined data will tell you whether a property's list price is low or high, and whether the price you want to pay is close to market value. Obviously you want to make sure you're buying low, not high, so you can sell high later.

▶ **STEP 3: Calculate potential rent.** Similar properties in an area also rent for similar amounts. So note the rent in the MLS listing and see how it compares to nearby rent for similar properties. A quick Craigslist search will give you a sense of what units are renting for. Also search the local university's off-campus rental listings. If the rent noted in the MLS listing is lower than what you're seeing in your search, the property might have underpriced rents that you could increase over time to milk cash flow.

How to Find a Better Deal and the Right Seller

Everyone who owns real estate is a seller, whether they know it or not. The trick is to find a seller who didn't even know they wanted to sell. Once you've done your research on a particular area, and you know what average costs and rental incomes are, you're well equipped to try door knocking.

Once I found an area in my college town that I liked, I'd quickly shave so I could use my baby face to my advantage, put on some college clothes, then hit the streets to knock on doors.

I'd knock and say: "Hey, I'm studying here and looking for a good place to lease, do you have any open rooms in this building?"

If the person answered yes, not a good sign. It means there are vacancies and maybe not a strong rental market. Vacancies will kill your cash flow.

If they say no, ask if they can introduce you to the owner of the property so you can think about renting from him/her when a vacancy does open. Bonus points if you sneak in a question like: "I'll need to rent in this area in the next few years, do you mind me asking what you pay for rent?"

Once you have the owner's contact info, invite them to coffee and see if they'd be willing to sell. Offer 100x what they are making on rent per month. If their unit makes them $2K per month, offer $200K.

As a general rule to quickly analyze a real estate deal, rental income should be 1 percent of the total cost of the unit. If the seller wants $100K, monthly rents should be around $1K. This rule works because if you can't get a rent that is 1 percent of deal value, it's unlikely you'll be able to make cash flow each month after paying your financers (banks, mortgages, or other expenses we'll talk about later).

Once you figure out the price, remember to use the magic rule to figure out if you should make an offer or not. Never offer more than 100x the monthly rent. If monthly rent is $2K, don't offer more than $200K.

Let's talk about why that rule makes sense if you're looking to do a deal that generates passive income for you every month.

Finance: How to Do Your First Deal Even with No Money

Old-school people will say you need $20K up front if you want to buy a $100K piece of real estate, about 20 percent. That's not true at all. You can buy real estate without putting down any cash, or very little. To do that, you first need to analyze different funding partners. They each require different amounts of money down.

If you have a family member who will loan you the mortgage amount, they may make you put no money down, whereas a bank will make you put down a minimum of 5 percent and a maximum of 25 percent.

If you can't turn to family and must work with a bank, you can shrink your down payment if you're willing to find a multifamily house and live in one unit while you rent out the others. Or if it's a one-family house, aim for a four-bedroom, then live in one and rent out the other three.

Living in the property enables the bank to classify the loan as a "home-owner" loan versus an investment. The benefit to this is banks typically require 25 percent down on investment properties, but only 5 percent down if you're buying something you plan to live in—sometimes less.

I'll walk you through funding sources and then give examples of deals with no money down, 5 percent down, and a recent deal I did where I chose to put 25 percent down to maximize cash flow.

Partnering with a Bank

The key terms in a bank loan are:

Percent down: The amount of money the bank will require you to pay on closing day. On a $100K purchase, expect additional closing costs on top of the percent down to be about $4K and include things like lawyer fees. These are real closing costs from my last deal. I purchased the property for $425K and had $6,811.53 in closing costs:

Closing Cost Details

				Borrower-Paid		Seller-Paid		Paid by
	Loan Costs			At Closing	Before Closing	At Closing	Before Closing	Others
	A. Origination Charges			$1,840.00				
01	0% of Loan Amount (Points)		to					
02	Application Fee	to	Everett Financial, Inc. dba Supreme Lending	$150.00				
03	Closing Fee	to	Everett Financial, Inc. dba Supreme Lending	$345.00				
04	Processing Fee	to	Everett Financial, Inc. dba Supreme Lending	$695.00				
05	Tax Service	to	Everett Financial, Inc. dba Supreme Lending	$89.00				
06	Underwriting Fee	to	Everett Financial, Inc. dba Supreme Lending	$561.00				
	B. Services Borrower Did Not Shop For			$585.00				
01	Appraisal Fee	to	MYAMC, LLC		$425.00			
02	Appraisal Management Fee	to	MYAMC, LLC		$100.00			
03	Document Preparation	to	Black, Mann & Graham, L.L.P.	$60.00		$100.00		
	C. Services Borrower Did Shop For			$3,076.40				
01	Title - Escrow Fee	to	Ishmael Law Firm, P.C.	$300.00		$300.00		
02	Title - Express Mail Fee	to	Ishmael Law Firm, P.C.	$30.00		$20.00		
03	Title - Lender's Title Insurance	to	Independence Title Co.	$2,735.90				
04	Title - State of Texas Policy GARC Fee	to	Texas Title Insurance Guaranty Association	$4.50				
05	Title - Tax Certificate	to	Texas Real Tax Services, Ltd.			$43.30		
06	Title - eRecording Fee	to	Independence Title Co.	$6.00		$3.00		
	D. TOTAL LOAN COSTS (Borrower-Paid)			$5,501.40				
	Loan Costs Subtotals (A + B + C)			$4,976.40	$525.00			

Other Costs

				Borrower-Paid		Seller-Paid		Paid by
	E. Taxes and Other Government Fees			$124.00				
01	Recording Fees	Deed: $34.00 Mortgage: $90.00	to Independence Title Co.	$124.00		$30.00		
02	Transfer Tax		to					
	F. Prepaids			$1,988.98				
01	Homeowner's Insurance Premium (12 mo.)	to	Nationwide	$633.93				
02	Mortgage Insurance Premium (mo.)	to						
03	Prepaid Interest ($48.3947 per day from 01/04/2018 to 02/01/2018)	to	Everett Financial, Inc. dba Supreme Lending	$1,355.05				
04	Property Taxes (mo.)	to						
	G. Initial Escrow Payment at Closing to Everett Financial, Inc. dba Supreme Lending			$2,086.56				
01	Homeowner's Insurance	$52.83 per month for 3	mo.	$158.49				
02	Mortgage Insurance	per month for	mo.					
03	Property Taxes	$627.30 per month for 4	mo.	$2,509.20				
04	Property Taxes	per month for	mo.					
05	City Property Taxes	per month for	mo.					
06	County Property Taxes	per month for	mo.					
07	School Taxes	per month for	mo.					
08	MUD Taxes	per month for	mo.					
09	HOA Taxes	per month for	mo.					
10	Aggregate Adjustment			-$581.13				
	H. Other			$223.50				
01	2017 Property Taxes	to	Travis County Tax Collector			$3,874.48		
02	Doc Prep Fee - Deed & Release	to	Ishmael Law Firm, P.C.			$210.00		
03	Home Warranty	to	Landmark Home Warranty	$1.00		$499.00		
04	Real Estate Commission - Buyer's Realtor	to	Varela Properties, LLC			$12,750.00		
05	Title - 70% of Title Premium	to	Ishmael Law Firm, P.C.					
06	Title - Owner's Title Insurance (optional)	to	Independence Title Co.	$218.00				
07	Title - State of Texas Policy GARC Fee	to	Texas Title Insurance Guaranty Association	$4.50				
	I. TOTAL OTHER COSTS (Borrower-Paid)			$4,423.04				

Interest rate: This is how the bank makes money. It's the cost of borrowing money. On a $100K deal where you get the bank to loan you $80K, you'll pay about $600 per month, of which $300 will go toward paying down your $80K loan (called principal) and the other $300 will go to the bank as an interest payment.

The interest rate on my last deal in Austin, Texas, was 4.375 percent on a loan of $403,750 so I could purchase the house for $425,000. That interest rate meant I'd pay $2,015.86 each month to pay down the loan and to cover interest payments to the bank. For context, I make about $5K/month on this unit, so it's cash flow positive to the tune of about $1K to $2K per month.

Closing Disclosure

This form is a statement of final loan terms and closing costs. Compare this document with your Loan Estimate.

Closing Information		Transaction Information		Loan Information	
Date Issued	1/2/2018	Borrower	Nathan Latka	Loan Term	30 Years
Closing Date	1/3/2018			Purpose	Purchase
Disbursement Date	1/4/2018			Product	Fixed Rate
Settlement Agent	Independence Title Company	Seller	Pendleton Plus LLC	Loan Type	☒Conventional ☐FHA
File #	1743565-ILF				☐VA ☐_____
Property	1005 Mansell Unit B Austin, TX 78702	Lender	Everett Financial, Inc. dba Supreme Lending	Loan ID #	830170738861
				MIC #	
Sale Price	$425,000.00				

Loan Terms		Can this amount increase after closing?
Loan Amount	$403,750	NO
Interest Rate	4.375%	NO
Monthly Principal & Interest See Projected payments below for your Estimated Total Monthly Payment	$2,015.86	NO
		Does the loan have these features?
Prepayment Penalty		NO
Balloon Payment		NO

Amortization: The amount of time you have to pay back the loan. The longer you have to pay back your loan, the lower your monthly payments will be, thus increasing your monthly cash flow. A twenty-year amortization on a $100K loan at 4 percent interest means your monthly payment is higher than the same deal on a thirty-year amortization schedule.

Cash at closing: I needed to bring $18,230.89 to close on this property that would make me $2K/month. I'd get paid back in nine months and then make $2K/month in perpetuity after that, or $24K/year forever, barring some catastrophe, which insurance would cover. Good deal!

If you had $18K today, would you sacrifice it if you could get it back in nine months, then make $24K/year forever?

Summaries of Transactions	Use this table to see a summar⟩

BORROWER'S TRANSACTION

K. Due from Borrower at Closing				$431,286.53
01	Sale Price of Property			$425,000.00
02	Sale Price of Any Personal Property Included in Sale			
03	Closing Costs Paid at Closing (J)			$6,286.53
04				
Adjustments				
05				
06				
07				
Adjustments for Items Paid by Seller in Advance				
08	Property Taxes			
09	City property taxes			
10	County property taxes			
11	School property taxes			
12	MUD Taxes			
13	HOA Dues			
14				
15				
L. Paid Already by or on Behalf of Borrower at Closing				$413,055.64
01	Deposit			$3,000.00
02	Loan Amount			$403,750
03	Existing Loan(s) Assumed or Taken Subject to			
04				
05				
Other Credits				
06				
07				
Adjustments				
08	Owners Title Policy Paid by Seller			$2,680.50
09	Seller Concession			$3,606.03
10				
11				
Adjustments for Items Unpaid by Seller				
12	Property Taxes	1/1/2018	thru 1/3/2018	$19.11
13	City property taxes			
14	County property taxes			
15	School property taxes			
16	MUD Taxes			
17	HOA Dues			

CALCULATION	
Total Due from Borrower at Closing (K)	$431,286.53
Total Paid Already by or on Behalf of Borrower at Closing (L)	-$413,055.64
Cash to Close ☒ From ☐ To Borrower	**$18,230.89**

Balloon: How many years your interest rate is locked in for. If something happens ten years from now and interest rates go up to 10 percent, the bank needs a way to increase your interest rate if they gave you something like 4 percent ten years ago. A balloon is the period that you lock in your interest rate for before having to reset the rate with the bank. To minimize risk, and to get more certainty, always try to negotiate for the longest balloon period you can. The best scenario is to get a fixed-rate mortgage, but banks are usually pretty tough about giving fixed rates.

MY REAL-LIFE BANK NEGOTIATION

Below is my actual email negotiation with a potential banking partner that I ended up using on one of my first deals when I was twenty-two. This will give you an idea of how all these terms work together.

Nathan,

Here is the best final deal I can do for you. Please review and let me and Aaron know your decision so she can inform the buyer's agent this morning. This gives you two additional years before the balloon and gives you the 25 year amortization you would like but requires you to fund 25% of the purchase price and increases your rate from 4.375% to 4.50% since the balloon is pushed out an additional 2 years. There are no additional changes I can make.

Borrower: Nathan Latka

Loan Amount: $161,250 (75% of the $215K purchase price)

Amortization: 25 years

Term: 7 year balloon

Rate: 4.50%

No Bank Origination Fee or Prepayment Penalty

Approximate Monthly Principal and Interest Payment: $900 (This doesn't include the taxes and insurance which we will escrow for you monthly)

Thanks, Jonathan

• • • • •

I decided to move forward with this loan because my goal was maximizing monthly cash flow, so I ended up putting 25 percent down.

Those of you reading this and thinking, "But you had to pay 25 percent! I don't have $55K to do a deal!" You would have negotiated to 5 percent down by buying a place where you could move into one of the rooms as discussed earlier. This would hurt your monthly cash flow but enable you to do your first deal with a much smaller amount of money down. I'll give a no-money-down example in a minute.

Before I give examples of zero money down versus 5 percent down versus 25 percent down, remember that the less money you put down up front, the higher your monthly payment and the lower your monthly cash flow will be.

Here are the two comparative deals from my Excel document that I use to quickly size up any deal.

Comparing percent down on a $215K unit with $1,800 in monthly rental income:

Putting 5 percent down (about $10K) leads to a $1,135.29 monthly payment:

Purchase Price	$215,000		Estimated Appraised Value		$215,000	
Loan Amt	$204,250.00		Interest Rate 4.500%	Term	300	months
First Mortgage (P&I)	$1,135.29					
Other Financing (P&I)						
Real Estate Taxes			Estimate - depends on sales price / assessment by county			
Hazard insurance			Estimated Yearly Premium		$840.00	
PMI						
HOA	$0.00					
TOTAL PITI	$1,135.29					

Putting 25 percent down (about $55K) leads to an $896.28 monthly payment:

Purchase Price	$215,000		Estimated Appraised Value		$215,000	
Loan Amt	$161,250.00		Interest Rate 4.500%	Term	300	months
First Mortgage (P&I)	$896.28					
Other Financing (P&I)						
Real Estate Taxes			Estimate - depends on sales price / assessment by county			
Hazard insurance			Estimated Yearly Premium		$840.00	
PMI						
HOA	$0.00					
TOTAL PITI	$896.28					

Remember, the more you can afford to put down now, the lower your monthly expenses will be, which will make your monthly cash flow higher. In this deal, I chose to put 25 percent down to maximize cash flow. With

$1,800 in rental income, subtracting $896.28 leaves me a big, beautiful $900 check every month, or about $11K per year on my $55K investment (20 percent cash on cash return!). I'll show you pictures of this unit later on, but first, let me show you a no-money-down example.

Putting $0 Down (0 Percent) to Buy a $200K House

Now let's talk about what you really want to know if you're a broke college student or just have no extra money.

There are several strategies for getting a deal without putting money down. We need to figure out a way to make the 5 percent down requirement from the bank disappear (about $10K on a $200K multifamily house).

1. **Partner with a family member.** If you have a family member who has money sitting in a savings account, look at what current bank interest rates are to see what they are making on that saved money. If they have $100K saved, and interest rates are only 1 percent, you might be able to help them earn more by paying them 2 percent on a $5K loan they give you as long as it still makes financial sense for your real estate deal.

2. You may feel guilty about taking money from family members, but remember, you're helping them make more money through the interest you'll be paying them. You may not be able to get a favorable deal with a bank, but family members trust you, so use that relationship to your advantage—you're helping them make more money and they're helping you. Just be reliable in paying them back. (Otherwise Thanksgiving will not be fun.)

3. **Ask the seller to loan you money after the deal is done.** Use this script: "Seller, I just closed and put about $200K in your pocket. Would you be willing to loan me $10K of that? It'll really help me out because coming up with the cash for the down payment was tough—but I got it done! I'll start paying you back with interest immediately."

4. **Ask the owner of the property management company you'll use to write you a loan after the deal.** Property management companies take care of things like broken toilets on your rentals so you don't even have to think about them. They typically charge 10 percent of rental income ($180/month of the $1,800/

month rent in this case). In other words, they get more business if you use them—that's a strong incentive to have them write you a loan. "Property Management Company, I'll have you manage the property I just bought if you write me a $10K loan, which I'll start paying interest on immediately."

The chart below gives you an idea of what your monthly mortgage payment would be if you put 0 percent down to buy a $200K house at a 4.5 percent interest rate that you pay back over thirty years.

It doesn't matter if you're paying a family member the 4.5 percent interest rate or a bank the 4.5 percent interest rate.

% DOWN	MONEY UP FRONT	MONTHLY MORTGAGE	INCREASE MONTHLY CASH FLOW	INCREASE ANNUAL CASH FLOW
0%	$-	$1,013.37	$0	$0
5%	$10,000.00	$962.70	$50.67	$608
25%	$50,000.00	$760.03	$253.34	$3,040

This unit does $1,800/month in rent, so if you put 0 percent down, you have only about $800/month left over after paying your mortgage to cover management, repairs, property mortgage insurance, and other expenses that cut into your cash flow, which we will discuss later.

Putting $10K Down (5 Percent) to Buy a $200K House

If you get your mortgage through a bank and you're unable to use any of the strategies above to finance the 5 percent down the bank requires, a $962.70/month mortgage payment is your most likely scenario.

By coming up with an extra $10K today, the day you do the deal, you'll save about $608 per year over the life of the thirty-year loan. Big savings. If you have the capital, I recommend you use it to put it down.

Putting $50K Down (25 Percent) to Buy a $200K House

If you're fortunate enough to have $50K cash now to buy a $200K house that does $1,800/month in rental income, you're going to reap more rewards over the long term. I recommend you put down as much as possible if you have no other ways to earn a return on your $50K (e.g., other business deals, investments, etc.).

Each year of your thirty-year loan you'll make $3,040 more in cash flow. A hidden benefit of putting more than 20 percent down on any unit is that you don't have to pay PMI (private mortgage insurance).

PMI is one of many additional monthly expenses you need to consider when calculating the total amount of take-home cash you'll make each month from your investment. Let's take a look at those other management expenses now.

Manage: How to Collect Monthly Checks Without Spending Time with Renters or Fixing Toilets

Many things will cut into your monthly cash flow from a real estate investment. We already discussed the first, and biggest—your mortgage payment. These will also cut into your monthly cash flow:

Property Management Fees: This is what you'll pay someone to deal with renewing tenant leases, fixing toilets, taking tenant phone calls and complaints, cutting the grass, and more. Typically ranges between 5 and 10 percent of the monthly rent.

Real Estate Taxes: What you pay the government for your property. On a $200K property, depending on where you live, expect to pay $2K–$4,600/year on property taxes.

Hazard Insurance: This will protect the property owner against damage caused by fires, storms, earthquakes, and other natural events. Expect to pay $50 to $80/month for this on a $200K house.

Private Mortgage Insurance (PMI): This protects lenders against losses if a borrower defaults. If you partner with a family member you can avoid this. If you partner with a bank and put less than 20 percent down, expect to pay PMI. This will range between $90 and $150/month depending on your situation.

Homeowners Association (HOA) Fees: If you're buying a building in a subdivision with an HOA, you'll owe them monthly fees. This is common in apartment complexes where a $10K roof repair benefits all tenants if it's fixed.

Repairs: I always assume I'll have to spend 2 percent of monthly rents on repairs. This could be as small as a clogged sink or leak, or as big as replacing the fridge. I've found 2 percent tends to average out nicely to accurately predict repair costs.

Let's break down each of these expenses, starting with **property management fees:**

Many people never start in real estate because they think they have to be good at fixing ovens, and fans, and doors, and toilets.

Remember, the New Rich focus on building passive income streams. Fixing stuff takes time and energy, so we need to find someone else to do it. This is what property management companies are for. They'll take care of your units in exchange for a percentage of the rent. They also make money by finding you new tenants, renewing leases, and managing repairs.

To maximize your monthly cash flows, you want to negotiate your property management fee down. Do this *before* closing on the property. Use this kind of leverage to get under 10 percent management fees:

1. I'll agree to put all future properties I buy under you if you cut me a deal and manage for 5 percent of monthly rent.
2. Unfortunately, I can't buy this place unless you agree to help me out and manage for 5 percent. Paying you 10 percent means I'd lose money.

You also want to use your property management company to get an idea of rental rates and potential increases in the future.

The quickest way to be certain your place will be rented is to bring in a property manager before you do the deal. By getting the property manager to commit early, you create a psychological influence on them where they feel like they'd better get your place rented because they told you before you bought the place that they can rent it at a certain price. They're going to keep their nose to the grindstone for that. That being said, you want to plan for the worst-case scenario. I generally plan for two months per year to go unrented. I don't count on that rental income. If you can't suffer that kind of cash flow hit, then you shouldn't do the deal.

I always loop in my property managers before I close a deal by asking them questions like:

Me:

OK, I'm fine executing either of these options:

1. 4 renters pay $600/mo. (total rent $2400) and I am responsible for utilities each month

2. 4 renters pay $550/mo. (total rent $2200) and they pay for utilities <—this is my preference

I'll have my phone next to me all day tomorrow. Let's work something out with them if you think it's going to be more expensive to try and replace their lease.

. . . . .

Property Manager:

They want to do the $2400 option with utilities included. Do you want me to finalize the lease for this? I know you are losing money short term, but if you have to turn the unit over and prepare for new tenants this late in the year I think you would lose more money. I would recommend going with this and we will send renewals with the firm higher rates for next year and prepare for them to vacate and re-lease.

Thanks!

. . . . .

Getting the property manager to either agree or disagree with you on what you think you can get for rents helps align them with your goal.

My property manager will fight harder for future increases in rents because they said they felt good about increasing next year to my levels: "We will send renewals with the firm higher rates for next year."

Property managers are your biggest allies. They help you keep expenses low and also help you drive rents up. They are your local feet on the ground for any deal. Treat them well. Send birthday cards.

Real estate taxes are the next expense that can eat into your monthly cash flow. You'll pay different taxes depending on what state your deal is in.

According to WalletHub (https://WalletHub.com/edu/states-with-the-highest-and-lowest-property-taxes/11585/), the states with the lowest real estate taxes are:

Rank ⬍	State ⬍	Effective Real-Estate Tax Rate ⬍	Annual Taxes on $176K Home* ⬍
1	Hawaii	0.28%	$489
2	Alabama	0.43%	$764
3	Louisiana	0.48%	$841
4	Delaware	0.53%	$929
5	District of Columbia	0.57%	$1,005

States with the highest real estate taxes are:

46	Connecticut	1.91%	$3,357
47	Texas	1.93%	$3,392
48	Wisconsin	1.97%	$3,459
49	New Hampshire	2.10%	$3,698
50	Illinois	2.25%	$3,959
51	New Jersey	2.29%	$4,029

Take these into consideration when forecasting your monthly cash flow.

The other expenses, such as hazard insurance, PMI, HOA fees, and repairs, are generally fixed or don't have good benchmarks. So for these, educate yourself up front by finding out the real numbers before agreeing to a deal. You don't want to learn the hard way that your expenses are way higher than you'd estimated.

Now that we know more about average monthly expenses, let's take a look back at what monthly cash flows look like with 0 percent, 5 percent, and 25 percent down on a $200K house.

The following chart assumes a **best-case scenario** of 5 percent paid to property manager, 0.4 percent in annual real estate taxes, no HOA fees, minimum hazard insurance, and no repairs needed:

% DOWN	0%	5%	25%
Rent	$1,800.00	$1,800.00	$1,800.00
Mortgage	$(1,013.37)	$(962.70)	$(760.03)
PMI	$(100.00)	$(80.00)	$-
Property Manager	$(90.00)	$(90.00)	$(90.00)
Real Estate Taxes 0.4%	$(66.67)	$(66.67)	$(66.67)
HOA	$-	$-	$-
Hazard Insurance	$(70.00)	$(70.00)	$(70.00)
No Repairs	$-	$-	$-
Total Expenses	$(1,340.04)	$(1,269.37)	$(986.70)
Monthly Cash Flow	$459.96	$530.63	$813.30
Annualized Cash Flow	$5,519.56	$6,367.60	$9,759.64

Worst-case scenario might have 2 percent repairs, 10 percent to property manager, 2.3 percent property taxes:

% DOWN	0%	5%	25%
Rent	$1,800.00	$1,800.00	$1,800.00
Mortgage	$(1,013.37)	$(962.70)	$(760.03)
PMI	$(100.00)	$(80.00)	$-
Property Manager	$(180.00)	$(180.00)	$(180.00)
Real Estate Taxes 2.3%	$(383.33)	$(383.33)	$(383.33)
HOA	$-	$-	$-
Hazard Insurance	$(70.00)	$(70.00)	$(70.00)
2% Repairs	$(36.00)	$(36.00)	$(36.00)
Total Expenses	$(1,782.70)	$(1,712.03)	$(1,429.36)
Monthly Cash Flow	$17.30	$87.97	$370.64
Annualized Cash Flow	$207.56	$1,055.60	$4,447.64

Monthly cash flows are so much lower in the second scenario because real estate taxes went from $66/month to $383/month and monthly property management fees went from 5 percent to 10 percent. When looking at any deal it's always good to look at best- and worst-case scenarios.

If the worst-case scenario does not generate cash flow (monthly income greater than $0), do not do the deal. This is called "stress testing" a deal.

Don't forget that in any deal you have two ways to drive more cash flow: decrease expenses or increase revenue. Use your property manager to drive up rents each year.

In our worst-case scenario above, with 0 percent down we make only $17.30 per month ($207.56 annually). If we increase rent by $200 next year, we make $217.30 per month or $2,607.60 per year—still a win! Yes, it's a 10 percent increase, but I've done it in the past!

Three Common Questions

Is Now the Right Time for Me to Buy Real Estate?

The best time to buy real estate you'll never let go of is before you are married with kids and two dogs. It makes it easier for you to move into one of your units, which lets you get away with putting only 5 percent down.

As a general rule, always keep six months of your living expenses in a savings account. The rest? Invest!

What If I Have to Pay for Costly Repairs?

A new roof might cost $5K to $10K. Minimize your risk of having to pay for repairs by getting a home inspection done. Actually, get a home inspection no matter what. You'll get a big report back with every potential repair or building code violation, which you can ask the seller to take care of before your purchase.

How Do I Make Sure My Place Stays Rented?

Do not buy a place unless you are certain you or your property management company can get it rented. Use a site like Revestor.com to see cash flow opportunities in your area. But even in the best scenario, I like to assume a property will be vacant for two months out of the year to put a cushion in my budget.

Comparing My First Two Deals: Big Winner and Big Loser!

I was twenty-four when I did my first deal on January 8, 2014. It was a six-bedroom, four-bath duplex for $215,000 that I found through my real estate agent:

Monthly Overview:
Rental Income: $1,990
Mortgage Payment: ($1,060.57)
Management Fees: ($100)
Lawn Care: ($45)
Repairs: ($35) Net Income: $750

This unit continues to make me $750 in cash flow today. Over the past three years, it's made me almost $27K ($750/month × 36 months) in free cash flow on my initial $55K investment. Additionally, I've grown my equity position in the unit, which is as good as cash. Remember, that $1,060.57 monthly mortgage payment goes toward paying down the loan and paying interest on the loan.

If I pay down the loan, $500 in a given month, that means I own $500 more of the $215K property debt-free. After thirty years, I'll own the full $215K building plus all the rental cash flows ($750/month × 30 years as back of napkin, or about $270K). This is conservative.

Once you have a cash machine like this set up and working for you, you can begin to consider where to invest your rental income to create even more passive income.

But First, Let's Talk About My Not-So-Good Deal

I was twenty-six when I did my second deal on April 14, 2016. It was a five-bedroom, four-bath house for $328K that I found by door knocking.

Monthly Overview:
Rental Income: $2,400
Mortgage Payment: ($1,747.45)
Management Fees: ($144)
Gas: ($29) Water: ($136.96)
Electricity: ($398.48)
Lawn Care: ($45)
Repairs: ($35)
Net Income: ($136)

My mistake here was that I assumed a typical utility arrangement when I closed this deal (tenants pay). When I realized this fell on me, it cut into my cash flow significantly.

The good news is, even with losing $136/month in cash flow, I'm gaining more than that in equity in the property with each mortgage payment.

Additionally, when we renew these leases, it'll increase rent to about $3K per month and the tenants will pay utilities:

Rental Income: $3K
Mortgage Payment: ($1,747.45)
Management Fees: ($200)
Lawn Care: ($55)
Repairs: ($60)
Net Income: $947.55

I put only 10 percent down on this deal, so cash on cash returns are not horrible. There's value in the negotiation I had back and forth with the bank on this deal. Here's the thread:

Bank:

I skipped watching the tournament games and looked over your info. How about we talk at 11:55 a.m., I eat lunch and you are approved by 3:30. Here you go.

Borrower: Nathan Latka

Loan Amount: $295,200 (90% of $328,500 Purchase Price)

Repayment Terms: Monthly Principal and Interest Payments based 30 Year Amortization (P & I $1,496) GNB will escrow taxes and insurance. (Approximately $248/month) Monthly payments will be auto debited from your checking account monthly. No PMI. (Private Mortgage Insurance)

Interest Rate: 3/3 ARM—4.00%, 5/5 ARM—4.50%, 10/10 ARM 5.25% (You can pick, let me know)

Origination Fee: $350—Borrower responsible for typical closing costs. (Title Insurance, Deed of Trust Recording Costs, Appraisals, Attorney Fees)

Collateral: 209 Otey Street and 710 E Roanoke St Blacksburg VA. Subject to appraisals on both properties with minimum combined value of no less than $543,600.

If you say you are good to go I'll order the appraisals and title insurance and closing through the attorneys office. Should be able to close 1st week in April but I need to hear back quickly.

Thanks,

• • • • •

Me:

Thanks for getting this back so fast.

I could say yes to this super fast:

7% down (if you won't budge on the 10%, I'd probably pull equity out of roanoke street place—pain in ass)

5 years locked interest rate at 4%, int rate cap of 5.5% over 30 year amort schedule

I'm fine on you using both of my properties as collateral.

. . . . .

Bank:

I don't have a lot of wiggle room on this one pal, trying to get you in this easily.

I need the 10% cash down payment, we are basically using the equity in the rental house as the additional down payment since we are taking both properties. Our loan to value will be 80% total which is what makes it doable for me. Obviously if you have cash in your rental bank account you can pull that out and use it.

From a rate standpoint I'll play ball a little but again gave you a decent deal.

5/5 ARM at 4.25%, we will cap how much it adjusts every 5 years when it resets, it won't change more than 2%, won't change more than 8% over the start rate for the 30 year term.

Rate resets every 5 years are additional 5 year fixed rates equal to 1 year T-bill + 3.72% which today is 4.25%.

In reality this loan probably is not outstanding with us 5 years from now, some point your income will be simple and consistent and you'll refinance to the secondary market so the resets are not as important.

That's as far as I can stretch pal. You know I'll get it done smoothly and timely for you and your time is too valuable to go through the pains of document gathering and BS question answering with a bunch of other secondary market brokers to maybe not even get it to the finish line.

Let me know. That's the best offer I have bud.

. . . . .

Me:

Deal:)10% down

5/5 4.25% with cap of no more than 2% increase each time reset with max 8% over 30 year term

What's next? Paperwork?

• • • • •

Now, you'll look at this and see just a bad deal. However, over time this turned into a great deal when cash flows swung the other way in early 2018. Today I make about $600/month in free cash flow from this unit because of two things:

1. We increased rents.
2. We shifted utility expenses from me paying to the renters paying.

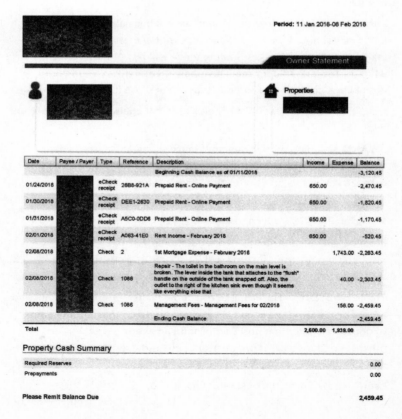

Period: 11 Jan 2018–08 Feb 2018

Owner Statement

Properties

Date	Payee / Payer	Type	Reference	Description	Income	Expense	Balance
				Beginning Cash Balance as of 01/11/2018			-3,120.45
01/24/2018		eCheck receipt	26B8-921A	Prepaid Rent - Online Payment	650.00		-2,470.45
01/30/2018		eCheck receipt	DEE1-2630	Prepaid Rent - Online Payment	650.00		-1,820.45
01/31/2018		eCheck receipt	A5C0-0DD6	Prepaid Rent - Online Payment	650.00		-1,170.45
02/01/2018		eCheck receipt	A063-41E0	Rent Income – February 2018	650.00		-520.45
02/08/2018		Check	2	1st Mortgage Expense - February 2018		1,743.00	-2,263.45
02/08/2018		Check	1086	Repair - The toilet in the bathroom on the main level is broken. The lever inside the tank that attaches to the "flush" handle on the outside of the tank snapped off. Also, the outlet to the right of the kitchen sink even though it seems like everything else that		40.00	-2,303.45
02/08/2018		Check	1086	Management Fees - Management Fees for 02/2018		156.00	-2,459.45
				Ending Cash Balance			-2,459.45
Total					2,600.00	1,939.00	

Property Cash Summary

Required Reserves	0.00
Prepayments	0.00

Please Remit Balance Due	2,459.45

Now rental income is $2,600 and expenses are about $1,939.00. A $661 check to me every month on autopilot!

When thinking about real estate investing you should always think about how to maximize cash flow. In the above negotiation you see me do a few things:

1. Lock in a 4.25 percent rate (or whatever the current rate is) for as long as possible (five years). Lower rate means lower cost of capital, which means more cash flow for me.
2. Cap the potential interest rate increase at 8 percent (this would be a worst-case sort of deal but important to protect downside).
3. Minimize cash down at 10 percent.

So there you have it. Two of my early deals: one good, one not as good!

Now let's get you your first deal and let's make it really good. Follow these steps.

SUMMARY

▶ Step 1: Find a great deal. Go to a real estate agent in your market and ask them for direct access to their "Back-end MLS." They'll put your email in their system and anytime a new deal comes on the market, you'll get an email.

▶ Step 2: Figure out how much money you can make. Peek at these deals every now and then and compare the selling price to the rental income. The MLS will have rental income listed if it exists. Look for deals where rent makes up at least 1 percent of the total deal value. If the sale price is $200K, you're looking at a good deal if rents add up to about $2K.

▶ Step 3: Finance the deal with no money down. Minimize the cash you need. The largest chunk of cash you pay in a real estate deal is the down payment. If you're living in the place you're buying, expect to put 5 percent down. If you're renting, expect to put down 20 percent. Our next step details how to get out of paying this money down.

▶ Step 4: Manage your property without spending time. Find the property management company you want to use to manage your unit after the purchase. Your business is worth about 10 percent of rental income per month. If you make $2K in monthly rent, the property management company will take $200 per month or $2,400 per year. If you intend to hold the property for life, let's say fifty years, that money starts to add up. Ask your property management company to write you a $4,800 check (two years of property management fees); otherwise tell them you won't do the deal and they'll miss out on a lifetime of 10 percent of your rental income.

► Step 5: Close the deal. Sit back and collect your monthly payment. In my example that's $500/month.

9

SPOTTING BUSINESSES TO BUY FOR VERY LITTLE MONEY

(HOW TO FIND THEM, NEGOTIATE A DEAL, AND PUT THEM ON AUTOPILOT ONCE THEY'RE YOURS)

"Invest in businesses any idiot could run because someday one will."

—Peter Lynch

I know some of you plan to skip this chapter because you think it doesn't apply to you. You're convinced buying businesses is for "other people"— people with disposable income to throw around; people who've been making business deals for decades. It's the classic mind trap that will rob you of major revenue streams. The New Rich realize this and they love you for it. More opportunity for them to play and get wealthier.

Most of the New Rich would never tell you this, but I'm on your team so I'll clue you in: You can.

So let's get the misconceptions out of the way so you can start thinking bigger.

. . .

▶ Broke Thinking: You need to have tons of money to buy a company.

▶ New Rich Truth: It's possible to buy a company with no money at all.

▶ Broke: You need to have experience making and negotiating business offers.

▶ Rich: You can make an offer with a basic email (I'll give you a template) and negotiate with just a few strategies (which I'll share).

▶ Broke: You need to know how to run a company.

▶ Rich: The companies you buy will have simple infrastructures that run themselves. You won't be in the weeds with day-to-day operations and you won't need employees because there *won't be any* daily upkeep. A company that needs daily attention is not one that you're going to buy.

▶ Broke: You need to know something about the industry you're buying into.

▶ Rich: All you need to know to buy a company is its financials, its infrastructure, and its reach. It doesn't matter what industry it's in or how much you know about that industry.

I'll be your first case study:

▶ I bought three companies by the time I was twenty-eight.

▶ I didn't pay anything for one of those companies, The Top Inbox. In fact, the founders paid me $15K to take it over. I bought an identical company that same year, SndLatr, for $1K.

▶ All three of my companies are in the tech space, but I know nothing about coding.

▶ Each acquisition began and ended with a short email. No lawyers, no painful red tape.

Here's how the deal for SndLatr started. First outreach was this email in June 2016:

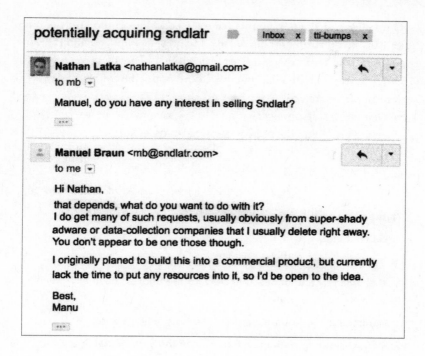

THE NO MONEY, NO LAWYERS WAY I BUY COMPANIES

Four days later, we had a deal. No lawyers, no accountants. Just an email agreement and me sending $1K via PayPal. It was an incredible setup because that $1K included a working Chrome extension and a 75,000-person email list. A lot of marketers would pay $20K to $30K or more just to build an email list of that size. I was getting it as a side product for free. Here's how the full conversation played out:

2016–06–17 15:51 GMT+02:00

Nathan Latka ▇▇▇▇▇▇▇▇▇▇

I'd be interested in buying it then investing more time energy and money to commercialize it.

Let's chat via Skype? Username?

· · · · ·

Our call was just a few minutes and I asked Manuel the kinds of questions I walk you through later in this chapter—I inquired about annual revenue (it was zero, since SndLatr was a free tool at the time), user base (75,000), how much time he spends on developing the software each week (just a couple hours), his team size (Just him. I like! He was willing to sell because it was a side project that he didn't know how to monetize. I did).

Then we picked up the conversation again on email:

2016–06–20 14:40 GMT+02:00

Nathan Latka ███████████████████████:

Great chatting!

To sum up what we discussed:

Nathan will pay a total of $1000 USD for the SndLatr business which includes but is not limited to:

1. Manuel making Nathan admin of the Chrome Extension

2. Manuel sending Nathan an Excel file of the approximately 75,000 users

3. Manuel sending Nathan the source code as is (Manuel will not be expected to update/change code)

The payment will be $500 when this document is signed (Manuel replying "I agree") and will be to Manuel's PayPal account. After the transition of 1–3 has occurred, the second half of the $500 will be deposited into Manuel's PayPal account.

Manuel, if you accept this, sign by replying with "I agree" and we can move forward.

Best,
Nathan
· · · · ·

He came back with a minor technical snag, which I didn't see as a problem because it didn't affect my ability to run the software and commercialize it (my whole purpose in buying it).

On Mon, Jun 20, 2016 at 8:10 AM,
Manuel Braun ▮▮▮▮▮▮▮▮▮▮▮ wrote:

Hi Nathan,

There is one concern that I did not think of before. Sndlatr uses some common source code that I use in some projects as well. So we'd have to make sure I can continue to do so. Would it work for you to agree that the source code is licensed under a permissive open-source license (APACHE2), instead of being sold completely?

Best,
Manu
. . . . .

2016–06–20 15:16 GMT+02:00

Nathan Latka ▮▮▮▮▮▮▮▮▮▮▮▮▮ :

Yes. I'm ok to agree that the source code is licensed under a permissive open-source license.
. . . . .

We jumped on Skype once more to talk through the details, then I followed up with this email:

Done. SndLatr started printing money for me just a few weeks later (more on how in the pages ahead).

I'll walk you through everything you need to do to buy companies, from finding them to negotiating a deal. Stick with me even if you're worried this is over your head. It's not. I'd like to believe my mom when she tells me I'm brilliant and special. That's why I'm so successful at this while you aren't, right? Maybe . . .

Or more accurately: I just had the balls to make these companies offers and see what happened. It doesn't always work—like the time I tried to buy *Success* magazine for $5M—but even when I fail I learn something from the experience. The only thing separating me from you (if you're still doubtful) is my willingness to try.

LET'S TALK CASH

If we're going to talk about buying businesses we have to talk cash. There's good news and bad news here.

The good: People tend to get stuck on the idea that "you need to have money to make money." That's true, but not as much as you'd think. You don't need a million dollars to buy a million-dollar company. You legitimately don't need any cash at all to *buy* a company. I'll show you how that works in this chapter.

The (potentially) bad (for some): You don't need cash to buy a company but you do need cash to get things set up. You're not going to buy a company you'd need to rebuild from the grave, so I'm not talking about hundreds or even tens of thousands of dollars here. But you'll have to front, say, $65 an hour per week to pay a developer from Toptal to spruce up an app you just bought, or a team of freelancers that you hire from Fiverr to maybe improve the company's website. These are your start-up costs, but they'll be infinitely less than any start-up costs you'd need to launch a business from scratch.

The problem is that most people lack the discipline to build up even $500 in savings. There's no silver bullet for that. You need to make sacrifices today so you can have cash to make these small investments that will give you huge payoffs. When you get paid you have to immediately set aside what you can—anywhere from 5 percent to 50 percent of your check. I still do that with every one of my income streams so I can keep putting money back into my companies. The good news is, once you have as little as $500 saved, you can leverage that to buy your first company.

Cue the victims' whine here: "But Nathan, I have two kids, a mortgage, a car payment, student loans, blah blah blah. Must be nice to be free to do whatever you want with your money!"

People who say these things drive me crazy.

(continued)

Your kids were a choice you made. You chose your house, so your mortgage was a choice. Your car was a choice. Your student loans were a choice. People love to see themselves as victims of their financial situation, but nearly all of their bills (or lack of bills) are a result of decisions they've made. Yes, there are exceptions, like surprise medical bills, but I'm talking here about voluntary spending.

I've chosen not to have kids until I'm thirty-five-ish so I don't have those expenses. The first house I bought wasn't for myself; it was 710 Roanoke Street, a rental property that now makes me $1K+/month in cash. I paid cash for my Prius when I was eighteen years old using my savings (mainly earned from refereeing soccer at $40 per game), so no car payment.

You get the picture. Your current money situation is a result of your choices. But your future will be, too.

You decide: Use your present reality as a bundle of excuses that lock you into poor-world, or accept it and focus your energy on working with your reality.

Some things you can change, some things you can't. I choose to have an abundance mindset and to focus on what I can change.

Your parental status isn't going to change, so you have to work around your reality. Nothing else to do about that.

But you *can* change things like how much you eat out, the car(s) you drive, or what you spend on unlimited data so you can stream episodes of *The Bachelor* on your phone.

I'm not here to school you on budgeting. Bottom line: If you're serious about joining the New Rich but don't have $500 saved to kick off a venture that could make you six figures, you need to check your spending priorities so you can start building a nest egg.

WHAT TO BUY

Buying companies is so simple. Actually, that's the most important tenet to follow when doing this. Keep it simple. If a deal or company looks too complicated, it's not worth your energy. Eventually your wealth will be nicely diversified with ten, twenty, even thirty passive income streams (I have about thirty). Owning companies can make up a huge part of your portfolio, but not if you take on complex projects.

So my nonnegotiable rule to buying: only pursue businesses that have a natural unfair advantage. It's a clear path to finding simple, cash-printing assets. The companies I buy have these innate advantages over the average business:

▶ **Digital over brick-and-mortar.** Digital companies give you a huge advantage over brick-and-mortar on overhead alone. You don't have to pay rent, utilities, and insurance on a retail space. You don't have to deal with inventory. You're not bound to regular operating hours. It's also much easier to get traffic online than it is to get feet in your store.

▶ **No employees.** Employees are usually an organization's biggest expense, so I avoid business models that rely on them. Digital products are perfect for this because you can tap the huge talent pool of freelancers on Toptal.com, Freelancer.com, Fiverr.com, etc., to do the work you need on a project basis. When the work is done you put the product on autopilot and print money until you decide to do another update (then tweak, test, and back on autopilot).

▶ **Already-established user base.** You don't want to spend time building an audience from scratch, or learn the hard way that there is no audience for your product.

▶ **Have a monopoly over a distribution channel.** I look for companies that have a monopoly over a free distribution channel so I don't have to pay for Facebook or Google ads to get traffic. For digital, these are usually marketplaces like Google Play, the Apple App Store, the Chrome Web Store, or the Salesforce AppExchange. There are millions of companies lurking in those free distribution channels waiting for you to buy them. You just need to know how to look. More on this on page 162.

Free apps and web extensions are perfect buys for beginners. They hit all of these criteria and you can usually get them for little money because the owners aren't making substantial income off them. (Hello, The Top Inbox and SndLatr.) Another bonus: the owners are often individuals or tiny companies that built the software as a side project. Because the asset is not their main focus, they're more likely to let it go.

So, my basic strategy, step-by-step:

1. Buy free digital properties with a big user base.
2. Hire a Toptal developer to put up a pay wall that appears after someone uses the product a certain number of times.
3. Reinvest the revenue back into the company as needed. Also use the income from this business to buy other companies (and to fill my pockets!).

Sound too simple? It is. The only reason everyone isn't doing this is because they haven't thought of it, or they think it's more complicated than it is. Keep reading—I'll unpack my approach in greater detail and show you how I did it with The Top Inbox.

A PEEK AT MY MONTHLY REVENUE STREAMS

I want you to see the ways I make money so you can get a clear understanding of how diversified I am. My income sources range from food trucks to hostels to software companies. But the trick lies in one key word: momentum. Don't get lost in all my revenue streams and try to copy them all immediately. Focus on getting one thing going, then use the momentum from that to start diversifying into others. That way you're not using your own money. You're using cash you've generated from things in which you invested an initial $500. Here are some things that I invested very little in to start and that are now printing money for me:

(continued)

Real estate: $1,600/month

GetLatka.com database: $50K+/month

eTools: $10K/month

TopInbox/SndLatr: $6K/month

Airbnb: $2K/month

Helping my friends buy/sell software companies via
    retainers: $50K+/month

Hostel dividends: $800/month

Royalties on food truck: $800/month

Royalties on meal prep service: $800/month

Podcast sponsorships: $50K+/month

Reality show on Facebook: $20K+/month

LOOK IN THESE THREE PLACES TO FIND A COMPANY TO BUY

In his book *Zero to One*, Peter Thiel talks about how important it is to launch a company that has a monopoly. He means you want a Google—a company so good at what it does that no others can compete with it. It owns the market. We'd all love that, but those companies are hard to find and hard to buy. But what's close, and much easier to acquire, is a company that has a monopoly over a distribution channel. That's the number one thing I look for when analyzing a business to take over.

The Top Inbox (originally called Mail2Cloud) and SndLatr are perfect examples of this. Both are Google Chrome extensions that help people use Gmail more efficiently. They do the same thing, but they started out as two separate companies that I bought independent of each other. This was strategic. By buying two tools that do the same thing, I can run them on the same code base and save half the developer costs. I also knocked out a good chunk of competition by buying two companies that dominate the same distribution channel.

When I discovered Mail2Cloud it had already been in the Chrome Web Store for five years. It was rated as a top recommendation in the store's Productivity category and had more than two thousand five-star reviews.

It was no Google, but Mail2Cloud clearly had a solid spot in a specific distribution channel—the Chrome Web Store's Productivity corner. Mail-2Cloud's user data on ChromeBeat.com also showed that it had been consistently adding one hundred new users every day for the last four years. That was enough information to make me want to keep exploring.

There are lots of different ways to monopolize a channel. A company might be one of the most popular apps in the Apple App Store for document signing. It might be number one in its category on G2 Crowd or another review site.

If a business has a natural monopoly on a distribution channel, it's a great sign that the company is running itself, or at the very least, that it's not a complete disaster. People wouldn't constantly download an app and give it strong reviews if it weren't functioning smoothly. That's huge. You don't want a company that requires you to be smart or work hard. You want one that you can put on autopilot with just a few tweaks by freelancers.

What's even better is if you find a company that hasn't monetized its top spot in that distribution channel. That's what happened with Mail2Cloud and SndLatr. Both company owners weren't charging users, so as soon as I took them over I hired developers to put up a simple $5/month pay wall that pops up after fifty uses. I immediately started making money from it. Now, less than two years after acquisition, The Top Inbox and SndLatr have made more than $130K in revenue. This is so easy to do. You can hire freelance developers at NathanLatka.com/toptal (site I use, and I get a kickback) to build something like a pay wall for a few hundred bucks.

This is the only change I made on SndLatr and The Top Inbox to go from no sales when I acquired to $130K over the first eighteen months. If someone clicks Choose a plan they pick $5/month or $50/year.

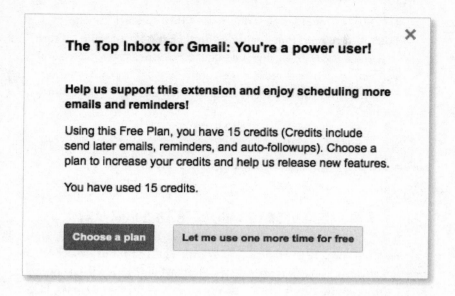

I didn't have to know anything about software development to do this. It was the perfect scenario. Minimal work and brainpower. Effortless cash flow. I keep winning.

Companies like this are hiding in plain sight. Try searching these free distribution channels and see what turns up. Megacorporations like Google, Apple, etc., will own the top results. They're not what you're looking for. Scroll down a bit until you get to the tools being offered by small to midsize companies. When you find an app or a tool with strong reviews and a large user base, check to see the last time it was updated (more on this in a moment). Start searching:

- ▶ Browse sites like AppAnnie.com, the Chrome Web Store, the Salesforce AppExchange, the Intuit App Center, or the Apple App Store for the top mobile apps in different industries and categories.
- ▶ See what companies rank high on G2 Crowd.
- ▶ Search CrunchBase.com for companies that raised capital but haven't gotten new funding in the last three years. They're probably failing, and you're likely to get them for a great deal. I have several friends who have bought companies for $30K or less af-

ter those companies raised at least $10M in start-up capital. I don't recommend that beginners do this, but if you build up the experience to take on this kind of acquisition, always make sure you can identify the reason the company is failing and whether it's something you can easily turn around (see page 170 for more on this).

You can also send an email to your list, if you have one, or post on Facebook to let people know you're looking for a company to buy.

I WAS PAID $15K TO TAKE OVER THIS COMPANY

I already told you a little about my deal with The Top Inbox. Many of my smartest advisers said it was brilliant. So simple, I didn't even need lawyers. And I had to know very little about running the business to make it instantly profitable.

I just went to the Chrome Web Store and browsed extensions under the Productivity category. Mail2Cloud was at the top with more than two thousand five-star reviews and thirty thousand active users. Its profile data showed that the extension hadn't been updated in more than eighteen months. That was a signal to me that the developers and the owner were not committed to continuing to make it better. Maybe they forgot about it, or maybe they didn't see it as an asset. Whatever the case, it got me thinking I could maybe get it for a great price.

It takes time and tedious searching to find these deals, but they are out there. If they were easy to find, everyone would do them.

When searching for apps or Chrome extensions I go entirely by reviews, number of users, and the date the software was last updated. If reviews and users are high and the last update was more than a few months ago, I consider it a prospect.

When you find something promising put it in a Google Doc and be sure to touch base with the creator once every six months. That way when they think about selling, they'll think about reaching out to you. I have a spreadsheet of two hundred companies, apps, and extensions I'm actively tracking. Here's my file, which you saw earlier:

Likley to acquire?	I	L	Notes/Type		Type	Link	users	Action		Next Step	Acq. Price	F
3			B2B Leads		Buy	https://gainful.io/		Emailed 1/27/2017			$22,000	0
10		In	Dhruv chatting w		Buy			Emailed 10/26/2017		Dhruv chatting w	$100k	$
Done Deal			Direct		Buy		35,094	Emailed 6/20/16			$1,000	
Done Deal			Direct		Buy	https://chrome.go	7000	Emailed 10/28/2016			$100	
Done Deal			Direct		Buy	https://chrome.go	39493	Emailed 7/5/2016			-$15k	F
7			churn saas redu									
		1/	Direct		Buy			Called 1/9/2018				
			B2B leads									
8			Direct		5/5/2016	https://chrome.go	378,000 users 1/	Emailed 10/29/2017		com	1.4 cents per ma	$
8			Direct		5/5/2016	https://chrome.go	11964	Emailed 8/7/2017			$1,200,000	
7			Direct			https://chrome.go	1700	Emailed 1/27/2017			$10,000	
7		S	Direct		sold scripted to S			Emailed 8/7/2017		He's holding on t	$200k	
7			Direct		Buy	https://chrome.go	2337	Emailed 1/27/2017		Asked Trever Fa	like nothing	
7			Direct					Emailed 8/7/2017			$250k total rever	
7			Direct			https://chrome.go		Emailed 8/7/2017		One of them goi		
6			Direct			https://chrome.go	15,000	Called 1/27/2017		He's thinking for		
5			Direct		Buy	https://chrome.go	98000	Emailed 11/10/2016				
4			Direct		not sure							
4			Direct			https://chrome.go	26109					
4			Direct			https://chrome.go	3439	Meet in SF, 212-729-7551				
1			Direct		5/5/2016	https://chrome.go	1107530 users					
1			Direct		5/5/2016	https://chrome.go	54300					1

Once you find a company you really like, use the email below to reach out. It's the script I use every time.

First, get the CEO's email using a tool called Etools.io (I own this tool, too).

For my Mail2Cloud deal, I sent the CEO this cold email:

Subject: Potentially Acquiring Mail2Cloud

Message: Hey, [CEO's name]—Would you be open to a chat about me potentially acquiring Mail2Cloud?

• • • • •

That was the start.

Originally he said no. So I told him to keep me in mind and left it alone.

A few months later the CEO was raising capital for a different project and investors saw Mail2Cloud as a distraction. So he reached back out to me and said he was interested in selling. I was in.

During a Skype call Mail2Cloud mentioned they had a $100K liability on their balance sheet. They called it a "partnership" with another company, but the bottom line is that it was a debt. I put a huge focus on this. I said, "Wow, so if I take this company over I'm responsible for paying off this $100K. That's a lot of money." I had the upper hand if I could renegotiate this debt.

Every company has liabilities. You want to find them and leverage them to get a great deal done. In this case I asked Mail2Cloud's CEO to introduce me to the person who owned their debt. I'd be making monthly payments to him, so this was a reasonable request. I then built a relationship with him and asked whether we could find a way to restructure the debt if I were to buy Mail2Cloud.

There are all kinds of ways to restructure debt, so use that to your advantage if you find it on a company's balance sheet. The debt owner would much rather work with someone who is going to grow the company than lose their investment (i.e., the money they loaned) if the company shuts down.

I struck a deal to extend Mail2Cloud's debt terms by two years. Now my monthly payments are smaller, making it easy to service that debt just from my revenue.

Meanwhile, I offered to take over Mail2Cloud, and their debt, if they'd pay me $18K. This was a great deal for them to get a $100K liability off their back. It was a win-win for everybody—but at first they declined. They said they loved the offer, but their board wouldn't approve it even though they knew it was a great deal. I cut that conversation off immediately:

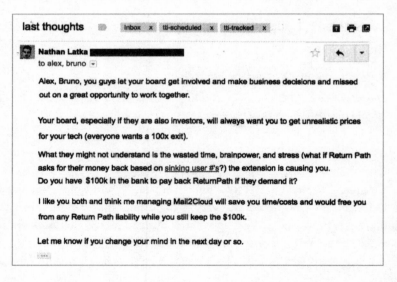

last thoughts   ☐   Inbox x   tti-scheduled x   tti-tracked x

Nathan Latka
to alex, bruno ▾

Alex, Bruno, you guys let your board get involved and make business decisions and missed out on a great opportunity to work together.

Your board, especially if they are also investors, will always want you to get unrealistic prices for your tech (everyone wants a 100x exit).

What they might not understand is the wasted time, brainpower, and stress (what if Return Path asks for their money back based on sinking user #'s?) the extension is causing you.
Do you have $100k in the bank to pay back ReturnPath if they demand it?

I like you both and think me managing Mail2Cloud will save you time/costs and would free you from any Return Path liability while you still keep the $100k.

Let me know if you change your mind in the next day or so.

When you buy a company, especially if it's a mature company with an established board, the founders will often try to use the board as the bad guy to kill deals. And the founders will try to stay on your good side. You have to know how to manage how they're using their board in the deal and cut that off. Your goal is to not let them use the board as an excuse to kill the deal or to get you to pay more.

Sure enough, a couple months later they came back and said, "Yes, Nathan, let's do the deal!"

They negotiated down to $15K and we had a deal ($3K less than my initial offer was not much in the grand scheme of things). Once we agreed on the terms, they paid me the $15K, transferred all of the company's files to me, and it was done. It took about two hours.

When I closed the deal it was literally six bullet points in an email. Any of you can copy this. It will hold up in a court of law. And frankly, it should be this simple. You don't want to buy someone's company if you think they're going to screw you over with a convoluted deal.

This was my deal-closing email thread with Mail2Cloud:

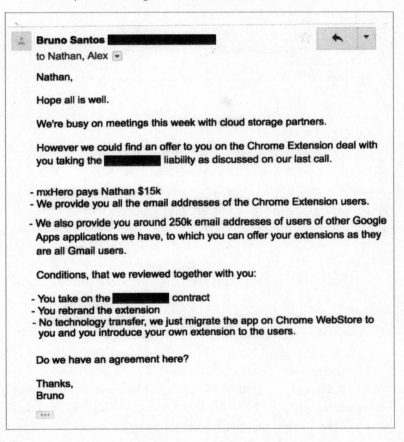

Bruno Santos

to Nathan, Alex ▾

Nathan,

Hope all is well.

We're busy on meetings this week with cloud storage partners.

However we could find an offer to you on the Chrome Extension deal with you taking the ███████ liability as discussed on our last call.

- mxHero pays Nathan $15k
- We provide you all the email addresses of the Chrome Extension users.

- We also provide you around 250k email addresses of users of other Google Apps applications we have, to which you can offer your extensions as they are all Gmail users.

Conditions, that we reviewed together with you:

- You take on the ███████ contract
- You rebrand the extension
- No technology transfer, we just migrate the app on Chrome WebStore to you and you introduce your own extension to the users.

Do we have an agreement here?

Thanks,
Bruno

After a couple follow-ups we had this final exchange:

GOLDEN GOOSE OR TRAIN WRECK?

A company acquisition usually goes through these steps. It doesn't always happen in this order (when I offered to buy *Success* magazine I jumped straight to the letter of intent, or LOI) but this is the basic breakdown:

1. **Inquiry**—"Hey, are you interested in selling X company?"
2. **Offer and Negotiations**—Back and forth until you agree on a sale price.
3. **Letter of Intent (LOI)**—I usually make this a quick email outlining the terms I want, but it can be an official letter. Once all agree to the terms in the LOI you will usually sign a nondisclosure agreement (NDA).
4. **Due Diligence**—Post-NDA, when you scour their books and internal systems. This is where you'll discover any liabilities that will give you leverage to decrease your purchase price or renegotiate other deal points. If both sides can't come to an agreement, you walk away. Nothing lost except your time.

Keep your "train wreck" radar on high alert at every step. You want to buy companies that are easy to run, and that means their financials and infrastructure need to be sound. If no red flags appear during steps 1 to 3, keep sleuthing during Due Diligence.

When reviewing their books, pay close attention to how the selling price they agreed to compares with their last twelve months' revenue. A sale price that's anything less than half of their last twelve months' revenue is generally a good deal. You just need to understand why they're willing to sell at such a cheap price and then figure out if you're able to fix the problem.

Great questions to ask that will uncover red flags during Due Diligence include:

- How long do customers stay with you on average?
- How are you getting customers?
- What does the average customer pay you per month?
- Is there any one customer that makes up more than 10 percent of your revenue?

Also ask the seller about any debt or signs of decreased revenue on their books. As you uncover these details you'll start to see where you can get leverage, where the business is weak and where it's strong. It also helps you start to figure out how to craft a revised deal with that leverage in hand.

If you're buying a digital property, you also want to make sure the product already runs well. The easiest way to do this: download and use it. Is the interface intuitive? Is it a useful tool? Does it seem like something you could get addicted to, or something you'd quickly forget about? Do you notice any bugs?

And the biggest question to ask yourself as you tinker on the user end of a free digital tool: What changes do I need to make to generate my first dollar of income? You can usually accomplish this by simply putting up a pay wall where you see the most addictive behavior happening. For The Top Inbox and SndLatr, I had a hunch that I could drive my first dollar if I put up a pay wall at a certain number of uses. Sure, I'd lose some of the current thirty thousand users, but enough of them would be hooked after fifty uses to drive solid income. Then I could use that revenue to reinvest in additional developers as needed.

If the user experience is good, you still need to uncover how much work (and money) you'd need to put into the product once it's yours. You can figure this out even if you're not tech-savvy. Remember, I know nothing about coding. I just know how to ask the right questions.

HOW TO BUY A TECH COMPANY IF YOU HAVE NO TECH EXPERIENCE

The most revealing detail is the number of hours they spend on development. If they spend only an hour a week, then you know it's a pretty simple tool. You can assume you're going to hire someone about an hour a week to take over. If they say they have a team of ten people and they work full time on it every day, you don't want to touch it. It's going to be really expensive. So ask questions like:

- ▶ How much time do you spend on coding?
- ▶ How many bugs are there?
- ▶ How many support tickets do you get every week? (If they get a lot of support tickets it's a sign that the software is buggy and that the user base is not happy.)
- ▶ How frequently do you push out updates to the code? (You ideally want something that doesn't require monthly updates.)

If everything checks out and you've come to an agreement with the seller, go for it. You can always work a clawback provision into your agreement as an added safety net if surprises pop up postacquisition. (See page 174 for more on clawbacks.)

NEGOTIATING THE BEST DEAL: ASK THIS ONE QUESTION

When I started buying companies in my twenties no one took me seriously. I had capital to buy whatever I wanted, but it was tough to get big, powerful executives to engage with me at all. Until I tested one question. To get people to throw out their first number, I asked, "What is a number that, if you got it, you'd be totally shocked and really excited?"

The question gives the potential seller permission to be unrealistic, but you're at least getting them in the habit of thinking about selling, and throwing out a number.

When I acquired The Top Inbox, I asked the question and got back a number I would never have paid. I then followed this script:

Me: Well, I'd love to make you really happy, but you're right, I would be dumb if I paid that price. If you Google "What do free software tools sell for?" what prices do you see? How does the number you threw out match up?

The trick here is to use market data to let the CEO you are negotiating with convince themselves of a lower price. Lead them in a direction that you know will benefit you. In the case of sale prices for free software tools, they'll see a bunch of answers like $0, $1K, or other very low numbers, which will help them come around to accepting your lower offer.

Getting a good deal involves a lot of art and science. Here are some things that combine both art and science that you should make sure you talk about on every deal to figure out where your leverage is.

Find out why the founders own the company. Is it a big focus in their life right now? If it's not, why is that? Ask questions like, "Is this project your full-time gig or is it a side project?" You want them to say it's a side project because that means they're not living off the revenue. They have a full-time job. Good news for you, because they're more likely to sell it cheap if they aren't relying on it.

Find out what's going on in their life. You can say, "Tell me more about where you live. What are you working on?" If they say they live in San Francisco but are looking to move to DC, or that they are having a kid, etc., it's a good sign. Any life stresses that are going to take time make it more likely that they will sell you their business now so they have less to focus on.

Get a feel for company size. Ask, "Is the company just you in your basement or is there a team of people backed by millions in funding?" If they have a big team with millions in funding you're probably not going to be able to get a deal done, so walk away.

Show how you'll make their customers happy. Start by asking something like, "What would you do to this tool if you could spend more money on the company?" Then tell them that when you buy it you're going to put more resources on it to make it better and that their customers are going to love it. A lot of founders obviously care about their customers. If you can help them see how you're going to give their customers a better product after the acquisition, they're more likely to do a deal.

Understand the emotional triggers driving the deal. This is the number one thing you can do to close at a price you like. One of my favorite things to ask a CEO or founder is, "After you sell this company, what are you going to do next?" They start convincing themselves by telling you what they want to do. It makes them want to go do that thing more, which gives you leverage because then they want to get rid of their current company more. You can also ask questions like, "If I pay you $10K to acquire your business, what would you spend the money on?" They'll reveal things like, "I'll use it to pay off my mortgage!" Knowing this, you can negotiate a more favorable deal: "How about I give you $1K now and then pay your last ten mortgage payments over the next year? That way you and your family don't have to even think about it." This saves you cash up front and still helps the founder get what they want! It's why the most powerful question you can ask in negotiations is, "What will you do with the money once I pay you?" Roger Fisher and William Ury argued in *Getting to Yes* that you must be "hard on the problem, soft on the people." This is a great way to end up doing a crappy deal. If anything, ignore the thing you're trying to buy (soft) and focus on the person (hard) and why they want to do the deal. Negotiate exclusively around that. In the example above it was a mortgage, but it could also be college tuition for kids, a car, medical bills to pay off, or a variety of other things. Figure out what the key decision maker wants to use the cash from the deal on and then help them get that while lowering the cash you pay.

Do something shocking to reset their perception of you. I start many negotiations where I am buying a company with: "If I buy this company, I will immediately shut off the pay wall, kill the revenue stream, and focus on growth." I say this because I want the CEO to understand that I'm not going to value the company based on the revenue stream, because I don't care about the revenue stream (to start). I'm going to focus on growth. That's really important because a lot of CEOs will tie their valuation to a very unrealistic multiple of their revenue. They'll say, "I did $100K last year, so I want $1M, or ten years' worth of revenue." That argument is dead if you tell them up front that the revenue stream is meaningless to you. After I buy the tool at a great price, and once the other CEO is working on their next thing, *then* I put up a pay wall where I think it makes the most sense. *Then* I focus on revenue. But I'm not buying it for the revenue.

THE DEAL AND PAYMENT TERMS ARE VERY DIFFERENT THINGS

I keep promising that you don't need cash to buy a company. This is absolutely true—and it all comes out in the payment terms. There's a big difference between the deal size and payment terms. For example, you can buy a company for a million bucks and hand over no cash on the day of the deal. Here's how that might work:

Say a company is making $30K/month in revenue. You can offer to buy it for $1M, which makes the current owner look good. He can tell all his friends he sold his company for $1M. Then your payment terms can look something like this:

You pay nothing, or maybe a few thousand, up front.

You agree to pay the seller 50 percent of revenue in perpetuity until you've paid him $1M.

Win-win: The seller can ethically say he sold the company for a million bucks. It's a great story line for him. You're minimizing your out-of-pocket cash and creating leverage for yourself.

Once you negotiate the deal price, you can sweeten the deal with any combination of terms, like:

- ▶ A chunk payable now, and some over time.
- ▶ Paid all over time.
- ▶ Paid all over time and only if the business doesn't start declining postacquisition.
- ▶ Clawback funds. A clawback is a provision in your agreement that says if X happens within a certain time frame after you've taken over a company, the seller has to pay you back X amount. So say, for example, you buy a company that has ten thousand users. And let's say that right after you buy it, something happens where you

lose five thousand of those users because of something the previous owner did that is out of your control. If you suspect there is a risk of something like this happening you can put a clawback in the deal that says the seller has to pay you back 50 percent of the deal if the number of users declines by over 50 percent in the first six months that you own the company.

DO THESE SIX THINGS AFTER YOU BUY A COMPANY

Once I take over a company I run it through my playbook to get it operating at top efficiency. I've accumulated this playbook over nearly a decade of taking over and running companies, and The Top Inbox and SndLatr are prime examples of how these moves can turn a mediocre company into a golden goose.

You can juice revenue from a newly acquired business by focusing on these five steps from my playbook, which I apply every time I take a company over:

> ▶ **STEP 1: Double pricing.** Do this the moment you take over a company—only for addicted users. If the product was free, start charging. If pricing was already established, double it. As consumers we love "free," but we also believe that we get what we pay for. And we're willing to pay for something that brings us value.
>
> Zendesk SVP Matt Price and his team witnessed this when they experimented with adding free features to their customer service platform. They discovered that doing this made customers feel they were overpaying because they were getting things they didn't want. So now they use a pricing structure that allows companies to pay for the value they're getting out of the software. Their Answer Bot feature follows this model. Answer Bot automatically answers customers' questions by tapping into available resources. The value to customers to not have to send that query to a support agent is very high—they'd usually have to spend $10 to $20 per query for a human to answer it. So instead of bundling Answer Bot with the features customers get in their software subscription; they price it out separately, at $1 per resolution.
>
> Zendesk also spiked revenue by matching price tiers to the value

a product brings to customers. "You can enter into pricing decisions with your eyes very wide open as to what people are using and set thresholds based on types of businesses," says Price. "Typically there's an opportunity to add a premium price into features that have very specific utility to a small number of customers."

Today Zendesk has two thousand employees, but start-ups can easily adopt similar strategies. One that's doing this is Gus Chat, a customer service company that specializes in chatbots—that is, automated customer service reps. CEO Pablo Estevez is growing the company by specializing in Spanish-speaking chatbots for enterprise clients. Gus Chat started with small-scale clients paying around $1,500 a month for their service, but now Estevez is scaling by offering those same services to larger clients who pay $10K to $25K a month. Estevez explains, "One of our focuses has been finding a niche in the market. We're realizing there's a big demand in enterprise deals for us to come in, get to really know the company, and create a custom solution."

It's fine to start small when you're still getting the kinks out, but aim to scale by finding new customers who are willing to pay a premium for the value you offer.

▶ **STEP 2: Focus on getting current customers to pay more.** Step 1 is about scaling your prices for new customers. But you can double your business without adding a single new customer by getting your current user base to pay you more, or to buy more from you. It's why your Netflix and Amazon Prime subscriptions creep up by a few dollars every year. But aside from raising prices, top CEOs know it takes less energy to expand their footprint with current customers than it does to find new ones—and the success rate is much higher.

Manny Medina, CEO of the sales engagement platform Outreach, has made this his growth mantra: "Reduce your land and accelerate your expand." He grew Outreach from $0 to $10M in annual revenue over just two years (from 2015 to 2017), and today he has more than doubled revenue year over year by focusing on current customers alone. "Our job is to land as fast as we can in the smallest thing that we can and then expand," says Medina. "The phrase we have here is 'make them a customer.' The moment you make them a customer the magic shows up." Once a customer is in,

Medina and his team obsess over making sure active users are getting the most out of the platform. "If you keep that user active and successful, you're going to retain them forever." From there, they drive growth by adding product lines, finding adjacent sources of business, and expanding the number of users within a company.

When you think about growth, think from within. Ask yourself: What else would my current customers be willing to pay for? Where does the value lie for them? Jump to chapter 12 for more on growth strategies with current customers.

▶ **STEP 3: Optimize SEO.** The options for search engine optimization (SEO) tools are endless but you can optimize your SEO for free, so make this a focus as soon as a company is yours. Nikos Moraitakis, CEO of the recruiting software company Workable, got his company to $10M in annual revenue before ever hiring a salesperson. As of July 2018, Workable has six thousand paying customers and adds four to five hundred every month. It's also the most popular HR website in the world, with twenty-three million unique annual users. In those early days Moraitakis just focused on creating great content around the question: What do people look for when hiring? He and his team started by posting descriptions for the one hundred most popular jobs, along with templates for offer letters, sample interview questions, and recruiting templates. "A lot of people found us by searching for interview questions or offer letter templates, then discovered the software and became customers," Moraitakis says.

If you want to spike your SEO beyond organic content I recommend using SEMrush. It's the platform I use and understand despite knowing very little about SEO. It's a great tool for beginners to get an edge.

▶ **STEP 4: Change where your payment pop-up shows.** If you don't have a pay wall yet, you already know you should add one. But also make sure you're adding it in the right spot. Tying payments to usage metrics is such an effective approach because the more someone uses something, the more likely they are to get addicted to it, or rely on its utility, and be willing to pay.

If a simple pay wall doesn't work with your business model it's still smart to tie price to usage—this ties back to step 1. Josh Haynam, cofounder of Interact Quiz Builder, charges clients based on the amount of data they capture every time someone interacts with their quizzes. Companies rely on Quiz Builder to collect data, so the more data they capture, the more value the product brings to them, the more willing they'll be to pay a higher price.

▶ **STEP 5: Understand the actions that turn leads into customers.** For a brick-and-mortar store, you always want customers to walk to the back of the store. That action gets them to see more products and potentially pick things up off end caps. It's why the most alluring section in the store—the sale rack—is always at the back.

Digital properties also need customers to do certain things to become sticky. Facebook knows they need to get you to add seven new friends in the first seven days for you to get addicted to the platform. Dashlane, a password management app, knows that free users are most likely to turn into paying customers if they do two things within the first five hours of installing the app: add ten or more passwords, and install the app on at least two devices. So Dashlane CEO Emmanuel Schalit and his team doubled down on getting new users to do these things with as little effort as possible.

Their tactics: When someone installs the app they're prompted to link it to their email account. That lets Dashlane identify, through the user's emails, all the accounts they have. But nobody wants to manually add all their passwords to the app. So from there, users are prompted to install Dashlane on their computer so the program can import all the passwords from their browser. It's a double bonus—the user doesn't have to deal with inputting passwords, and Dashlane removes the passwords from their unsecured browser. As of October 2017, Dashlane has roughly 650,000 customers paying $3 to $4 a month to use its product ($23M per year in revenue!).

▶ **BONUS STEP 6: Launch an affiliate program or partner network.** This incentivizes others to help you drive sales by giving them a cut of revenue for customers they send your way. The most important thing about an affiliate program is to make sure you set up an offer that other people are likely to then sell through to their audience—30 percent of the sale price is a motivating number, for example. Once you have that structure set up you can decide whether you want to use software to manage the program. I use

Ambassador. Nikola Mircic bootstraps his drag-and-drop CMS software, Sitecake (Sitecake.com), by partnering with white label clients who then use the software to build websites for their customers. He charges clients a percentage of their annual sales revenue in exchange for tech support. This model works so well that he hasn't had to raise capital (so he keeps full control of the company) and he can scale it as much as he wants. His clients range from mega corporations to "tech guys" building websites for their local small businesses.

The Top Inbox and SndLatr had no revenue when I took them over but had huge user bases and email lists associated with them. I got all that for free. In fact, I made $14K doing it. (Remember, I got paid $15K to take over The Top Inbox, and I paid $1K for SndLatr.)

Between May 1, 2016, and April 6, 2018, I used my playbook to sign up 1,327 customers who pay me every month. Total sales have passed $130K. Not bad considering I didn't start either company.

MY STRIPE ACCOUNT SCREENSHOT

These are the kinds of returns smart investors go after. Infinite returns, actually. Below is a screenshot from Stripe, the payment system I use for these tools, which shows customer sign-ups and sales:

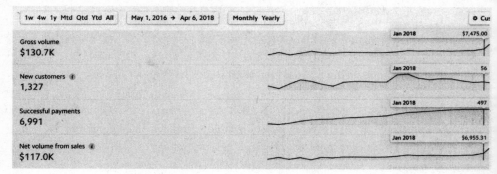

I then pumped this $130K back into the companies, or into my own pocket. Remember, this is all "house money" at this point since I paid nothing to get it. Moving forward, I want to buy only companies that have a recurring revenue stream so that I keep getting richer and richer each month.

It's why I got excited when the founder of Etools.io sent me this email in March 2017:

The partnership he proposed didn't work out because I was more interested in buying the whole company. At the time he wasn't interested, and he went dark for six months. Then I got this email:

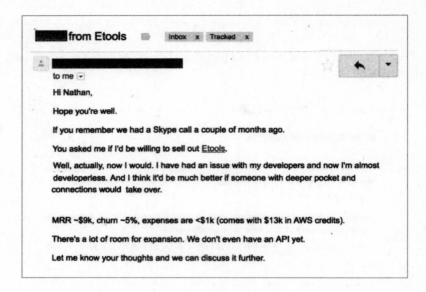

(Note: MRR = Monthly Recurring Revenue; Churn = annual percentage of customers who stop paying for the service.)

In January 2018, I ended up buying Etools for 1x annual revenues, or about $125K—all money that came from my other ventures. I didn't have to make any changes to the company after buying it. It was a clean takeover that immediately started pumping revenue into my bank account.

Now SndLatr, The Top Inbox, and Etools, my first three acquisitions, altogether are doing about $18K per month in sales. I take about 60 or 70 percent of that to the bottom line. All from companies that I didn't create.

It's why I argue that it's much smarter, cheaper, and less risky to buy companies than it is to start them.

$5M FAILED TAKEOVER ATTEMPT

Make a habit of spending one hour a week prospecting for new deals. Make offers. Do things when you don't have to. Don't wait until you have money lying around to start building relationships to do a deal. Start negotiating when you don't have to, when you don't care about it, when you always planned to walk away anyway.

(continued)

I will buy many media companies over my life. One that I never cared to own is *Success* magazine. While some say its owner might be smart, the magazine had been poorly run until recently by out-of-touch people who still put CDs in its jacket cover. Because I couldn't care less about doing a deal with *Success* (nothing to lose if they say no!), it was the perfect opportunity to drum up some deal flow by issuing a $5M letter of intent and posting it on my blog.

This did a few things:

- It signaled to other media properties that I'm a buyer.
- *Success* might have responded and negotiated with me. Because I never wanted the deal, it allowed me to stay emotionally removed from it and drive a good bargain if I ended up wanting to close the deal at the end.
- Many ex-employees at *Success* reached out to me saying they'd love to rejoin the company if I owned it. Now I have a stable of sharp media minds ready to work for me should I ever launch my own media venture. Talk about a cheap way to recruit! Most recruiters charge $30K+ (30 percent of first-year salary).
- The press loves this sort of story, so many big, talented outlets like Entrepreneur.com wrote about it. Saved me $7K that I would have had to pay a PR firm to get me the same exposure!

When I initially reached out to the CEO he wouldn't even return my emails. So I thought, How can I get his attention? That's when I posted my letter of intent directly on my blog, and within minutes the CEO's lawyers reached out, he reached out, and I had direct contact. He would not sell the company to me, which turned out to be a good thing because about six months later he shut down the whole magazine (though it later rebounded).

(continued)

By the way, at that time I did not have $5M, but if I had negotiated to buy *Success* for that amount I knew I could reach out to my network and raise enough money to do the deal. But in this case I got rejected and moved on to the next deal. There will always be another deal.

Also, my new magazine is a massive hit. Sometimes you have to bet on yourself and go from scratch! Take one look at the magazine landing page and you can probably figure out why it's doing so well: http://NathanLatka.com/magazine.

The Top Entrepreneurs in Money, Marketing, and Life
Nathan Latka brings you entrepreneurs who...

The Latka Agency LLC– The Top Podcast

Stuart Johnson, CEO, Success.com (Success Partners)
5800 Democracy Dr
Plano, Texas 75024

Dear Stuart,

As host of the fastest growing business podcast of 2016 "The Top Entrepreneurs" on iTunes, I'm writing this letter to express my intent regarding the offer to potentially acquire substantially all of the assets of **Success Magazine** (the "Business"), which are used in the business of operating **Success.com** for **$5,000,000** on and subject to the following terms and conditions, and subject to the execution by Seller and Purchaser of a mutually acceptable definitive asset purchase agreement (the "Definitive Agreement") and related ancillary documents.

1.   Acquisition of Assets; Purchase Price.

(a)   At the closing (the "Closing"), Seller will sell, transfer and

BUYING BUSINESSES VERSUS STARTING OR INVESTING IN ONE

If buying a business sounds intimidating, know that it's actually way smarter, easier, and less risky than starting one. I'm not saying you shouldn't launch a new venture. Most of this book is advice on starting and running a business. But buying a business, by comparison, is much more efficient. Once you take a company over, all the groundwork is done. Your systems are in place and running themselves. You have a built-in customer base. All you have to do is tweak and monetize what's already there. If a company needs more than that, you're not going to buy it. It's that simple.

You might wonder why you would ever start a company if I'm advocating for just buying. Well, remember, I started Heyo from scratch when I was nineteen. And while I was building Heyo to eventually do more than $5M in sales, I learned things like how a team works; how vesting and equity work; how to get ten thousand customers from the ground up; and how to deal with pricing.

Starting a company from the ground up teaches you what's needed to run one well. I recommend that before you buy a business, try starting one yourself just so you can learn. If you never obsess over creating a system that kills inefficiencies and generates cash flow you won't know how to recognize one when you see it in another company. It also helps you appreciate what you're getting when you do buy one. These companies already have systems set up. They already have customers. You're just running tweaks on them.

But remember that the goal isn't to be a prolific entrepreneur. It's to be rich. And you get there by having several revenue streams that you've put on autopilot. Buying businesses is a smart and fast way to multiply your cash flow if you do it wisely.

One way to *not* do it wisely: getting stuck in a business. A lot of people will buy a company and their ego is so big that they think they have to do everything themselves. So they end up in the weeds every day, answering support emails, returning phone calls, recruiting people, updating designs, pitching salespeople, traveling to get clients. That's working *in* your business and that is *not* what you want. You're buying companies to build up revenue streams that free up your time, not hijack it. The only way to do this is to buy a business with an infrastructure that lets the business run itself, like an assembly line that prints you money.

Buying is also much more of a beginner's game than investing. It sounds counterintuitive, but you need more cash in hand to invest in a business than you do to buy one. CEOs won't waste time talking to someone offering a $1K investment in their company. They want at least six figures. Even very small businesses need a good chunk of cash before they'll consider forking over equity. Ming's Yummy Thai Food, a two-person operation, needed $6K for my investment to have a meaningful impact on their cash flow. Firehouse Hostel needed $11K.

By comparison, you can buy a company for very little money, or no money at all, if you find a motivated seller. So focus on buying companies if you're just starting out. As you keep doing it, you'll eventually start writing investment checks with the extra cash flow. One revenue stream spawns another. Exactly what you want.

HOW THE NEW RICH BUILD BUSINESSES

10

UNCONVENTIONAL INVESTING

"Fortune sides with he who dares."

—Virgil

In May 2017, I fired up Facebook Live on my phone and filmed myself walking around Rainey Street in Austin with my checkbook in hand. I was at the city's food truck hub and I wasn't leaving without writing an investment check to one of them.

1.2M WATCHED ME DO THIS FOOD TRUCK DEAL LIVE ON FACEBOOK

About 1.2 million people watched while some cheered and gave advice in the comments. Others called me a con man. Just as many said I should stop being so obnoxious as I flashed my checkbook and complained about having so much money in the bank and nowhere to invest it. I'm sure I was annoying as hell to some. But I don't care—especially since my afternoon ended with an investment deal that's still one of my best to date. I hope the trolls stopped watching in time to miss that part. Less competition for the rest of us chasing off-the-beaten-path investment opportunities.

That day I wrote a $6K check to Ming, owner of the Yummy Thai Food Truck. She'd pay me $0.75 per meal until I earned back my investment, and if we liked doing business together, I would get $0.10 per meal in perpetuity.

Our partnership started with me randomly walking up to her, ordering Pad Thai (Ming's recommendation), and striking up a conversation about her business. The whole deal was done in less than twenty minutes.

Ming now sends me checks every month that I don't have to think about. And my Facebook Live video that captured the deal was picked up as a reality show called *Latka Money*. New episodes post every Tuesday at 8 p.m. EST on Facebook. You can watch at NathanLatka.com/facebook.

Most people who hear this story have one of two reactions:

Dude, you're an idiot.
Or
Tell me more—I want to do that.

Then there are the people who want me to write *them* a check. If that's you, we're casting for *Latka Money*. Send your pitch to sarah@nathanlatka .com. I'm always looking for ways to invest my money that the herd isn't thinking of. It's a big part of how I—and most megamillionaires—got rich.

If your dream is money in the bank and an empty calendar, you'll have to start thinking this way, too. Your business ventures will get you far, but remember the goal is to do as little work as possible. That won't be because you're lazy. It will be because you're smart with your work *and* your investments.

This is the part where you say, "Sure, Nathan, easy for you when you have so much cash burning up your checking account."

I feel you—I hate when rich kids whine, too. But you should know by now that I'm not a trust-fund baby. And I didn't always have this "too much money" problem. I got to this point by starting small and finding opportunities where others didn't think to look.

Think about this: the average net worth of people under thirty-five years old in the United States is $4,138.* If the typical person is this poor, you have to do the opposite of what everyone else is doing to get rich. People will call you an idiot, or crazy, but that's a good thing. The more your ideas sound insane to the masses, the more you're likely to be onto something. Remember, the masses are broke!

Most poor people brush off the rich as just being lucky. Who hasn't heard: "Oh, how lucky was she for investing in Apple back in the day?" "Who'd have thought that start-up he dumped his money into would go anywhere?" "She's so lucky the sketchy neighborhood where she bought that apartment is now trendy and expensive."

It's not luck. Rich people purposely plant seeds off the beaten path, and when a few of them bloom they create their own luck. I've said this for business, but it's especially relevant when it comes to investing. The rich get richer because they're not thinking like the herd.

Keep reading even if you're just scraping by financially. Your dream of that extra $10K or $20K in your bank account isn't as far off as you think if you follow this movement. And when you get there, you'll do yourself a huge favor by investing that extra cash in unexpected places with 20 percent+ annual returns.

HOW TO SPOT UNCONVENTIONAL INVESTMENT OPPORTUNITIES

The best way to find off-the-beaten-path investments is to source them yourself. You can literally put up a Facebook status that says, "I have $5K

---

* "Wealth, Asset Ownership, & Debt of Households Detailed Tables: 2013," United States Census Bureau, www.census.gov/data/tables/2013/demo/wealth/wealth-asset-ownership.html.

to invest. I can't find any good investments. Do you know of any?" Then see what responses you get. Most will be crap, but some might turn into real conversations and real opportunities for you.

Otherwise, just keeping the mindset that you're looking for fresh investment opportunities will help you see them where others don't.

RICHES IN HOSTELS

One of my favorite investments is with Firehouse Hostel in Austin. I met Collin, one of the owners, during a meet-up Firehouse was hosting at their bar. As we talked, I started complaining about the fact that I couldn't find any good places to invest my money. The stock market and real estate were booming and I didn't want to buy high. So I asked him what he was doing, and sure enough, he said he was raising capital for Firehouse and asked if I wanted to invest. He had my attention.

I'd heard about Firehouse before. When I first moved to Austin a few months earlier, I was searching for a good drinking hole, and everyone raved about this bar with the bookcase door. After talking to Collin at the meet-up I went to check it out.

I walked into the lobby and put all my weight on this little rusted handle tucked in a bookshelf. It moved to reveal a dimly lit bar with a seductive band playing in the corner. The liquor shelf looked like it belonged in the Hogwarts teachers' lounge, with elaborate craft cocktail accessories surrounded by drips of candle wax.

That night I ordered two Moscow mules and found myself chatting with travelers from all over the world who had come down to drink from the hostel upstairs. I overheard languages I couldn't identify. I immediately wanted to invest. Prime location. Great vibe. Interesting mix of locals and travelers. Totally Austin.

I ultimately invested $11K, which earns me about $1,200 per quarter, or $4,800 per year. Almost a 40 percent annual cash on cash return. Daddy likes. The trouble with this kind of investment is that there's not enough of it. Your tongue gets hungry for more returns like this, but there just aren't enough "bar and hostel" deals to buy.

I milked this as much as I could and asked the founders for introductions to other equity holders and proceeded to buy out someone else's

3 percent stake to increase my quarterly dividends since I knew returns were so great.

I'm a big fan of Kent and Collin, the two blue-collar guys who launched the bar. They know how to hustle, and because of that the business is growing fast. I also like when investors and founders are aligned, and Kent is a perfect example of that. Firehouse is Kent's main source of income, and he and his wife just had a baby. His family is absolutely dependent on making this business work. I like that. The founders are all in, so I'm happy to put more money in.

Most people looking to invest would miss an opportunity like Firehouse because they just don't think to ask. They're busy trolling stock prices and picking index funds that will *maybe* get them the average 7 percent return over too many years of waiting. They're thinking the average way and because of it they're missing the high return opportunities their last bar chat could have led to if they had been thinking about it.

So keep your investment radar on at all times. Forget index funds, financial advisers, and all that. They have their place, but you won't get rich through them. It's the unconventional investments that will set your portfolio on fire. Just pay attention to the companies or entrepreneurs you encounter in your everyday life. It could be your local hot dog stand, the coworking space you work out of, the indoor play yard where all your friends host their kids' birthday parties, the new microbrewery in your town. . . . You get it. Pay attention to what's working. When a business looks hot to you, and you have money with which to experiment, introduce yourself to the owner. Tell them you're looking to invest in a business and see if they bite. At worst they'll say no, but you'll make a new friend. At best you'll be on your way to a cash-printing investment.

PLAYING WITH JUDGMENT-CALL INVESTMENTS

Sexy as it sounds, I don't actually walk up to people and just hand them checks—well, not all the time. I did it with Ming, but that's because I could afford to lose the $6K investment if everything went up in flames. For most people and most investments, writing a check without running due diligence is way more stupid than it is sexy.

The smarter thing to do, and what I do when I'm interested in making a larger investment in a company, is ask to see their numbers. I need them to show me at least a three- or four-year financial history before I consider investing. Anything less is too risky. And if they don't have a structure for reporting that lets me look at their historical financials and see growth, I'm out. I also need to have confidence that once I put money in, I'll get updated financial reports every month. If that doesn't exist I stay away from the investment.

You should absolutely do all these things if you're investing a sizable percentage of your net worth (your definition of "sizable" will depend on your comfort level). But do also give yourself room to make judgment-call investments like the one I made in Ming's food truck. On paper my approach to that deal is a grand example of what not to do. I did not verify financials with Ming or get anything in writing. I just took her at her word and we moved forward on a handshake—strangers to $6K check in twenty minutes.

Anyone will tell you this investment strategy is insane. And it is if you're risking the only extra money you have. Don't ever do that. But it can be a huge time and money saver, and open you up to opportunities that others can't see, if the money is small enough that you can afford to lose it.

I took the risk with Ming because the six or so hours it would have taken me to analyze her financials, go back and forth on details, etc., was not worth $6K to me. Six hours of my time is worth way more than that. So it was easier for me to just write the check and use the $6K to figure out if Ming was someone I could work with over the long term, which she has proved to be. She's a good person. She's given me the monthly report of meal volume and written me the monthly checks. I took the same approach with Firehouse, and Kent and Collin are also proving to be great partners.

These judgment-call investments are a quick, efficient way to run a test and see if you get a good cash return. Once you do earn your money back you can make even bigger investments. At that point, you'll have been working with the person for many months. You'll know their financials; you'll know if they're someone you can work with. But initially the investment is based entirely on your gut impression of the business and its owner. You can learn a lot about someone in the first twenty minutes of meeting them, so I just trust my gut and go with it. Sure, there are times when I lose money, but nine times out of ten my judgment call is dead-on.

I won't try to teach you how to read another person's demeanor. That's a whole field of study in itself. You probably already have a sense of how well you can read people anyway. I'll just emphasize that if you're going to take a risk like this, only do it with a very conservative percentage of your net worth. Also consider putting together a one-page agreement that outlines your investment terms and have everyone sign it. I didn't sign an agreement with Ming or Firehouse, but I was willing to take that risk. I won't officially advise you to do the same, but it's obviously your call.

Even though these investments are quick and simple, they shouldn't be thoughtless. One of my key strategies is to look for a business that is making a big monthly payment on something. If I can pay for that thing up front, erasing the payment, it frees up their cash. I'll then tie my return to the growth of the business, which I know I can help drive with my distribution channels.

That was exactly the case with Ming. As we talked I learned that she was paying $600/month on the truck she worked out of. She could buy the truck outright for $6K and lower her monthly expenses by not having to make that loan payment. So I wrote her a $6K check to buy the truck in exchange for her paying me $.75 per meal until I earned my investment back, and then $.10 per meal in perpetuity if we kept working together after that. She was doing about five hundred meals a month, but I knew I could help her grow that pretty quickly. So I estimated it would take about a year to get my money back and learn if Ming and I could work together in an advantageous way. So far, so good.

My distribution channels immediately helped—getting those 1.2 million eyeballs on Ming's food truck boosted her sales that same day. I also helped her negotiate with the owner of the land to get her truck moved right up on the street. Previously it was three trucks back, so fewer people walking on the street saw it.

WHAT MY DIVIDEND CHECKS LOOK LIKE

Ming has written me seven checks over the seven months we've been working together, totaling $4,307. I almost have my $6K back and she's now doing about 1,200 meals per month.

Ultimately, Ming wants more money to expand. I'd be happy to write a $100K check and tie my return to growth: $2 per meal until I'm paid back, then $.25 per meal in perpetuity. The numbers might change, but I'd keep that same structure. I make money if Ming makes money. And like the guys at Firehouse, I know Ming is all in on growing her business. It's her only source of income and she's built her legacy on it.

FINDING CASH WHEN THERE'S NONE TO SPARE

I know the idea of investing sounds impossible if you're just getting by. But if that's you, the fact that you're reading this book proves you're itching to break your slump. You can do it immediately, and while you're at it build contacts who can later turn into business partners.

My top suggestion for bringing in cash builds on the idea of trading exposure that I talked about in chapter 7. If you have a big email list or online following you can sell email spots to build your income. But what if you don't have a big following? That's when you play the broker.

You can do this with no money. Literally anyone can profit from being a broker between two groups that each want what the other has. You're just smart enough to have thought of it. Here's what you'll do:

1. Reach out to people with big email lists.

2. Offer to sell placement in their emails for them, and negotiate yourself a good cut. I send emails like this all the time:

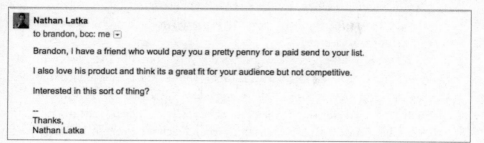

Nathan Latka
to brandon, bcc: me ▾

Brandon, I have a friend who would pay you a pretty penny for a paid send to your list.

I also love his product and think its a great fit for your audience but not competitive.

Interested in this sort of thing?

--
Thanks,
Nathan Latka

That's really it. If you target people in your industry you'll get the added bonus of learning both sides of the marketplace. Then, eventually, when you have your own email list, you'll know who to sell it to. Or if you want more exposure for something you're working on, you'll know the people with lists who are willing to take payment for exposure.

How you find people with big lists will depend on your industry. I'm in software, so I'd go to sites like G2Crowd.com or Siftery.com and see who has the most users. Obviously if they have a lot of users they have those users' email addresses. Then I'd do cold outreach to those companies. Paved.com and Sponsored.tech are two more outlets for access to big email lists.

You can also do this with contacts from other projects you're already running. I've pitched my podcast sponsors, asking if they're interested in being featured in an email blast to 100,000 marketers. It's a separate fee from their podcast sponsorship. On the back side of that deal I've negotiated a 60 percent cut of the fee to the person who owns that 100,000-person marketing list. So if I bring them a sponsor, I get 60 percent of the revenue. Here's an email I've sent that led to a deal:

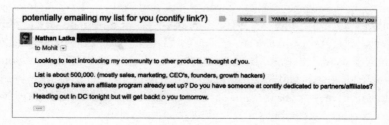

potentially emailing my list for you (contify link?) ▶   Inbox x   YAMM - potentially emailing my list for you

Nathan Latka
to Mohit ▾

Looking to test introducing my community to other products. Thought of you.

List is about 500,000. (mostly sales, marketing, CEO's, founders, growth hackers)
Do you guys have an affiliate program already set up? Do you have someone at contify dedicated to partners/affiliates?
Heading out in DC tonight but will get backt o you tomorrow.

Make the note sound really personal. Saying something like "Heading out in DC tonight but will get back to you tomorrow" gives it the feel of a one-to-one note, which will increase your response rate.

For good measure, throw in a spelling error or two so they clearly understand it's not a mass email.

In terms of finding people who'd want to buy access to lists, listen to podcasts and notice who is sponsoring them. Those same people are looking to pay for additional exposure. Also Google keywords associated with your industry, or whatever the list is about that you're brokering a deal with. Notice who is running ads for that thing, then reach out to them and say:

> Hey, I noticed you're spending money on Google ads. You might get a
> better return if you spend some money with me and email this list,
> which is catered to the same keywords that you're running on Google.
> . . . . .

There can be huge money in brokering emails if you really get into it. Invest what you make into a few businesses and see where it takes you. Even if you can't quit your day job and live off the profits, you'll start building up those passive income streams that add up over time.

Obviously there's more you can do to bring in cash than brokering email deals. I'm suggesting it because it's worked for me, it's superefficient, and it requires no cash. Any of the cash-generating strategies I mention in chapter 6 will also work. One other option I'll highlight, and this one is more mainstream, is driving for Uber or Lyft. This is a great alternative if your schedule is limited and you want to control when you turn your work on and off. Anytime that you don't have some other responsibility, you have the ability to make money. The hourly rate isn't high, but you can hustle your way to some savings by driving when you want and keeping full control of your time. It's grunt work. It's not easy. But it's a good way to build up a nest egg that you can start using to do other deals. And depending on your location, Uber and Lyft driving *can* be surprisingly lucrative. Some people are literal millionaires just from driving in big cities with lots of surge pricing, like Los Angeles or New York. Sure, they're working twelve-hour days or longer, but they're doing it on their terms.

11

HOW TO GET RICH BY COPYING YOUR COMPETITORS

(AND WHY INVENTING SOMETHING NEW IS A SURE WAY TO LOSE)

"People are going to copy your product if you build great stuff. Just because Yahoo has a search box doesn't make it Google."

—Evan Spiegel

When I show up to an entrepreneur meet-up and ask someone what their idea is, I often hear: "I can't share my idea until you sign this NDA."

This person thinks their idea is so good they'll win over the whole market. Couldn't be further from the truth. Brand-new ideas almost always lose and cost boatloads of money.

You already know what I think about copying other people's ideas. Do it. You're stupid if you don't. (See chapter 2 if you need a reminder why.) In this chapter I'll show you exactly how to copy, add your own twist, and then out-execute.

Winners don't have new ideas. Rather, they copy the heck out of their competitors, then add their own flavor or unique angle to win. This way you're just making a new move on the board, not inventing a brand-new board game. Every successful player does this.

Facebook released Marketplace, which is a better-designed version of Craigslist. Stripe is a payment processor with an easier-to-use API. Venmo, PayPal, Square Cash, and Google Pay all do the same thing with a twist. Rockefeller copied other people's steel mills, then changed one procedure related to oil refining and sulfur to print money.

Have you seen those sections at the bottom of major blogs that showcase sponsored content, or "related posts"? Companies like Outbrain and Taboola have dominated this space for years, but it didn't stop John Lemp at Revcontent from throwing his weight into the competition.

In 2017, Revcontent processed $184M of ad spend through its platform, collecting 25 percent of that as revenue. This is a prime example in which a big thinker ignored the conventional wisdom that "you must have a new idea!" Instead, he went right after business models already proven and is now chipping away at their lead.

Don't let your ego be so big as to think your idea has never been done before. If no one else is doing it, there may be a reason. And even if you do have a brilliant new idea, you'll make a profit much quicker by building on something that already exists. You'll have plenty of time (and money) to launch your genius invention *after* you've made bank by copying.

FROM AFFILIATE TO COMPETITOR
($18M BIZNESS APPS VS. $2.4M BUILDFIRE)

Copying your competitors can make you rich even if you never scale to their size. Ian Blair proved this when he launched BuildFire while still in college. BuildFire is drag-and-drop software that lets people create mobile apps without any tech expertise. Think WordPress for apps. BuildFire is a lot like another company, Bizness Apps, which Ian previously used to build apps for small businesses. After about a year of creating one-off apps, Ian realized that the big money was not in client work, but in building a software competitor to Bizness Apps.

I love the story that the numbers here tell. Since launching BuildFire in 2012, Ian has raised $2.5M in investor funding and has thirty-one employees at age twenty-five. His annual revenue in 2017 was $2.4M and his current monthly recurring revenue is $300K. When we chatted on Skype, Ian called me from his $850K apartment with a full view of the San Diego skyline behind him.

While Ian built his empire by copying a competitor, Bizness Apps' numbers show that they're still killing it. Andrew Gazdecki launched the company in 2010 with $110K in investor funding. Today Andrew, at age twenty-eight, has ninety employees, with $18M in 2017 annual revenue. His current monthly recurring revenue is $1.5M.

	BIZNESS APPS	BUILDFIRE
CEO/Founder	Andrew Gazdecki	Ian Blair
Year founded	2010	2012
$ Raised	$110K	$2.5M
# Employees	90	31
2017 Revenue	$18M	$2.4M
Monthly recurring revenue	$1.5M+	$200K–$400K
Revenue per employee	$80K	$77.4K
# Customers	3,000+	1,000–5,000
ARPU (avg. revenue per user)	$500+	$400–$500

I'm a numbers geek so I can go on (if that's you, too, you can see the full Bizness Apps versus BuildFire comparison above). The takeaway here is that even though Andrew's business is more successful, Ian was still able to create a multimillion-dollar enterprise by directly copying Andrew's idea. And Andrew's idea wasn't all that new, anyway. Other drag-and-drop app builders existed before Bizness Apps and the whole concept is a riff on drag-and-drop website software like Wix, Squarespace, and Weebly.

I'm going to show you how to do the same, and how I did it with my past two companies. Much of my advice in this chapter is related to the software space since that's where I do most of my work, but you can apply these tactics to any industry, whether you're running a restaurant, knitting company, professional services business, or software.

Whatever you do, your first step is to find an idea to copy. And ideas are lurking everywhere—you just need to know where to look.

FIND AN IDEA YOU LIKE IN A HOT INDUSTRY

If you win the game but there's no pot of money to win, you picked the wrong game.

The first step the New Rich take when thinking about new businesses is to make sure the winnings make the work worth doing. Start by looking at trends. What spaces are hot? It's always a good bet to go where a tide is already rising. Try these resources to find up-and-coming markets and industries.

Use These Four Websites to Find Best-Selling Physical Products

The quickest way to build capital if you're launching a physical product is to presell it. Crowdfunding is perfect for this because it's essentially a way to presell your product and get press for it at the same time. In general, it's a great option if you:

- ▶ **Are launching a consumer product.** It's much harder to crowd-fund B2B stuff since those audiences tend to be smaller. Crowdfunding is all about mass appeal.
- ▶ **Care about keeping all of your equity.** Backers don't get a cut of equity like investors do, so you get the cash and 100 percent of your company. That also means you're not at the mercy of investors who get to tell you what to do.
- ▶ **Don't want to take out a business loan to fund your launch.** Please don't take out loans. Presell until you have the money you need.
- ▶ **Are not rich enough to personally fund your launch.** Again— presell, presell, presell, and then put it back into the business.

You get two chances at copying with physical products. You can swipe ideas from existing items *and* from their crowdfunding campaign if they had one.

So get copying. Go to Kickstarter or any crowdfunding site and sort by "Most raised" to "Least raised." Study the "Most raised" campaigns and try to figure out why they were so successful. Was it the storytelling on the crowdfunding page? Is the product a genius idea? Why did these Vue glasses raise more than $1M from 5,500+ people?

Why did this neck pillow do so well? What about the ladle?

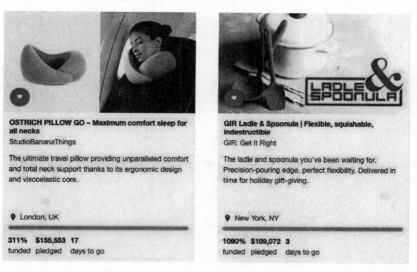

Each of these products, despite being drastically different, succeeded by leveraging the strategies you can copy:

Set goals you can hit and then seed your campaign. These products all hit their fund-raising goals early by setting low targets and building momentum fast. You do this by seeding your campaign—get people you know to commit to making a contribution before launch. Then tell them the moment you go live so they can jump in and pledge. So if your goal is $5K aim to get fifty to one hundred people to commit to $50 to $100 so you can hit that in the first couple days.

Once you crush your goal it's easier to get free press, which begets more money and more press. *Business Insider* featured Vue Smart Glasses mid-campaign, when they'd raised $780K on a goal of $50K. They were also featured in *Forbes, TechCrunch, Computerworld, Digital Trends, The Verge,* and *Wareable.* Ostrichpillow Go was plugged in *USA Today* mid-campaign.

Tell great stories. People want to connect with you emotionally when they invest in your product and the best way to do that is through great stories. Use video to show potential backers that you have character. Inject humor. Vue's promo video showed how awkward other smart glasses look by having a guy wear a big VR set while answering the door for the pizza guy. The Spoonula folks connected with cooks by showing how perfectly it scoops up every drop of beef stew. Ostrichpillow Go commiserates with us on the ridiculous ways we try to get comfortable sleeping on airplanes.

Geek out on specs and design. Backers love to see how you got to the end product. Break down how it works, why it works, and how you arrived at the design. Show pictures of early prototypes and whiteboard idea sessions. Vue shows people using the glasses while explaining how they use bone conduction audio technology to transfer stereo sound to your inner ear. Ostrichpillow Go shows us their whiteboard design ideas. Spoonula gets obsessive on geometry, dimensions, and the wonders of pharmaceutical-grade platinum silicone.

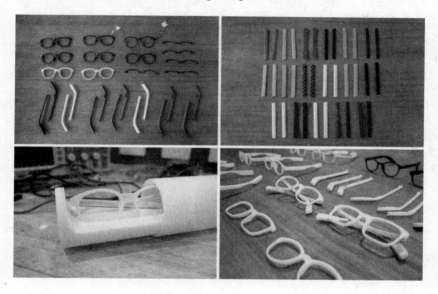

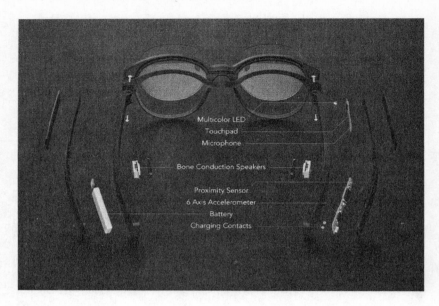

Battery

2-3 days standby time on a single charge

7 days standby with charging case (3 charges)

Talk time: 5 hours

Size: 3.7V 90mAh Lithium Polymer

Water Resistance

Rain, splash and sweat-resistant

Sensors

6-axis accelerometer & gyroscope

Infrared proximity sensor

5 field capacitive touch pad

Audio

Stereo bone conduction speakers

Patent-pending sound leakage prevention design

Frequency range: 20–20,000Hz

Impedance 8.5Ω, Distortion <5.0, SPL 88dB

MEMS digital microphone

Charging

Wireless charging via case

Charging time: 2 hours

Case is charged via USB

App Compatibility

iPhone 5+ running iOS 8+

Android 4.3+

Bluetooth

Compatible with all devices

Bluetooth 4.2

A2DP profile

30ft / 10m range

Processor

ARM Cortex-M3

Weight

28 grams

Use value + scarcity to create urgency. People love to be the first to get something, especially if it's at a discount with limited supplies. Use your rewards to appeal to those tendencies in all of us. Vue fueled momentum for early orders with an early bird reward: 41 percent off a pair of prescription smart glasses with only 350 spots available. When that sold out, 6,833 people paid $179 for the same reward—their most popular tier. Each of these campaigns leveraged scarcity to drive action. They also set up stretch goals to keep momentum up. So if they hit $200K in funding, $500K, $1.2M, they would add additional features to their products. And they don't have to be expensive. The $1.2M stretch goal for Vue was adding attachable nose pads to the glasses. Not crazy.

Buy us a coffee		**$5**
T-shirt		**$29**
Vue × 1 (Early bird)	41% off Sold Out	**$159**
Vue × 1	33% off	**$179**
Vue × 1 (Custom Etched)	ONLY ON KICKSTARTER	**$229**
Vue × 1 (Polarized / Transition)		**$259**
Vue × 2		**$329**
Vue × 1 (Progressive lenses)		**$379**
Vue × 5		**$799**
Vue × 10		**$1499**

Product Hunt is another great resource for scouting physical products. It's a place where folks can post new products and get up votes from the community. Assume there is large demand for products that get lots of up votes. You can't use Product Hunt to fund-raise, but it's still a great leading indicator to what's hot.

In addition to Kickstarter, Indiegogo, and Product Hunt, check out these crowdfunding sites to get ideas of other hot markets: Pozible.com, Ulule .com, and Fundable.com.

Eight Places to Find Digital and Software Products Selling Fast

If you're thinking about launching a software business, try looking in these places for industries that are hot.

1. **Siftery.com** allows you to see what companies are actually getting new customers. The site then ranks tools (mostly software) that have landed the most new customers over the most recent time period. Money doesn't lie. If people are becoming customers of a new product in droves, you know it's a hot space.

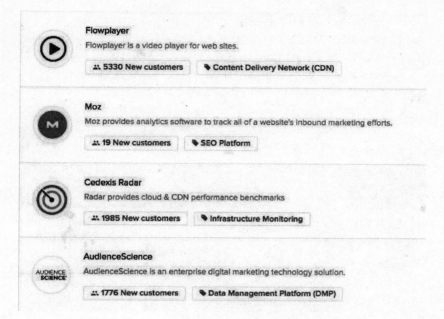

Siftery covers several software categories, including Marketing, Sales and Business Development, Customer Support, Product and Design, Analytics and Data Science, HR, Finance and Accounting, and Productivity.

2. **GetLatka.com** allows you to see the customer counts, revenue figures, pricing metrics, and other data points on private software companies. If you're thinking about launching a piece of software, check this site out to see how others with similar sorts of software are doing.

3. **BuiltWith.com** is a site that will tell you what technologies other websites use. In other words, it lets you see what pickaxes the gold miners are using. If you were interested in the e-commerce space, it'd be valuable to know who currently has how much market share. You can then reverse engineer why the winners are winning and losers are losing to increase your chances of success in the same space. Go to BuiltWith.com and click TOOLS in the dropdown to start exploring trends.

I got to the screenshot below by clicking on WEB TECHNOLOGY TRENDS in the main menu and then ECOMMERCE from the column on the left. The following chart pops up, which shows me that

WooCommerce has 10 percent, Magento 11 percent, Shopify 9 percent, and other platforms 44 percent of the e-commerce market. Understanding who has what percentages of e-commerce technology allows you to decide whom to go after. Why does WooCommerce have 10 percent? Why does Shopify have 9 percent? Is there a company in that 44 percent that you can buy to jump-start your entry into this space? These are the kinds of things you can learn using BuiltWith.com.

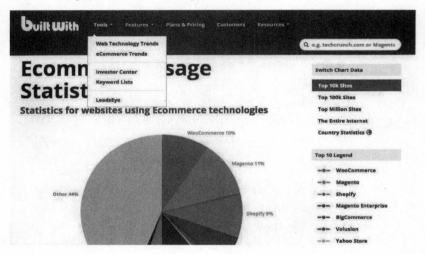

4. **TechCrunch.com** is a blog focused on the technology sector. Across the bottom you can view all recent rounds of funding. If you see a large amount of money going into a particular company, you can assume that space is hot. Venture capitalists don't invest unless they see $1B+ opportunity. Hijack their research by looking at what they are investing in.

M-sense	BABBLER	Zapnito	DigitalX
Not available Venture	**$2.5M** Private Equity	**442K GBP** Seed	**$1.6M** Post IPO Equity
HQ: Not available	HQ: Paris, Ile-de-France	HQ: Not available	HQ: Perth, Western Australia
Categories: Apps	Categories: Journalism, Email, Public Relations	Categories: Internet	Categories: Not available
Investors: Not available	Investors: Not available	Investors: Not available	Investors: Not available

You can also use *TechCrunch*'s side navigation to look at funding sorted by the investors, the funding size, and the industry. A closer look at Babbler reveals the following:

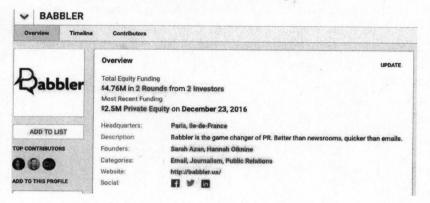

After you understand that Babbler is in the PR space, you might use the product to figure out if they have some special twist that other companies in the PR space don't have. Remember, VCs invest only where they think they get can 10x or higher returns. You're hunting for the reason investors see 10x opportunity in the business so you can copy the best parts and then invent your own twists to make it better.

5. **Listen to podcasts that feature entrepreneurs.** In my fifteen-minute daily podcast, I ask every CEO what their favorite online tool is. This helps me find great new tools and markets to research. If I like a space I'll decide if I want to buy a company in the space, build one myself, or invest in one that already exists. (To listen to the podcast, go here: http://NathanLatka.com/the-topitunes.) Other podcasts great for discovering new tools and markets are *Art of Charm*, *The Tim Ferriss Show*, and *The $100 MBA*.

6. **Search large LinkedIn groups.** If there are a bunch of members in a LinkedIn group around "Amazon analytics" you can assume there is interest in the space. If you choose to build a tool for the space, congrats, you already have your first distribution channel.

Let's say you're selling a digital product. You'd search LinkedIn for groups related to digital marketing and see that one of the biggest is Digital Doughnut, with more than 1.5 million members. From there, find the admins and message the group owner. Your goal is to build a relationship with them so that eventually they'll feel comfortable and excited to email their group about a product you might be working on. It's a huge distribution channel opportunity. This is my message exchange with the owner of Digital Doughnut:

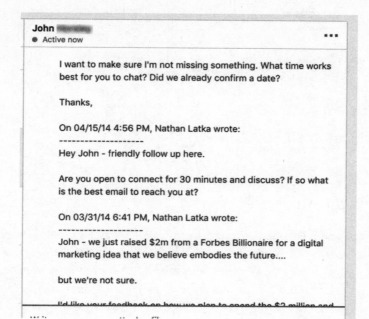

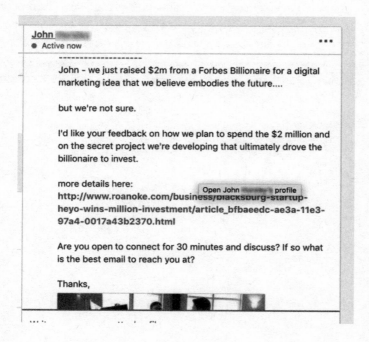

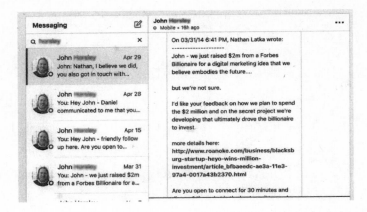

7. **Search Facebook groups.** Use Facebook search to find clusters of groups around a certain industry. Let's say you create a journal and decide that entrepreneurs are among your target audience. You'd search for entrepreneur-related groups and reach out to the group owners to try building a relationship. Eventually you'd try figuring out how to cross-promote your product into their group. That's obviously a delicate art, but these are clusters of people you can go after, distribution channels you can monopolize once you decide what market your product fits into.

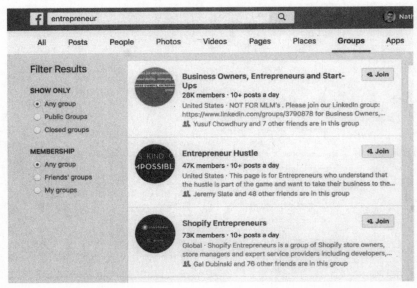

8. **Join Slack groups.** I'm part of a Slack group called Sales Hackers, where more than seven hundred account executives, C-suite executives, and other sales tool users talk about their favorite tools and why they use them. It's a great way to get a soft read on what products are hot or not. Use www.SlackList.info to find Slack lists in any industry.

The first software company I built was called Heyo.com, which helped companies drag and drop together Facebook applications. My sense that the space was hot came from the fact that many others were getting funding.

In October 2010, Buddy Media raised an additional $27M from top-tier investors. Wildfire (another competitor) raised $10M. Involver raised $8M in October 2010. It was very clear that the space would produce many winners—and it did, to the tune of $1B+ in exits in late 2012.

Many people would look at the space and conclude that they shouldn't compete because they don't have funding, or that the other guys were years ahead. Totally false. Think about it this way. If investors are sinking all that money into one industry, they're growing the industry and making it easier for you to find future customers. You turn their resources into yours when you join the space they're pouring money into.

Following this sort of playbook will help you consistently create business wins. Once you identify an industry that you think is hot, plot out who is leading and reverse engineer their growth.

Reverse Engineer: The Easy Way to See Your Competitors' Systems

Companies use all sorts of methods to drive growth, ranging from free content marketing to $1M+/month paid marketing campaigns. In order to beat a competitor, you have to understand where they get their food from. Then slowly siphon their food supply. If you can't figure out where they eat, don't attack. Here's how I figure out why companies are growing and how they are getting customers.

SimilarWeb is a tool that tells you where websites get most of their traffic from. If I wanted to build a competitor to Todoist.com, I'd go to SimilarWeb, type in "Todoist.com," and this report would generate:

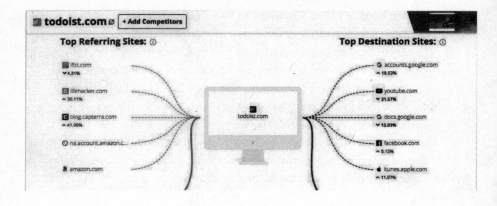

I immediately learn that the majority of Todoist.com traffic comes from LifeHacker.com and Ifttt.com. Go make friends with the CEOs/authors of those blogs/websites. It's a double whammy to persuade those people to write about your new tool while at the same time hurting your competitors' traffic. Later in this chapter, I'll show you how I did and got more than fourteen new customers to pay $360 each in under twenty-four hours.

Ahrefs is a tool that tells you which Google searches make your competitors pop up. Going to https://Ahrefs.com and typing in "Todoist.com" generates this report:

Fifty-three thousand organic keywords means there are fifty-three thousand words people type into Google that Todoist ranks for—meaning Todoist.com will appear in the organic search results for those terms. You can quickly look at what those terms are by clicking "Organic keywords":

Keyword	Position[i]			Volume[i]	KD[i]	CPC[i]	Traffic ↓[i]	URL[i]
▪ 14,717 ▬ 3,927 ▦ 3,528 ◉ 2,417 More ▾ 14,717 results								
outlook	20 ↑1		▮	4,100,000	79	1.36	28,618	🔒 en.todoist.com/outlook ▾
todoist ⌀ 🐦	1		▮	67,000	48	3.42	23,861	🔒 en.todoist.com/ ▾
todoist ⌀ 🐦	3		▮	67,000	48	3.42	9,865	🔒 todoist.com/Users/showLogin ▾
to do list 🔲 💻 ⌀	1		▮	34,000	76	1.69	4,600	🔒 en.todoist.com/ ▾
to do list 🔲 💻 ⌀	2		▮	34,000	76	1.69	3,987	🔒 en.todoist.com/chrome ▾

Todoist.com gets 4,600 unique views per month from the keyword "to do list." Now you've quantified your potential gains and their potential losses if you outrank them for the words "to do list." This book is not about content marketing or SEO, but those are the tactics you'd Google and use to outrank Todoist for any keyword.

Use **App Annie** if you're trying to study a market in the mobile app space. For example, if I were analyzing the document signing space, I might explore how HelloSign ranks so well in the App Store. Going to App Annie and searching "HelloSign" creates this word cloud that tells me what people search in the App Store to find HelloSign:

App Store Optimization

signature jotnot electronic or import scan sign hello docusign

What words do people use when trying to find an app?

The right keywords can help an app to get discovered more often, and increase downloads and revenue. App Annie tracks millions of keywords so you can get more downloads for your app, and understand what keywords your competitors are using.

LEARN MORE

Keyword optimization in the App Store is a fine art. Nobody quite knows how Apple ranks apps, but it's certainly a combination of the title of your app, the subhead, the description, and the number of reviews you have. So you'd want to make sure your subhead and your description contain the same keywords that drive people to HelloSign.

At the end of this chapter, I'll show you how I built Heyo.com to $5M in cumulative revenue, ten thousand customers, and $2.5M raised using these tactics.

First let's talk about how you get your product built. Again, I'm going to focus on the tech space in this example, but many industries could follow this same process.

Use Toptal or Upwork to Build a Version of Their Tool with Your Own Twist

The number one question I get is from business-minded founders who can't get a developer to join them. The businessperson doesn't want to give up a portion of their company—usually tough because if you're building a tech company, you need deep technological expertise.

The way to keep most of your company's equity and the fastest way to find developer talent is via Toptal.com. Another version of Toptal, with less developer talent, is UpWork.com. Use these sites to hire freelancers who work on a fee basis. You get the expertise you need on your project without having to give up equity.

Help your freelancer get an idea of what you're looking for by pointing them to projects you want to copy. I recently interviewed Jim Fowler, who sold Jigsaw to Salesforce for $120M+. During our interview Jim shared his new venture with me, Owler.com. I had been looking for a way to present business data I had collected, and I liked how he did it. It's much simpler for me to point to this example when communicating to my Toptal developers what I want versus wireframing my own new version for GetLatka.com.

GetLatka is my site where I help founders make the most money selling their companies, investors get the best deals, and business development teams at large companies find acquisition targets. The layout is very similar to Owler. The data source is very different.

HOW TO BUILD A COPYCAT FAST

Here's how I used Toptal to launch GetLatka.com:

1. Post a job and let Toptal recruiters go find you development talent. I used Balsamiq.com to wireframe different user flows for the new tool, which helps my developer better guess how much time (and money!) a project might take:

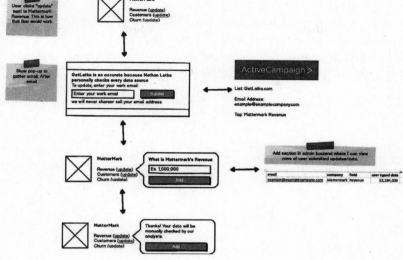

2. Interview the talent via Skype and either hire them or turn them down. I had two interviews and hired a guy named Steven who lives in Ukraine because he asked me the best questions about the wireframe I sent him.

3. Use Toptal to pay your developer and use something like Bitbucket, Asana, or Trello to manage tasks.

4. Toptal makes money by paying developers $50/hour and selling that time to you for $65/hour (or some markup). They save you a ton of time from having to go find contractors yourself.

The reason I much prefer using a site like Toptal to build my initial prototype is twofold:

1. You keep 100 percent equity in your company.

2. You don't increase your fixed monthly expenses as you would if you hired an employee. Also, you don't have to worry about health coverage, birthdays, or office parties (which usually waste time).

Last note on building your prototype: set yourself a budget and stick to it.

There are plenty of resources on how to get a minimum viable product built so I won't go into detail here. You should force yourself to spend no more than $5K before getting your first customer. Ideally less.

I brought in my first $5K with GetLatka by selling this initial, very ugly prototype of my database as a CSV file:

#	Space	Company	Episode	Conference Spe	Source	Date Data	Growth Tactic	Gross Margin	Customers	Raised	2015 Revenue	ARPU	MRR as of Column	Gross Churn (/mo)
144		ErterCastle.com							500	$3,000,000	$100,000	$174	$31,000	1.00%
145	Amazon	etailinsights.com			Darren Pierce	12/6/2016			150	Bootstrapped	$1,000,000	$750	$112,500	2%
146		Execvision			Steve Richard	12/5/2016			50	$1,000,000	$500,000	$1,417	$70,833	1.00%
147	Search for Sales	Findo.com	002		Gary Fowler	1/22/2017			700	$7,000,000	$0	$10	$6,983	6.00%
148	HR	Frontapp.com			Mathilde Collin	6/9/2016			1210	$13,000,000	$1,000,000	$200	$242,000	3.02%
149	Misc	geekatoo.com			Kevin	7/13/2016			40,600	$2.7M		$130 per project	$275,000	
150		Gearapp							300	$100,000			$300	
151	Marketing Auto	GetAmbassador.com				12/1/2015			300	$2,900,000	$3,500,000	$1,600	$320,000	1.25%
152	Real Estate Tool	Giraffe360				1/5/2017			60	$500,000	$168,000	$1,400	$84,000	0.00%
153	Sales Automati	Handshake			Glen Coates	12/7/2016			1000	$24,000,000		$	$800,000	
154	Contact Data	HGData			Mark Godley	12/6/2016			200	$24,000,000	$6,000,000		$833,333	<1%
155	Contact Data	HipLead			Conor Lee	12/7/2016			30	$200,000	$900,000	$4,000	$120,000	1.00%
156		http://hrois.com/	636		Amarpreet Kalka	2/2/2017			18	$290,000	$250,000	$2,667	$41,000	2%
157		http://www.smartboat	619		Paul	1/23/2017			5	$260,000	$20,000	$98	$495	too early
158		http://www.winmo.com	624		Dave Currie	1/26/2017			2000	Bootstrapped	$12,096,000	$583	$1,196,667	1.20%
159		InfusionSoft	837		Clate Mask	2/2/2017			45,000	$125,000,000	$100,000,000	$250	$11,000,000	2.00%
160	Content	Issu			Joe Hyrkin	7/13/2016			100,000	$21,000,000		$35	<$3,500,000	2.00%
161		KarmaCircles.com				7/20/2016			Running pilots	$100k		$2-3/user/mo	$0	too early
162	Business Intelli	Klipfolio	710		Allan Wille	5/14/2017			8500	19,900,000		$67	$570,000	3.8%
163	Business Intelli	Klipfolio	810		Allan Wille	1/22/2017			7000	19,900,000	3,000,000	$71	$500,000	3%
164	Contact Data	Lead Genius							200	$8,000,000		$3,333	$700,000	2.75%
165		Leadfuze			Justin McGill	12/5/2016			175	$150,000	$250,000	$175	$30,625	20%
166	HR, Find Freela	LessDoing.com			Ari Meisel	6/13/2016			170	$0	$200,000		$45,000	
167	Email Marketing	MadMimi												
168		Meistertask.com							5,000	$600,000	$20,000		$30,000	
169		Mention.com	630		Matthieu Vaxelai	2/27/2017			4,000	$500,000		$60-400	$240,000.00	2%
170	Project Manage	Mindmeister.com							30,000	$600,000	$2,500,000	$6	$220,000	6.00%
171	$3-5M	Nimble	643		Jon Ferrara	2/6/2017			10,000	$3,000,000	$1,500,000 2016	$20	$200,000	3.00%
172		Nova.ai	597		Will Dinkel	1/21/2017			100	$3,250,000		$150	$180,000	too early
173	$13m pre money	Nowinteract	591		Magnus Astrom	1/20/2017			19	$7,000,000	$3,500,000, 201	$10,000	$220,000	small sample size
174	HR, Accouting	Numbrarz.in	577		Aditya Tulsian	1/19/2017			1200	$650,000	$65,000 2016 to	$15	$18,500	3.00%
175	Website Builder	PageCloud	809		Craig Fitzpatrick	1/22/2017			8400	$8,500,000		$16	$150,000	6.00%

My first customer started paying $1K/month on June 12, 2017, for access to my database of company metrics and deal flow:

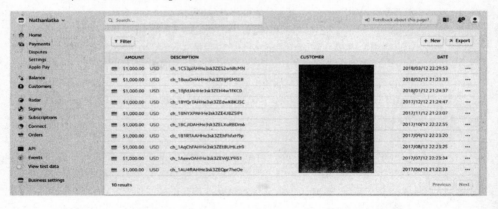

Include early customers in product discussions so they get emotionally invested in you and the product. You want them to be proud that they were first. If you do this right, they'll brag to their friends about how they "discovered" you. When I pushed new updates on GetLatka.com I'd always ask my early customers what they thought:

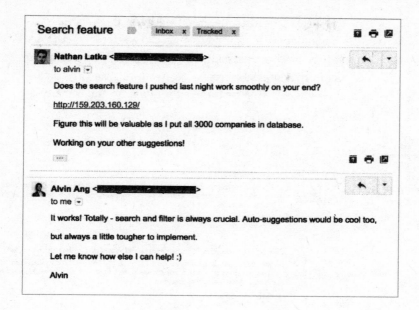

Then sign up new customers and always be increasing your price. My second GetLatka.com customer paid $2K/month:

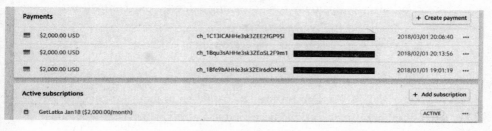

Today I'm charging $20K a month for this kind of data. And I increase my costs on the company only in tandem with revenue growth. For every dollar in revenue, I'll spend $.10 on developers to improve the product. I've easily invested $50K into growing GetLatka.com without ever dipping into my personal cash.

Once you're done using Toptal to build your minimum viable product, you want to start figuring out ways to attack your competitors.

1. Read their support forum if they have one and see what their most requested features are that don't exist yet. I call this the "support-driven business launch guide." You can literally launch

a business based on the intel you find here. If you wanted to create a competitor to Cratejoy, you could go to their feedback request page, www.cratejoy.ideas.aha.io, and develop a solution to something their customers are clearly asking for (fifty-six up votes for giving existing customers the ability to add something to their cart).

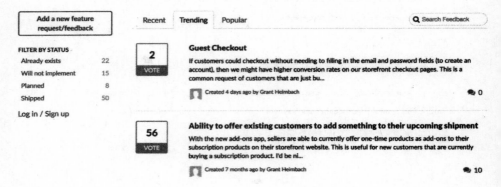

If you build a tool that includes just this one added feature it allows you to slowly start chipping away at your competitors' dominance in the marketplace.

2. Go to comparison and rating sites like G2 Crowd to see what negative reviews your competitors get.

These will help you find features you could build that your competitors don't offer, but remember, the best products rarely win. That's where distribution comes in.

ATTACK THEIR DISTRIBUTION CHANNELS: HOW I GOT #1 SPOT ON POPULAR INDUSTRY BLOG POST

In 2014, when I was researching how Heyo.com competitor ShortStack .com was getting so much traffic, I saw that a lot of inbound traffic (via Ahrefs.com lookup) was coming from a blog post on GuavaBox.com titled "Facebook Contest Apps: Top 5 Apps for Your Next Contest." The list did not include my company, Heyo.com.

The following is the email back and forth between the GuavaBox co-founder and me where I ultimately persuade him to put a link to "Heyo

Free Contest Builder" at the top of the article. My initial reach-out was through the GuavaBox.com website contact form:

Me:

Hey guys, I saw you wrote this article on the Facebook Contest space. I'm building a tool in the space and had 2 questions for you about a new design we're about to roll out. Open to a call so I can show you the private stuff?

GuavaBox:

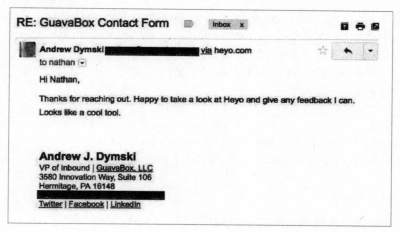

Me:

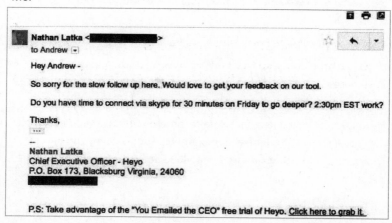

Once I got them on Skype, I asked them loads of questions to get them emotionally committed to the product, such as:

What are you currently selling to your customers?
What tools are you currently using? What do you like about them? What do you dislike about them?
Are you using any of our [Heyo's] competitors?

Then I started to get them connected to our product by asking things like:

What do you think about this feature on our toolset?
Do you think, if we gave you the ability to use this widget, you could upsell that to your customers?
Do you see how you can make more money from your customer by using our tool?

Having these kinds of conversations lets partners feel like they own the product because you let them in behind the scenes.

After the call, I followed up with Gray (Andrew's cofounder):

Hey Gray,

On the call we discussed putting Heyo text above "Wildfire Promotion Builder" on this article to which you agreed. I'm thankful you're willing to go back into your archives and make these updates and I look forward to working together more in the future!

_____

Section header: Heyo Free Contest Builder

Heyo is a drag and drop Facebook contest platform that many businesses are using to drive engagement, capture emails, get likes, and convert sales.

Heyo also makes contest template recommendations that they know convert across all industries. For example, Squaw Valley ran a Facebook contest that captured over 4500 email addresses in under 10 days.

Another business, Nicolette Island Inn, captured 25% of all their fans' email addresses using the Heyo Contest Template which asks users to enter their email, then click "like," "share" and "tweet" for their chance to win.

One of our favorite aspects of Heyo is that with every contest you build, they automatically make it mobile optimized and even provide a smart URL for you to use in your marketing. Click here to start the free trial.

Gray—feel free to change this up as you see fit. You know your audience way better than I do!

Please note that this does not have your affiliate link embedded. You can log on at Lujure.Zferral.com (our program) and grab your link here: OR

You can wait to update the links until we release our $100/signup program in about 4 weeks. Let me know if you have any questions. Thanks,

. . . . .

Several days later, Gray updated the blog post to put Heyo right at the top:

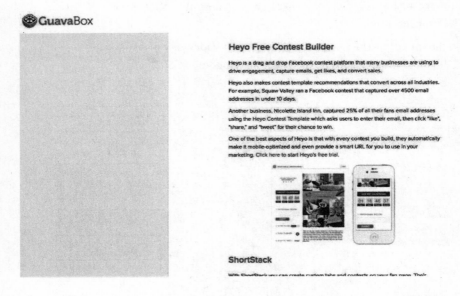

In the first thirty days of this article being live it drove us fourteen new $30/month customers. I knew customers stayed with us for well over twelve months ($360+ lifetime value) so we had no problem paying Gray $100 per new customer. He makes $1,400 (14 new customers × $100), Heyo makes $5,040 (14 new customers × $360 lifetime value).

There are thousands of battles out there like this for you to win. By the way, these opportunities don't exist if you're trying to create some brand-new idea. This worked only because GuavaBox had posted a list of the top tools already created in my space. I just hijacked the list by incentivizing GuavaBox more heavily than others.

Actively reach out to the authors of old articles written about your competitors and try to build relationships with those authors. Many times they can go in and change old content, which can help you win over new monthly traffic. Icing on the cake is you're stealing it from your competitors!

These sorts of investments grow more valuable over time. Once you set them up, they pay back in small pieces, like five to ten unique new website views per month. Think of this like stacking paper. Looks like nothing at the start, but if you add one sheet per day for 365 days, your pile starts to get tall! As you layer on these distribution techniques while having your product do the same thing, most consistently, over the longest period of time, you'll start to emerge as the clear leader in your space.

It's also a great investment to buy distribution channels—if you can—instead of paying to be put through them. So instead of paying, say, $5K for someone to mention you on their email list one time, try to buy the whole company so the list becomes yours. That's exactly what I did with The Top Inbox. You can do this with anything—a curation website, a reviews website, a YouTube channel, or any other distribution channel you can think of.

SUMMARY

▶ Step 1. Find a hot industry: Use crowdfunding sites like Kickstarter to see what is getting the most funding and sites like Siftery .com to figure out which businesses are adding the most customers the fastest.

▶ Step 2. Figure out why leaders are leading: Use Ahrefs, SimilarWeb, and other tools to see how competitors get traffic.

▶ Step 3. Build your own version: Use Toptal or Upwork to build your own version of your competitor's product. Start by copying what works, then read their support forums to add quick improvements.

▶ Step 4. Attack their distribution channels: Reach out to bloggers, influencers who previously shared your competitors. Use my script to persuade them to promote you.

12

MULTIPLYING YOUR BUSINESS

"Being clever was when you looked at how things were and used the evidence to work out something new."

—Mark Haddon

People often think I make all my money through media—especially my daily podcast and Facebook Live show since they have audiences in the millions. That's true to a point, but it doesn't tell the full story. What people don't realize is that my biggest revenue streams come from projects going on behind the scenes.

Much of my "hidden" income is the result of multiplying. I talked about this on page 18: multiplying is when you find the patterns that link different projects and then use those connections to make more money. It's how you make the magic of 1 + 1 = 3 happen. For example, CEOs interviewed on my *Top Entrepreneurs* podcast see the appeal in also getting promoted via The Top Inbox, so I set up a sponsorship package that gets them exposure in both channels (a new revenue stream for me that wouldn't exist without the original two projects).

Don't worry if you feel you don't have enough revenue streams going to start multiplying them. You can uncover new ideas pretty easily. The most direct approach is so simple, I do it all the time and it never lets me down.

ONE QUESTION I ASK CUSTOMERS THAT GETS THEM TO PAY 2X MORE

Use my script and ask your customers.

There's a specific way to do this to get the information you want: immediately after one of your customers checks out, ask them what other products they buy that are similar. You can do this whether you have one hundred, one thousand, or three customers. Just send them an email asking: "What other tools have you bought to help you X?"

X is whatever space you're in or problem you're solving. So if you're selling tax software, you can ask your customers (whether they're paying or in a free trial) what other tools they've bought to help manage their taxes and money.

Now to be clear, this is totally different from asking customers *what they want*. There are lots of things people say they want that they won't actually buy. Knowing what they have actually paid for tells you what they're willing to spend their money on now.

You'll get a bunch of answers back. Sort through them and look for the patterns in everyone's responses. Do they keep mentioning the same products, or the same need? From there, you can decide to:

- ▶ **Buy the other company.** If I keep hearing that my customers also buy Company X's product, I'll use what I taught you in chapter 9 to figure out how to buy that company. It's easier than launching a new venture if you have room in your portfolio for another company. Then you can cross-sell your new company's products to your current customer base.

- ▶ **Partner with the other company.** If you can't buy the other company, join forces with them. If so many of your customers like their products, there's a good chance that their other customers will also buy your products. It will be a win-win if you can cross-sell with them.

- ▶ **Add a similar product to your current company's offerings.** No need to launch a new business here. Just make the product an add-on to what your customers are already buying. So if your tax software customers say they also pay for invoicing or inventory tracking tools, you can sell similar items and bundle them with your original product.

A famous example of this approach with a physical product is McDonald's. They realized early on that people like to buy fries with a burger, so they bundled them together. Now customers are more likely to buy both every time. McDonald's also discovers new revenue streams by copying popular items at other chain restaurants. When Starbucks took off, McDonald's launched McCafé and started offering elaborate coffee drinks. When they noticed nobody wanted their pale iceberg salads they copied Panera and Chick-fil-A by using more colorful, nutritious ingredients.*

Most of this chapter will focus on how to add products to what you're already doing. It also ties into what I've found to be the most effective growth strategy for launching new revenue streams so you can start multiplying: going deeper on current customers, not wider with new ones.

GROWING REVENUE: HOW TO GET TO $1M

People often think the only way to grow a business is by expanding their customer base. Not true at all. Bringing in more customers is actually the last thing I try to do when strategizing revenue growth. It's much more effective to think about how you can drive new income from people who are already paying or following you.

Let this be your mantra anytime you think about growing your business: Go deeper, not wider.

One way to do this is by launching a new product that your customers say they also buy. Even if they already have that thing and don't buy it again, new customers are likely to buy more from you because all your products appeal to them. So yes, new customers do play a role here, but your main focus is on going deeper, not wider, by getting all of your customers to pay you more.

Think about how you can get your current customers paying you more money for more value. There's a balance to strike here—you don't want one customer making up more than 10 percent of your revenue. That's risky. But if you can get a small group of people paying a lot for something they want, your earning potential will be huge.

---

* www.businessinsider.com/mcdonalds-is-changing-its-salad-2016–6.

# CUSTOMERS	PRICE PER CUSTOMER	ANNUAL REVENUE
5	$16,600 per month	$1M
100	$833 per month	$1M
5,000	$16 per month	$1M
100,000	$.80 per month	$1M
Pause and consider what business model you would use if you could have only five customers versus the model you would use if you could have 100,000.		

Challenge yourself by putting a creative limit on your customer number. Ask yourself:

- How would I build a multimillion-dollar company if I were only allowed to ever have fifty customers?
- What products would I sell to them?
- What would I charge them?
- How would I manage pricing increases over time?
- What would they be happy to pay more for?

I realized that GetLatka.com was never going to be a product that I could sell to a million people at $30/month. There just are not that many people interested in B2B SaaS data. But it offers a lot of value to a very small group of people in venture capital. So I decided I would draw in customers, and keep them, by limiting the number of people I would let in. Maintaining a small circle also allows me to give each customer white glove service and build a waiting list.

Today I cap my customer base at around fifty. Every few months I'll send out an email letting them know my monthly price is going up. About one to three customers churn as a result of the increase, so those spots open up to the waiting list. Then I email the waiting list saying, "Hey, we have three spots available at $X [the new price]." They fill up immediately.

My audience knows I will only ever have fifty customers at a time. That fact creates an urgency that drives folks on the waiting list to jump in the moment a spot opens up. And I'm going deeper, not wider, to grow cash flow by charging every customer more with each price hike.

Clate Mask, CEO of Infusionsoft, also used a deeper-not-wider approach to growing revenue. He told me how, back in 2014, his customer churn was 8 percent every month. That means out of every one hundred customers who signed up for his software, he'd drop to ninety-two the following month. That churn is really high if you're trying to build a software business.

So he did something counterintuitive: he started charging customers more money and fewer of them left. How did that work? Well, he discovered that churn was high because people were signing up for his software as a free trial but didn't start using it right away. Then, when their trial was over, they left.

When Clate added a $2,500 service fee at the beginning of the sales process, his customers became more invested. He also started attracting more serious customers while weeding out those who never intended to pay for the service. He could also afford to put one of his people on each customer to help them have success quickly. Churn dropped from 8 percent to 2 percent. He signed up fewer customers, but at a higher price, and those customers were more likely to pay for longer periods of time.

If you're still getting to know your customers, you can cast a wide net first, then study their behavior over a few months: Who has reordered already? Who has paid the most money? As you start recognizing trends you can tweak your approach to serve those high-paying customers more directly.

The image on the next page shows how many customers canceled their subscription to my first company, Heyo, depending on the month in which they signed up. We called this our cohort churn analysis. Out of the 443 customers who signed up in February 2014, 84.7 percent had churned by February 2016. If I were exploring new pricing options, I'd reach out to the 15.3 percent of customers who signed up in February 2014 who are still paying me to try to identify why they are so sticky.

I'd then update my pricing, or introduce an upsell, based on why these super-sticky customers keep paying. In Heyo's case, the customers who kept paying the longest were those who captured the most leads through our Facebook contests. So we started to tie pricing to the number of leads collected and immediately saw a revenue spike.

Anyone can do this with their business. Look at which customers have paid you the most historically, then figure out *why* they paid you the most and introduce pricing tiers around that data. Don't make decisions based on your gut alone, which is sometimes right but often wrong. You want gut + data.

		Totals	% of Cohort Churned
Feb-14		443	84.7%
Mar-14		401	82.7%
Apr-14		418	78.6%
May-14		304	79.2%
Jun-14		438	81.6%
Jul-14		396	77.5%

Be careful here: don't just upsell for upselling's sake. Customers have a low tolerance for that. Aim to upsell based on usage if it can fit your business model since customers will be hooked by the time they face the new pricing. We did that with Heyo and it's also how I monetize The Top Inbox—you hit a $5/month pay wall after using it fifty times. It's a no-brainer for customers to pay by that point since they're regular users.

When upselling physical products, think about how supermarkets use checkout lanes or how Amazon uses "people who bought this also bought this other thing." It's not annoying to put ping-pong balls on the beer end cap in a college town. The store knows that most college students buying beer ($9.99) will also buy ping-pong balls ($3.99) to play beer pong. You just increased your average checkout size from $9.99 to $13.98.

The annoying version of this is when you're at a Verizon store and the sales guy tries to sell you a bunch of extra stuff you don't want: cables, chargers, "new data plan for just $1/month." Make sure you're upselling things that the customer is already thinking they want.

THREE MULTIPLYING TACTICS TO FILL YOUR WALLET

Once you have multiple projects or products running you can get to multiplying. In all my business dealings I've discovered three multiplying tactics that, when used together, get me maximum returns.

Multiplying Tactic #1: Increase "Wallet Share" by Increasing the Time a Customer Is Under Your Control

Wallet share is simply the amount of money a customer spends on your products. You'll know your wallet share is growing when your cart value—the average cart checkout—starts to increase.

You want to maximize the amount of time a customer spends in your ecosystem so you can put more products in front of them. As customers we succumb to this tactic all the time, especially when we feel we're getting a better deal by doing most of our shopping in one place.

It's exactly why Costco requires memberships to shop there, or why Amazon has Amazon Prime. They know you'll shop with them more if you invest in the membership fee. It's why we get drunk on the all-inclusive cruise. You start drinking at 8 a.m. and you drink all day, every day, because you want to get your money's worth.

Walmart is valuable by itself, and so is any gas station. However, they are more valuable together because we spend more time "in their control." By the time we drive off Walmart property they've dipped into our wallets for everything from toilet paper and frozen pizza to the 5-hour Energy drink and car wash we got with our gas.

So you're not Walmart or Amazon or Costco—not even close—but anyone can grow their wallet share, no matter their business size. The key is to simply understand what else your customers buy that is most closely related to products you're already selling.

Let's say you sell iPhone cases. And let's say you've done the hard work of getting your case ranked high on Amazon and getting distribution in a retail outlet. However widely your product is available, the work you put into getting distribution has paved the path for any other related products you can sell. So what a waste it would be if you sold only iPhone cases.

To figure out what to sell next you need to know what other phone-related products your customers buy, and how much they're spending. If it's, say, $100 a month, your goal should be to get as much of that $100 as you can for yourself. So what else are they buying, and how can you sell that to them? The most powerful way to find out is to ask them. Runners-up: look at the "Customers who bought this item also bought" section on Amazon below your product, or similar products; for software, search Siftery .com or BuiltWith.com.

If you learn they're buying USB chargers with the cell phone cases, do you then go partner with a USB cord provider? Do you build your own? License it? You can approach it any way you'd like once you know what customers are buying.

A company doing a great job at increasing wallet share is BestSelf.co. The owners, Cathryn and Allen, are brilliant entrepreneurs. They created and sell the SELF Journal for $31.99. Since launching in 2015, they've sold more than two hundred thousand units. Part of the genius behind their journal is that it covers only thirteen weeks' time and you can start using it at any point in the year. So once you're hooked on using it you're going to buy another one after those thirteen weeks are up—you won't care about the expense. BestSelf.co even incentivizes customers to keep their wallets open by offering a journal subscription. You get a new one every thirteen weeks for 10 percent off.

They've recently expanded to selling related products like the SELF Shield, a cover for the SELF Journal that actually costs more than double the journal itself.

They're also selling T-shirts for $24, a WIN THE DAY hoodie for $55, SmartMarks (a combo bookmark and notebook) for $15, Sidekick (a mini-version of their SELF Journal) for $13, a wall RoadMap for $9 . . . and that's not even half their stuff. Today their average order value is $54— nearly double what it was two years ago ($28), before they started adding additional products. The wallet share they're going after is the money people spend on productivity tools—and they're doing a great job at that.

On the software side, ClickFunnels founder Russell Brunson keeps customers using his tools by making it as easy as possible for entrepreneurs to market, sell, and deliver their products and services online. Russell has studied his customer data and knows that churn will drop from 10 percent to 4 percent in the first two months if they do a couple key things, like setting up a custom domain—so Russell does it for them. He sets up a custom domain and covers the bill as part of the on-boarding process. He's also found customers are more sticky after they set up SMTP integrations. Once they're in, ClickFunnels' tools help customers execute every step of their business, from setting up a website to customer service, so they never have to use another service. Then the more their business grows, the more they use ClickFunnels to keep it running. The entire business model is built around increasing wallet share. I interviewed the ClickFunnels COO on my podcast, where he shared that they've passed sixty-five thousand customers and $60M in annual recurring revenue without raising any outside capital.

Multiplying Tactic #2: Once You Have More Wallet Share of Customers, Negotiate Discounts on Things You Already Buy

You can do this on anything, from supplies to software subscriptions that help run your business. Every dollar you save is a dollar you get to keep. If this sounds petty to you, remember that wealthy people are wealthy not just because of how much money they make, but how much they keep. Driving down expenses is just as important as growing your income. So once every three months or so, look at your expenses to pinpoint your ten biggest payments. Send an email to those companies and say:

"I need to find a cheaper option. I can't afford this anymore. Can you help me cancel my account?"

Say those exact words so they understand that you really might leave. Almost every company has a process in place where, when somebody asks to cancel, it unlocks the ability for the salesperson, or a team member, to incentivize you to stay with discounts, etc. This is especially the case with software and services. They just have to actually believe you're going to cancel.

A few times a year I email any software company that I'm paying more than $100 a month for and simply say, "I need to cancel my account. It's not doing what I thought it would."

I recently sent this email to ActiveCampaign, a company that I use for specific email marketing campaigns (Aweber is what I use for everything else):

"Hey, if you look at my account you'll see I haven't used it as much as I have in the past. I should probably cancel the $275/month payment. Can you help me do that?"

Christine, a customer success manager at ActiveCampaign, replied and offered to bring my monthly payment down from $275 to $182. I saved nearly 50 percent just by asking. You'll get these kinds of responses all the time when you threaten to cancel a service. It's the fastest way to save money.

This doesn't work with a huge company like Amazon or Facebook. You can't do this to get a cheaper iPhone. But you probably have many expenses that you're paying to smaller companies where you'll have power and leverage. They don't want to lose you because that means churn goes up.

This tactic won't be as easy if you're buying supplies for a physical product until you get some scale. It's still absolutely doable, though. If you have a food truck and reach the point where you're doing five thousand meals a month, you'll start to have negotiating power over suppliers. Just by virtue of increasing your order quantity you can drive down your unit costs on things like avocados or food containers.

This happens in every industry, on every level. Walmart gets its gas cheaper than anyone else because it can promise the gas supplier it will deliver huge volumes of sales. You have this same leverage. For example, I get software that I need to run TheTopInbox.com for free or at a big discount by offering to mention the software company on my podcast. Best Self.co gets better prices on paper the more their volume increases.

Multiplying Tactic #3:
Get Your Biggest Revenue Streams Working Together

You learned in math class when you were a kid that three small things multiplied together yield something small: $1 \times 1 \times 1 = 1$. But just level up by one degree and you start to see growth: $2 \times 2 \times 2 = 8$. The more things you multiply together, and the more powerful each of those things is, the bigger output you get. These are basic rules of nature and math.

Apply this thinking when growing your business. Find your biggest revenue streams, or the projects or skills with the biggest potential, and try to get them working together.

This approach led me to create GetLatka.com. My podcast was my first big asset—put that at a 10. I wanted to figure out what I could multiply it with to get a big output. So I thought about what I was really good at that could become a large asset. Well, Heyo was a software company. I'm great at building software. So I thought, How can I take my podcast, a media asset (10), and multiply it by another asset related to software (10) to get a 100 output?

Then I remembered a problem my podcast listeners had: they valued the info in my 700+ episodes but didn't have time to sift through every one to find the specifics they're looking for. So I decided to spend $50,000 without putting up any of my own cash (more on that in chapter 11) to create GetLatka.com so listeners could easily sort through my episodes to figure out which to listen to. They can also look up revenue data, customer counts, valuations, and more data on privately held software companies.

NO-COST SALES: FROM SPREADSHEET TO $2K
EACH MONTH IN MY POCKET

It all started with me preselling a simple Google spreadsheet. I filled the spreadsheet with data points my podcast guests gave me and then told my podcast listeners they could buy a version to download themselves:

Dec 16 MRR	Dec 17 MRR	Growth Rate	Space	Podcast Episode	Company Na	CEO Name	Custome	Raised	ARPU	Gross Churn	CAC	Location	LTV Months	LTV Dollars
$4,500	$55,000	1122%		678	Ripple Recruit	Andrew Myers	view on	$700,000	$300	0%		NYC		
$35,000	$350,000	900%		1051	marketmuse		view on	$4m	$5,000	0.01	9000	Boston, NYC,	84	
$65,000	$600,000	823%		984	hyprbrands.	Gil Eyal	view on	$8,000,000	$3,333		$20,000	Israel, NYC	6-7years	$200k
$10,000	$68,000	580%		970	tagove.com	Laduram Vish	view on	$750,000	$65,000	$70		SF, London, I	16	$700	1500
$10,000	$67,000	570%		1041	idealspot		view on	$2,500,000	$670	0.2	15000	Austin	5	
$20,000	$120,000	500%		829	demandjump	Christopher D	view on	$4,000,000	$82,500	$10,000			36	$135,000	5000
$67,000	$386,000	476%	$8m cap on o	799	leadcrunch.c	Olin Hyde	view on	$2,000,000			$14,000	Chicago, San Diego, SF		
$100,000	$550,000	450%	65% seas, 35	768	mobilewalla.	Anindya Datta	view on website	$172,000		Don't spend o	NYC			Don't spend
$22,000	$100,000	355%		895	Detectify	Rickard Carls	view on	$2,500,000	$80	2%	no paid	Sweden		
$10,000	$45,000	350%		998	publicfast.co	Vitalii Malets	view on	$400,000	$333	20%		Ukraine		
$17,000	$70,000	312%	Sales Automa	383	Prospect.io	Vincenzo Rug	view on	$60,000	$45	6%	$50	Belgium	16.66666667	$750
$10,000	$40,000	300%		748	komiko.com	Hal Howard	view on	$2,000,000	$30	<1%	too early	Seattle	too early	too early
$50,000	$191,815	264%		386	TravelFlan.c	Kenneth Lee	view on	$125,000	$10	too early	$20	Asia	too early	too early
$70,000	$268,000	283%	Data and Lea	523	Xiq.ai	Usman Sheikl	view on	$1,125,000	$7,000	0%	too early	Los Altos, CA	too early	too early
$9,167	$35,000	282%		403	PromoRepubl	Maksym	view on	$850k	$10/mo	8%	$100		12.5	$125
$50,000	$190,000	280%		735	Wurk	Keegan Peter	view on	$3,000,000	$20			Denver, Colorado		
$600,000	$1,833,333	267%		1069	jelli		view on	$46,000,000		<5% annually	100000	San Mateo, NYC, Boise Idaho		
$416,600	$1,520,000	265%		911	instapage.co	Tyson Quick	view on	Dec 2016 $5m	6%	SF		$1,200	166666.67	4 months
$75,000	$270,000	260%		1038	prezly		view on	bootstrapped	$900	0.012	7000	Remote	100	$40,000
$109,000	$375,000	244%		651	exponea.con	Peter Irikovsk	view on	$3,000,000	$269,187	$38,000	Slovakia dev,	300	11 months	106
$104,000	$350,000	237%	Marketing Aut	335	SocialProof	Nathan Laben	view on	$4,000,000	$50	5%	$100	Detroit	20	$1,000

Today GetLatka.com has come a long way from that spreadsheet. I multiplied my biggest asset (my podcast) with my high-potential skill (creating software) to create a cash-printing software that clients use to sort through my podcast data. Now I increase my prices incrementally. Here is an example of an early customer paying me $24K ($2K/mo) for the data (see "Retainer Fee" at bottom):

RETAINER AGREEMENT

This Retainer Agreement (this "**Agreement**") is entered into effective as of January 1, 2018 (the "**Effective Date**") by and between ▮▮▮▮▮▮▮▮▮▮ a Delaware corporation ▮▮▮▮▮▮▮ ▮▮▮▮▮▮ and The Latka Agency, LLC, a Texas corporation (the "**Latka Agency**").

RECITALS

A. ▮▮▮▮▮▮▮▮ is engaged in providing revenue-based financing loans ("**Revenue-Based Loans**") to qualified commercial businesses ("**Qualified Businesses**") on terms and in amounts that have been previously outlined to the Latka Agency.

B. ▮▮▮▮▮▮▮ desires to engage and authorize the Latka Agency to introduce certain Qualified Businesses to ▮▮▮▮▮▮▮ subject to certain terms and conditions, in return for certain fees to be paid to Latka Agency hereunder.

AGREEMENT

NOW, THEREFORE, in consideration of the foregoing and for other good and valuable consideration, the receipt and sufficiency of which are hereby acknowledged, the parties agree as follows.

1.   **Role of Latka Agency; Not an Agent of** ▮▮▮▮▮▮▮▮▮▮▮▮ retains Latka Agency to act as its non-exclusive intermediary to locate Qualified Businesses (each, a "**Prospect**") that may desire to have ▮▮▮▮▮▮▮▮ provide Revenue-Based Loans. ▮▮▮▮ shall be under no obligation to consummate any Revenue-Based Loan with any Prospect. LATKA AGENCY IS NOT AUTHORIZED TO ACT AS AGENT FOR ▮▮▮▮▮ ▮▮▮▮ OR TO OFFER TO FINANCE OR MAKE A LOAN TO ANY PROSPECT OR TO BIND ▮▮▮ IN ANY WAY WITH RESPECT TO THE MAKING OF ANY REVENUE-BASED LOAN. LATKA AGENCY IS AND SHALL BE AN INDEPENDENT CONTRACTOR AND NOT AN EMPLOYEE, PARTNER, AGENT, REPRESENTATIVE OR JOINT VENTURER OF OR IN ▮▮▮▮▮▮▮▮.

2.   **Information**. Latka Agency may make certain information available to Prospects regarding ▮▮▮▮▮ and/or to ▮▮▮▮▮▮ regarding Prospects, their qualifications and or conditions for financing in such Prospect, however the evaluation of such information is the responsibility of parties to the Revenue-Based Loan, and any information provided to either party may be accepted or rejected by the parties.

3.   **Retainer Fee:**. ▮▮▮▮▮▮ will pay The Latka Agency, LLC a monthly fee of $2,000 in exchange for curated introductions to Prospects. Payments will be made monthly via credit card on the 1st of each month. Any Retainer Fee payable to Latka Agency hereunder shall be solely the obligation of ▮▮▮▮▮▮ Notwithstanding any provision to the contrary in this Section 2 or elsewhere in this Agreement, ▮▮▮▮▮▮ shall not be required to pay any Fee

The goal here is to get all three multiplying tactics working at the same time: expand wallet share, negotiate discounts on things you use in bulk, and get your biggest revenue streams working together. If you get only one multiplying tactic working, it's like eating a sandwich with just the bread. You'll eat it (what most of you do your whole lives), but it tastes awful. Get all three working together and you have a big, beautiful sandwich with meat, lettuce, and tomatoes that dance in your mouth. Tastes much better. Welcome to the New Rich.

13

SELLING A BUSINESS

"I made my money by selling too soon."

—Bernard Baruch

Selling a business is as much of a strategy for growing wealth as launching or buying one. The decision to sell has everything to do with time—the time you spend running the business, the time you'd need to grow it, and market timing.

A packed scheduled is the biggest red flag telling you to sell. Remember, joining the New Rich is all about passive income. If you're spending all your time running a company, it's preventing you from generating other revenue streams. A lot of people lie to themselves about this. They think a project is passive when it actually eats tons of their time. If a company is truly passive and making you money, hold it. If it takes your time with no end in sight, sell.

Also look at growth. If numbers are flat or declining, sell. You may be tempted to push for growth, but that requires a lot of time. Or it requires you to hire a team and incentivize the team by giving them equity to grow it. You can do it, but it's an art.

And just as important: market timing. If you get the sense that the market is overvaluing the space that you're in, you might take advantage of that hype and sell. Cash in while it's hot.

ONE SENTENCE I USE TO GET OFFERS
WITHOUT SOUNDING DESPERATE

The old saying "You have to be bought, not sold" is just that—old. Forget the tired thinking that you can only get a great offer for your business if buyers woo you into selling. You need to make it known that you want to sell—with a reason people will believe—to get conversations going. Give this impression even if you're only curious about the prospect of selling. Email a few of your competitors and say:

"I really need to sell the business to take care of some personal stuff. Want to chat?"

Leave it at that. This sounds desperate, but that's the point. Your desperate vibes will get prospective buyers to engage in conversations that otherwise wouldn't have happened. They'll see it as an easy opportunity to take over a competitor that they won't want to miss. And they'll work on persuading their cofounders, teammates, and board to make an offer. That's where you want them. Once they sell their team on the idea, they're expected to get the deal done. If they don't, it puts egg on their face. Use this to your advantage. Everyone wants to get a good deal and then brag about it to their team. If you can give the potential buyer an initial "discounted" price that makes them feel good, they'll tell the world about it.

After they are hooked, you tell them others want to buy, thereby creating competition and getting them to increase their bid into a range you'd actually take.

Emotions start running high when prospective buyers issue a LOI. When they've reached that point it means they've persuaded their team to make an offer. They've taken the time to strategically think about the purchase; they're naming a price; they're naming a closing date. They're visualizing what the company will be like when they own it.

This is the foreplay that happens when companies are pursuing each other. When I'm looking at buying companies, I know that once I issue an LOI I'm significantly more invested. I've learned more about the CEO, the company's financials, and the systems the team uses. I can still walk away, but it hurts more to walk away at that point. That's the state you want to get your buyers into.

Once you have a few LOIs you'll have the power and the leverage to spark bidding wars. But how do you get prospects to push beyond that discounted price they thought they'd be getting? Keep them emotionally invested. I often give this response to an initial offer (when I believe it's true) to spark emotions:

"I have two responsibilities: One is a fiduciary responsibility to my investors. The other is making sure my customers are happy. You're at the top in terms of where I think our customers would be happiest. But financially, you have to increase your offer for me to feel I'm meeting my fiduciary responsibility to my investors." (If you don't have investors, say "advisers.")

Making the higher price tag about the investors keeps the money conversation objective. The financials are what they are. You're not just throwing out a pipe dream price. And mentioning customer happiness gets buyers thinking about personal fit and culture—intangibles that talk louder than money. Think about anytime you've shopped for a place to live. Weren't you more likely to push beyond your budget if you walked into a place that felt *just right*? Suddenly you're rationalizing the extra expense. It's a totally human reaction and it works in business, too.

I used this technique when negotiating with a potential Heyo buyer in 2015:

Nathan Latka <██████████>
to Don

this is how phone conversation went:
Me: You are at bottom of the pole in terms of deal value.

Them: how much?

Well, I have two responsibilities: Financial and Customer. You are at the top in terms of where I think our customers will be happiest but you're going to have to increase the deal value by a pretty massive amount.

Them: how much?

Me: You offered $200k, what is your best offer?

Them: ???

Me: I'm willing to give you a discount below the current best offer we have because you're a good fit for our customers but you're going to have to double or triple your deal size in order to get Heyo.com and it's assets.

Jim: Let me talk to Mike.

They then countered with an LOI with $200k cash and 100k earnout (with terms that make it almost impossible that we'll ever see it). Their offer is still too low. It needs to be more like $375k cash, 100k earnout. (still a financial discount - but they are best customer fit)

thoughts?

This conversation got them to triple their initial offer.

SELL PICKLES TO THE LETTUCE GUY

If you've never sold a company, it can be hard to know whom to approach with that initial email. Your first obvious group is your competitors. Most of them would love to swallow your business and get you out of the way. If you're a local brownie shop, approach other bakeries in your neighborhood. Or look up a national brownie brand. You never know if they're looking to expand in your area.

Another easy option is good old social media. It's a great way to find potential buyers you'd never have known were interested. And it makes it easy for people to spread the word. Just post the same thing you'd write in an email to prospects:

"Hey, everyone, I really need to sell the business to take care of some personal stuff. Let me know if you or anyone you know might want to chat."

This approach works best if you're selling a small business doing less than $10K per month. Otherwise, think of companies that play around you. If you're a software company that helps small businesses with invoicing, try approaching a company that processes payroll. Or a company like Vistaprint that helps small businesses create marketing materials and business cards.

Think of the market as a hamburger. There are several different but complementary players all around you like buns, tomatoes, onions, pickles, ketchup, cheese, and meat. If you're a cheese and can't find a direct competitor to buy you—another cheese—look for complementary companies, like the lettuce or the bun. Look around and understand what else your customers are buying. If they're buying footballs from you they're probably also buying air pumps. Maybe you can sell your football production company to the air pump company.

Also look at your product's distribution channels as potential buyers. Matt Rissell cofounded the payroll software TSheets in 2006 but struggled to turn a profit during the company's initial years. They didn't see major growth until they started selling the software through the Intuit App Center, eventually making their way to a number one ranking. Fast-forward to 2017: Intuit bought TSheets for $340M.

Square and Weebly followed a similar track. Square cross-sold many of Weebly's website-building products for years. In 2018, Square ended up buying Weebly for $365M.

Look at who is selling a lot of your products. If you're paying someone a cut and they're driving a lot of volume, you might offer to sell them your whole company.

So make sure to look at these three channels if you're not sure where to start your hunt for a good buyer: competitors, other players in the same space (the hamburger), and distributors. You'll likely find more options than you think.

SELL WHILE YOU'RE YOUNG AND HOT

By young, I mean you. By hot, I mean your company. (But it can't hurt if you're hot, too. You'd be shocked how many deals I get because of my hair.)

I learned this lesson the hard way with Heyo.com. Back in 2012, iContact offered me $6.5M to buy Heyo. At the time, all of our competitors were exiting with huge offers. Salesforce bought Buddy Media for more than $600M. Wildfire sold to Google for $350M.

Seeing those deals inflated my ego. I thought, If Mark Zuckerberg could turn down Yahoo's billion-dollar offer to buy Facebook in 2006, and my peers were getting nine-figure deals, $6.5M was nothing. I could do so much better. At the time I was twenty-two years old and new to all of this. I didn't try to negotiate or spark a bidding war. I just passed on iContact's offer.

5221 Paramount Pkwy Ste 200 | Morrisville, NC 27560 | (919) 433-0735 | www.icontact.com

October 20, 2011

Nathan Latka
CEO, Lujure Media LLC
220 N. Main St.
Blacksburg, VA 24060

Dear Nathan:

The purpose of this confidential letter (**"Letter of Intent"**) is to summarize our discussions and express our mutual intent regarding the acquisition by iContact Corporation, a Delaware corporation, or its wholly-owned subsidiary to be designated (**"Purchaser"**), of substantially all of the assets of Lujure Media LLC, a Virginia Limited Liability Company (the **"Seller"**), which are used in the business of operating Lujure.com (the **"Business"**), on and subject to the following terms and conditions, and subject to the execution by Seller and Purchaser of a mutually acceptable definitive asset purchase agreement (the **"Definitive Agreement"**) and related ancillary documents.

    1.   <u>Acquisition of Assets; Purchase Price.</u>

      (a)   At the closing (the **"Closing"**), Seller will sell, transfer and assign to Purchaser, and Purchaser will purchase and acquire from Seller, all of the tangible and intangible assets of Seller that are a part of, or currently or customarily used in connection with, or necessary for the conduct of, the Business, including any such assets acquired after the date of this Letter of Intent but before the Closing (collectively, the **"Assets"**), free and clear of all claims, liens, charges, security interests, encumbrances, and restrictions, for a price (the **"Purchase Price"**) as set forth below. The Assets will specifically include, without limitation, the assets set forth on Exhibit A attached hereto. Subject to due diligence, Purchaser anticipates that the Closing will occur on or before December 5th, 2011.

      (b)   The Purchase Price will be up to $6,500,000 and will be paid in the following manner:

- Total potential cash consideration will be calculated by multiplying the sum of Seller's September 2011, October 2011, and November 2011 GAAP revenues by 12.0; however, the cash consideration range will be bounded such that the minimum cash consideration will equal $2,000,000 and the maximum cash consideration will equal $2,500,000, subject to adjustment for claims against the escrow and the Key Hire Escrow Obligation (as defined below). Cash consideration will be payable as follows:
  - o 80% of the total cash consideration will be payable at Closing.
  - o ~~20% of the total cash consideration will be held in escrow~~

It was one of the biggest mistakes of my life.

Never underestimate the timing of a market. Salesforce bought Datorama in July 2018 for $800M. At the same time, Babak Hedayati crossed $15M in revenues and three thousand customers for his competing tool, TapClicks, which helps media companies like Scripps manage real-time reporting. Companies are using it for scalable deployment of client reporting, data aggregation and visualization, and workflow management to bring intelligence and automation to their operations. It would not surprise me to see Babak take advantage of market timing and exit for six to ten times his $15M in annual revenues in the near future.

I wish I'd realized how important market timing was back in 2011. So-cial media marketing platforms were hot at the time. That was obvious from all the deals happening around. But once my competitors got out of the game the market cooled. Google even shut down Wildfire in 2014. I'd completely missed my window to make a big profit because the cliché is true: timing is everything.

By the time I got another offer for Heyo, in 2016, it was much smaller. We got $300K for just a part of the company's assets and the $1.4M that we had in the bank was returned to investors. I had to sell because the com-pany was taking up all of my time. Being a young, single guy with no re-sponsibilities, I knew that putting all my effort into one business was not going to make me rich.

MY PAY STUB: I WAS TWENTY-SIX, CEO

It would have been so easy to stay at Heyo. At twenty-six years old, I was making more than all my friends but I knew I could never get *really* rich off a paycheck. It's funny looking back at when I was persuading the board to raise my salary from $80K to $100K, as if that would make a huge differ-ence to me.

Here was that beautiful $100K pay stub:

Lujure Media, Inc						Earnings Statement			
902 Prices Fork Road									
Suite 2100						Check Date:		October 15, 2014	
Blacksburg, VA 24060						Period Beginning:		October 01, 2014	
						Period Ending:		October 15, 2014	
Nathan W Latka	Employee Number		16	Dept	100	Voucher Number			1809
						Net Pay			2,770.18

Earnings	Rate	Hours	Amount	YTD Hrs	YTD Amt	Taxes	Status	Taxable	Amount	YTD Amt
Reg	0.00	86.67	4166.67	1646.73	75000.03	Medicare		4166.67	60.42	1087.50
Total Gross Pay		86.67	4166.67	1646.73	75000.03	OASDI		4166.67	258.33	4650.00
						Federal Income Tax	S/0	4166.67	856.07	15171.18
						Virginia SITW	S/0	4166.67	221.67	3972.13
						Total Tax Withholding			1396.49	24880.81

I felt very "good" about this income, but it didn't do much going from $80K to $100K since the government kept so much in taxes. It also made me see that I was an employee in a flat business. The potential upside of my equity (how you get rich) was very little because I missed our shot in 2012.

I quickly realized I needed to think about how to shut Heyo down, or sell it, so I could move from making money as an employee to making money as an investor. I went from fighting like hell to get the board to increase my salary to wanting out.

I was obsessed with Jim Collins's mantra: Good is the enemy of great. And I wanted big-time "great." I knew I had to get out of Heyo and free up my time so I could do the deals I'm doing now, which are making me millions. It was the right move.

This is a big thing to remember: if you're young and single and have no responsibilities, even if you're a student in a dorm room, now is the time to take big risks because if you fall, you won't fall far. You don't have a lot to lose. I missed out on a ton of cash when I didn't sell in 2012, but my losses would have been even bigger if I'd stuck with Heyo any longer. I was under twenty-five years old with no obligations to anyone. It was the perfect time to make bigger bets.

WEIGHING OFFERS: WHEN TO SELL, WHEN TO WALK

I know not everyone reading this is a dorm-dwelling, risk-taking twenty-something. It can be hard to know when you should stick to what you're doing (as Zuck did in 2006) or cash in while you can (what I should have done in 2012). Add big responsibilities to the picture, like a family that's counting on you, and the choice can be paralyzing.

But the decision comes down to simple math. If you're in a moneymaking business, think about the time value of money. Let's say you own 50 percent of a company that makes $500K a year and you're paying yourself an $80K salary. And let's say there's no money left over at the end of the year, so you're not paying yourself a dividend.

If you could sell the company today for 1x its annual revenue (that's $500K), that's going to put $250K in your pocket pretax (you own 50 percent). My general advice is that if selling will get money in your pocket now that would otherwise take you three years or more to earn by working in the company, take the deal. Then use the cash to start something new.

So if you're making $80K a year, pretax, with no dividends, take the deal that will put $250K in your hands now. You'll then have that momentum behind you. You can say you sold your company and you'll have $250K you can reinvest in your next idea.

Walking away from a moneymaking business is scary, but you have to trust yourself in these moments. You're smart. You will have another great idea. Bet on yourself. Use the momentum to create something else.

We always worry there will never be a better idea, but that's never true. You don't have to look past Elon Musk to see that. His first business was an agency that he launched in his twenties. He sold the agency and started X.com, which eventually morphed into PayPal. After he got out of PayPal he used his profits to launch SpaceX, then Tesla, and most recently The Boring Company. At the time of this writing Musk's net worth is $20B. Even if you never go that big, Musk is a great example of what can happen if you trust your gut and keep building on current successes.

So take the win. Momentum is a huge asset. Keep it, hold it, and create it. Sell your company if you get the chance and the cash makes sense. A lot of it comes down to emotions, too. When you look at your final offers, if you don't think there's one that's competitive, email everyone and say, "Sorry, I can't take the offer. I'm going to keep building the company." Many times when you really walk away like that, people will reply with a higher offer.

When you use this tactic, and it works, remember your buddy Nathan!

CONCLUSION

Many books written on money, wealth, and power are timeless. This is not one of them.

There are limited spots in the New Rich Boat, and if you don't grab your seat now, you'll miss out. When you look at history, the wealthiest people took advantage of big-time knowledge before "the broke masses" caught up.

Henry Kravis of Kohlberg Kravis Roberts (KKR) created the leveraged buyout (LBO) industry in 1976, using a company's own cash flow strengths to saddle it with debt, and take it over. In 1980, everyone started doing LBOs, making rich deals harder to find.

Billions of dollars of wealth were created when Bitcoin spiked to $19,205.11 in late spring of 2017. Those who had knowledge of the power of Bitcoin a year prior bought at under $3,000. Early mover's advantage.

Usually when the masses catch on to any idea, the strategies don't work anymore.

Why?

The top 1 percent are smart. When they climb the ladder of success, they want to hoard, which means they must destroy the ladder so others can't climb.

They invent "rules" and work very hard to sell these rules to you so that you get stuck working for them.

▶ Focus on one thing!
▶ Copying is bad!
▶ Make sure you set goals!
▶ Ask customers what they want and give it to them!

Over the past 200+ pages, I've showed you how I challenged these rules mentally, and then broke them spectacularly to create immediate wealth for myself.

At the beginning of this book I told you that you'd learn:

▶ How to unlock your hidden money by decreasing expenses
▶ The easy way to live like a king without owning a thing
▶ How to invest in real estate without any time, money, or knowledge
▶ Clever ways to buy entire companies without spending your own money
▶ How to turn $1 into $3 with unconventional investing ideas
▶ How to get rich copying your competitors
▶ Three levers you can pull to multiply your business
▶ How to sell a business whenever you want

I then showed you (screenshots and all!):

▶ How I got a $300K white Rolls-Royce Ghost for free
▶ The words I used to get my first real estate deal, which makes me $1,700/month in passive income
▶ How I used a liability to my advantage to take over a company (and have them pay me $15K to do it!)
▶ How I wrote a $6K check to a food truck owner and got back my money fast, plus a royalty stream for life
▶ Weird places online I look to find ways to copy competitors, steal their market share
▶ How I get current customers to pay me more, without extra work hunting down new customers
▶ Five words I used to sell my business: "Is that your best offer?"

Congratulations on investing in yourself and making the time to read this book. You're now part of a very unique group. The next step is to execute before everyone else catches on. I gave you the keys to the New Rich vault. Now you open the door.

I did.

Google search right now: "Nathan Latka Raises $1 Billion for More Software Buyouts" and you'll see what I mean.

ACKNOWLEDGMENTS

So many people deserve credit for this book.

First off, to my friend Allen Gannett who introduced me to one of the best book agents in the business, Jim Levine, who helped me turn my ideas into a winning proposal and then continued to play a crucial role in editorial development and launch strategy.

Thanks to the entire team at Portfolio/Penguin Random House, starting with my very patient editor, Leah Trouwborst; followed by president and CEO Adrian Zackheim; Will Weisser; Stefanie Brody; Helen Healey; Olivia Peluso; Taylor Edwards; Tara Gilbride; and Jamie Lescht for embracing my wild ideas and having the courage to publish a book that flies in the face of many conventional business ideas.

Maria Gagliano had an incredible ability to organize my ideas and drafts into a coherent flow. It's clear why Simon Sinek and so many other bestselling authors think of her as a total star.

Finally, I have so many friends to thank who helped me test chapter titles, book titles, cover images, and so much more. These friends include Pat Matthews of Active Capital; Tucker Max of Scribe; James Jacoby at Harvard; Bill Shaw, president at Entrepreneur.com; Dave Hamilton and Erika Hardin at Cineflix who saw the books potential to be on TV; and my TV agent Ben Levine at CAA.

Special thanks to my mom and dad for deciding they were going to "get wild" one night some twenty-nine years ago. My mom taught me the value of money, the power of a decision, and the upside of hard work; and my dad helped me build my competitive muscle and a truly remarkable hunger for winning big.

TOP 100 FACEBOOK GROUPS FOR ENTREPRENEURS

If you'd like to find private groups of entrepreneurs on Facebook in many different industries, try these top 100 I've found and used.

NAME	MEMBERS	LAST 30-DAY POSTS	ADMIN
Dream Catchers: LIVE RICHER w/ The Budgetnista	320,000	9,200	Kristina Spells
Freelancers	260,000	200	Mohd Danish
International Development Jobs for Young Professionals	177,000	240	Anna Okello
Professional Photographers	177,000	3,000	Elena Salvai Photography
RCCG Entrepreneurs' Network	170,000	200	Arise Arizechi
Professional Photographers	124,000	1,200	Manoj Eknath Chavan
Real Estate Investors	91,000	910	James Simmons
Mompreneur Circle	87,000	3,200	Latika Wadhwa
Learn Digital Marketing	83,000	120	Sanjay Shenoy
Digital Nomads Around the World	79,000	320	Joan Gaya
Shopify Entrepreneurs	78,000	350	Timothy Dann-Barrick

NAME	MEMBERS	LAST 30-DAY POSTS	ADMIN
Freelancers	77,000	440	Nilesh Yerunkar
Legit Entrepreneurship 2018	74,000	4,500	Roderick Allred
Women Helping Women Entrepreneurs	70,000	7,000	Christina Rowe
Amazon FBA Ninjas!	70,000	1,800	Kevin David
Graphic Designer/Freelance Design Group	67,000	3,300	Chuyênsi Temnhãn Hôpquà
It's Better Handmade Group	66,000	8,800	Natalie Shay Meiners
Startup Buddies	65,000	70	Abhinav Prashant
Millennial Entrepreneur Community	61,000	4,200	Frank Salas
Merch by Amazon	61,000	590	Chris Green
Women's Entrepreneur Network	60,000	385	Haley Lynn Gray
Artisan Indie—Etsy Sellers, Makers & More	58,000	2,000	Sarah Sewell
The Amazing Seller	57,000	720	Scott Voelker
Stash Investors	56,000	3,100	Keith Bridgeforth
Entrepreneur Lifestyle Group	55,000	50	John Golat
Start A Money Making Blog	52,000	3,000	Pete and Heather Reese
Entrepreneur Hustle	50,000	1,000	Danny Veiga
WORLD FASHION BLOGGERS	50,000	2,100	Erika Isalberti
Studio U	50,000	460	Alex Mozes
ETSY SELLERS ONLY	47,000	2,100	Elizabeth Liberty
Amazon FBA Rockstars!	46,000	800	Ariela Janeen Vianu
Remote Work & Jobs for Digital Nomads	45,000	150	Sergi Mateo
The Facebook Ads Group	45,000	230	Ben Malol
Award Travel 101®	44,000	720	Richard Kerr

NAME	MEMBERS	LAST 30-DAY POSTS	ADMIN
ClickFunnels Avengers (Affiliates)	43,000	630	Dave Woodward
QliqMedia: Digital Marketing Hub	42,000	20	Henshaw Jacobson
Travel Bloggers	42,000	5,000	Mark Monta
Stock Market Investing	39,000	650	Chris Smith
The Smart Passive Income Community	37,000	250	Timothy Moser
Value Investing	37,000	130	Tim Melvin
Work and Travel	36,000	440	İbrahim Kutsal
Sales Professionals Group	35,000	1,700	Jeremiah Cargle
Girls LOVE Getting Paid While They Travel!	35,000	970	Emmy Rogers
Digital Marketing Question & Answers	34,000	360	Sorav Jain
Amazon FBA Heroes	34,000	2,800	Derrick Struggle
Digital Nomad Entrepreneurs	32,000	100	Sergi Mateo
Digital Marketing Hub	32,000	110	Prateek Shah
Humans of Digital Marketing	32,000	2,100	Mahesh Gaur
Global Digital Nomad Network	32,000	100	Johannes Voelkner
Entrepreneurs, Startup & Business Association of New York	31,000	4,700	Shonali Sen
Social Media for Entrepreneurs	30,000	370	Josh Forti
App Entrepreneurs and Marketers Group	30,000	50	Ted Nash
Female Digital Nomads	30,000	1,100	Milou Van Roon
HEP—Etsy Shop Help & Support	25,000	400	De Shockney
Amazon FBA Domination	25,000	80	Andy Arnott
The Game of Networking	25,000	260	Rob Sperry

NAME	MEMBERS	LAST 30-DAY POSTS	ADMIN
Digital Marketing	24,000	1,000	Gajendra Patel
Digital Marketing	21,000	600	Amartya Sinha
Etsy Support and Guidance Group	21,000	40	Fiona Fletcher
The Intentional Entrepreneur	20,000	4,600	Jennie Rensink
Lifestyle Entrepreneurs	20,000	500	Yosef Ravaliere
Digital Nomad Jobs: Remote Job Opportunities	20,000	70	Steven Lin
Shopify, Ecom & Facebook Ads Community (Trackify 8-Figure Mastermind)	20,000	100	Thomas Bartke
Travel & Lifestyle	20,000	1,300	Sonit Soni
Airbnb Professional Hosts	20,000	1,200	Christina's
60 Second Persuasion	20,000	130	Bushra Azhar
Entrepreneur Exchange	19,000	150	Kendra Kroll
The Passive Income Lounge	19,000	70	Louise Henry
Facebook Ads Rockstars	19,000	220	Alex Fedotoff
Facebook Advertising for JEDI Entrepreneurs	18,000	470	Jason Tibbetts
Digital Nomad Accelerator	18,000	100	Mitchell Weijerman
Entrepreneur Insiders Club	17,000	340	James Bowen
Entrepreneurial Leaders	17,000	200	Amy Prueter
Digital Nomad Girls Community	16,000	350	Jennifer Lachs
Digital Nomads Hub	16,000	60	Rémy Lasset
Unlimited Success and Amazon Community	16,000	140	Rob Moore
Real Estate Investing For Beginners	16,000	60	Cody Sperber
FBA Tactical Arbitrage	16,000	370	Alex Moss

NAME	MEMBERS	LAST 30-DAY POSTS	ADMIN
Investing and Personal Finance Club	15,000	250	Robert Farrington
10xTravelcom Insiders	15,000	940	10XTravel
Social Media Influencers	15,000	60	Oliver Isaacs
AWE—Aspiring Women Entrepreneurs	14,000	280	Shaila Colaco
BALTIMORE ENTREPRENEURS	14,000	970	Candice George
Digital Marketing	14,000	120	Akansha Gautam
Online Publishers and Entrepreneurs Network	14,000	380	Edirin Edewor
eCommerce Dream Mastermind	14,000	30	Aristide Basque
Facebook Ads, Chatbots & Affiliate Marketing: Quit The 9 To 5 Group	14,000	130	Jeff Miller
JenPlanscom Budgeting & Personal Finance	14,000	300	Jen DuFore
The Poor Travelers: Support Group	14,000	380	Yosh Dimen
6 Figure Digital Marketing Hacks For Entrepreneurs W/ JR Rivas	13,000	60	JR Rivas
Digital Marketing Mastery	13,000	120	Saurabh Choudhary
The Entrepreneur Movement	13,000	30	Karl Commissariat
DigitalMarketer Engage	12,000	1,100	Justin Rondeau
VetpreneurTribe	12,000	2,100	Curtez Riggs
E-commerce & Shopify Pirates	12,000	80	Karlo Bradica
Thriving on Etsy and Beyond	12,000	260	DiEtte
GrooveLearning—an Entrepreneur Community	11,000	80	Rohan Gilkes
EcommerceMindset	11,000	150	Tim Sharp
The RV Entrepreneur	10,000	200	Alyssa Padgett
Seedly Personal Finance Community (SG)	10,000	460	Tee-Ming Chew

TOP ORGANIZATIONS FOR ENTREPRENEURS

If you're looking for local organizations where other entrepreneurs hang out, try one of these top organizations we've sourced from around the United States.

ENTREPRENEUR HOT SPOTS	PHONE NUMBER	TOWN	WEBSITE
Academies for Social Entrepreneurship	(949) 500-2381	Calabasas	http://www.academies-se.org/contact.html
Arizona Women's Education and Entrepreneur Center	(602) 601-7200 ext 4	Phoenix	http://aweecenter.org/
Ascend: Entrepreneurial Growth	(915) 351-1886	El Paso	http://www.ascendeg.com/
Bay Area Entrepreneur Center	(650) 738-7994	San Bruno	http://skylinebaec.org/
Bellevue Entrepreneur Center	(425) 564-2548	Bellevue	http://www.bellevuechamber.org/?page=BEC
Berkeley-Haas Entrepreneurship Program	(510) 642-4255	Berkeley	http://entrepreneurshipberkeley.edu/
Bexar County Small Business & Entrepreneurship Department	(210) 335-2478	San Antonio	https://www.bexar.org/SBED
Brooklyn Small Business Development Center	(718) 797-0187	Brooklyn	http://brooklynnyssbdc.org/

ENTREPRENEUR HOT SPOTS	PHONE NUMBER	TOWN	WEBSITE
Business Ownership Initiative—Source River West Entrepreneurship Center	(317) 464-2258	Indianapolis	http://www.businessownership.org/
Cal Lutheran Center for Entrepreneurship	(805) 493-3668	Westlake Village	http://www.callutheran.edu/entrepreneurship
Caruth Institute for Entrepreneurship	(214) 768-3689	Dallas	http://www.coxsmu.edu/web/caruth-institute
Center for Entrepreneurial Innovation	(602) 286-8950	Phoenix	http://www.ceigateway.com/
Charles D. Close School of Entrepreneurship	(215) 895-2566	Philadelphia	http://drexel.edu/close/
College of DuPage Center for Entrepreneurship and WorkNet Force	(630) 942-2600	Lisle	http://www.code.du/about/maps_and_directions/center_for_entrepreneurship.aspx
Columbus District Office SBA	(614) 469-6860	Columbus	https://www.sba.gov/offices/district/oh/columbus
Consortium-Entrepreneurship	(614) 486-6538	Columbus	http://www.entre-ed.org/
Dallas Women Entrepreneurs	(214) 971-5005	Dallas	http://www.dallaswomenentrepreneurs.com/
DePaul University Coleman Entrepreneurship Center	(312) 362-8625	Chicago	http://colemandepaul.edu/
Dublin Entrepreneurial Center	(614) 989-2429	Dublin	http://www.decindublin.com/
El Paso SCORE Mentors	[Phone Unknown]	El Paso	http://www.elpasoscore.org/
Elite Entrepreneur Organization	(310) 560-5603	Beverly Hills	http://eliteentrepreneursociety.org/
Entrepreneur Center of Austin	(512) 974-7800	Austin	http://www.austinsmallbiz.com/
Entrepreneur Dentist	(323) 240-7313	Los Angeles	http://entrepreneurdentist.com/
Entrepreneur Like a Boss	(551) 626-2813	Fort Worth	http://entrepreneurlikeaboss.com/
Entrepreneur Partners	(267) 322-7000	Philadelphia	https://www.entrepreneurpartners.com/
Entrepreneur Space	(718) 392-0025	Queens	http://www.entrepreneurspace.org/

ENTREPRENEUR HOT SPOTS	PHONE NUMBER	TOWN	WEBSITE
Entrepreneurs Foundation-Control	(512) 482-8894	Austin	https://www.entrepreneurs foundation.org/
Entrepreneurs Hub	(313) 887-0293	Detroit	http://www.entrepreneurshub .space/
Entrepreneurs' Organization—Los Angeles Chapter	(310) 447-1234	El Segundo	https://www.eonetwork.org /losangeles
Entrepreneur's Source	(773) 363-7790	Chicago	http://www.entrepreneurssource .com/
Entrepreneur's Source	(425) 746-1950	Seattle	http://www.esourcecoach.com/
Entrepreneurship Institute	(614) 934-1540	Columbus	http://www.tei.net/
Entrepreneurship Legal Clinic	(215) 898-8044	Philadelphia	https://www.lawupenn.edu/clinic /entrepreneurship/
Entrepreneur Works	(215) 545-3100	Philadelphia	http://www.myentrepreneur works.org/
Greater Seattle SCORE	(206) 553-7320	Seattle	https://seattlescore.org/
HBU's McNair Center for Entrepreneurship and Free Enterprise	(281) 649-3275	Houston	http://hbu.edu/McNair-Center
Innovation, Design and Entrepreneurship Academy	(972) 794-6800	Dallas	http://www.dallasisd.org/idea
Institute for Entrepreneurial Studies	(312) 996-2670	Chicago	http://iesuic.edu/
Institute for Environmental Entrepreneurship	(510) 665-5656	Berkeley	http://enviroinstitute.org/
Jacksonville Entrepreneurship Center	(904) 723-4007	Jacksonville	http://www.eecjacksonville.com /about-us/jacksonville-urban -league
Knapp Entrepreneurship Center at Illinois Institute of Technology	(312) 567-3000	Chicago	http://www.iit.edu/knapp_center
Lavin Entrepreneurship Center	(619) 594-2781	San Diego	http://lavincentersdsu.edu/
Lemann Center for Entrepreneurship and Educational Innovation in Brazil	[Phone Unknown]	Stanford	https://lemanncenterstanford .edu/

ENTREPRENEUR HOT SPOTS	PHONE NUMBER	TOWN	WEBSITE
Liu Idea Lab for Innovation and Entrepreneurship	(713) 348-0000	Houston	https://entrepreneurshiprice.edu/
Longhorn Entrepreneurship Agency	[Phone Unknown]	Austin	http://www.utlea.org/
Lowenstein Sandler Brooklyn Entrepreneurship Center	(212) 262-6700	Brooklyn	http://www.lowenstein.com/
Maestro Entrepreneur Center	(210) 952-6672	San Antonio	http://maestrocenter.org/
NASDAQ Entrepreneurial Center	[Phone Unknown]	San Francisco	http://thecenternasdaq.org/
NFTE	(212) 232-3333	New York	http://www.nfte.com/
North Texas Small Business Development Center	(214) 860-5831	Dallas	http://www.ntsbdc.org/
NYU Entrepreneurial Institute (Leslie eLab)	(212) 992-6070	New York	http://entrepreneurnyu.edu/
Pace University Small Business Development Center	(212) 618-6655	New York	http://www.pacesbdc.org/
Price Center- Entrepreneurial	(310) 825-2985	Los Angeles	http://www.andersonucla.edu/
Prison Entrepreneurship Program	(832) 767-0928	Houston	http://www.prison entrepreneurship.org/
Prison Entrepreneurship Program	(214) 575-9909	Dallas	http://pep.org/
Renaissance Entrepreneurship Center	(415) 541-8580	San Francisco	http://www.rencenter.org/
SCET	(510) 666-3735	Berkeley	http://scetberkeley.edu/
SCORE Mentors	(210) 403-5931	San Antonio	https://sanantonioscore.org/
SCORE Mentors Columbus Ohio	(614) 664-7267	Columbus	https://columbusohscore.org/
Small Business Development Center at Baruch College	(646) 312-4790	New York	http://www.nyssbdc.org/centers /centersaspx?centid=36
South Bay Entrepreneurial Center	[Phone Unknown]	Torrance	http://thesbec.org/

ENTREPRENEUR HOT SPOTS	PHONE NUMBER	TOWN	WEBSITE
South East Michigan Entrepreneurs Association	(248) 491-3146	Southfield	http://www.semea.info/home.html
St. Clair College Genesis Entrepreneurship & Innovation Centre	(519) 972-2727 ext 4033	Windsor	http://www.stclaircollege.ca/genesis
The Business Center for Entrepreneurship & Social Enterprise	(215) 247-2473	Philadelphia	http://www.thebizctr.com/
The Center for Urban Entrepreneurship & Economic Development	(973) 353-5987	Newark	http://businessrutgers.edu/cueed/about/contact-us
The Dallas Entrepreneur Center Coworking Space	(469) 480-4466	Dallas	http://www.thedec.co/
The Entrepreneur Option	(484) 278-4589	Narberth	http://theentrepreneuroption.com/
The Entrepreneurial MD	(310) 476-6116	Santa Monica	http://www.entrepreneurialmd.com/
The Entrepreneurship Lab (eLab)	(212) 618-6667	New York	http://www.elab.nyc/
The Institute for Innovation & Entrepreneurship at UT Dallas	(972) 883-5982	Richardson	http://innovationutdallas.edu/
The Introvert Entrepreneur	(253) 617-0779	Tacoma	http://www.theintrovertentrepreneur.com/
The Jim Moran Institute for Global Entrepreneurship	(904) 528-9722	Jacksonville	http://jmifsu.edu/
The School for Entrepreneurship and Technology	(858) 874-4338	San Diego	http://www.sethigh.org/
Tie Austin	(512) 305-0575	Austin	http://austintie.org/
Toilet Paper Entrepreneur	(973) 453-4534	Fair Lawn	http://www.toiletpaperentrepreneur.com/
UCLA Anderson School of Management Entrepreneur Association	[Phone Unknown]	Los Angeles	http://www.entrepreneurassociation.net/
US Small Business Administration	(206) 553-7310	Seattle	http://www.sba.gov/

ENTREPRENEUR HOT SPOTS	PHONE NUMBER	TOWN	WEBSITE
US Small Business Administration, Office of International Trade (US Export Assistance Center)	(415) 902-6027	San Francisco	http://www.sba.gov/international
USD Entrepreneurship	(619) 947-8040	San Diego	http://usdentrepreneurship.com/
VEDC Entrepreneur Center	(818) 330-1564	Los Angeles	http://www.vedcentrepreneur center.com/
WEtech Alliance	(519) 997-2857	Windsor	http://www.wetech-alliance.com/
Wolff Center for Entrepreneurship	(713) 743-4752	Houston	http://www.baueruh.edu/wce/
Women Entrepreneurs Of America Inc	(888) 871-3566	Indianapolis	http://www.weaincwebs.com/
Women's Center for Entrepreneurship	(973) 507-9700	Chatham	http://www.wcecnj.org/

TOP SCHOOL CLUBS

I f you're a student reading this, get active at your college or one nearby. Remember, you have the least to lose launching your own company while you're still under the umbrella of college (quick food, easy housing!).

UNIVERSITY	STATE	ENTREPRENEUR CLUB LINK
Arizona State University	AZ	E + I Ambassadors
Arizona State University	AZ	https://entrepreneurship.asu.edu
University of Arizona	AZ	https://entrepreneurship.eller.arizona.edu/
University of Arizona	AZ	https://www.facebook.com/groups/349204831936831/
University of Arizona	AZ	https://entrepreneurship.eller.arizona.edu/about/annual-events/mcguire-innovation-expo
University of Arizona	AZ	http://techlaunch.arizona.edu/nsf-i-corps
University of California, Los Angeles	CA	http://www.anderson.ucla.edu/centers/price
University of California, Los Angeles	CA	http://www.anderson.ucla.edu/about/clubs-and-associations/institutions/entrepreneur-association-(ea)
University of California, Los Angeles	CA	http://www.bruincubate.com/about/
California State University, Fullerton	CA	https://www.facebook.com/pg/escsuf/about/?ref=page_internal

UNIVERSITY	STATE	ENTREPRENEUR CLUB LINK
California State University, Fullerton	CA	https://business.fullerton.edu/Center/Entrepreneurship
California State University, Fullerton	CA	https://business.fullerton.edu/clubs/
University of California, Berkeley	CA	http://bea.berkeley.edu/
University of California, Berkeley	CA	http://www.haasventurefellows.com/
University of California, Berkeley	CA	https://berkeleyinnovation.org/contact_us
University of California, Berkeley	CA	https://berkeleyln.com/
University of California, Berkeley	CA	https://codebase.berkeley.edu/
University of California, Berkeley	CA	https://www.facebook.com/pg/innovate berkeley/about/?ref=page_internal
University of California, Berkeley	CA	http://www.ucberkeleysep.com/sponsorships.html
University of California, Berkeley	CA	https://scet.berkeley.edu/about/
University of California, Berkeley	CA	http://www.berkeleyvss.com
East Los Angeles College	CA	http://www.elac.edu/academics/departments/businessadmin/entrepreneur/
East Los Angeles College	CA	http://www.elac.edu/academics/departments/businessadmin/entrepreneur/
California State University, Long Beach	CA	https://www.csulb.edu/institute-innovation-entrepreneurship
California State University, Northridge	CA	https://www.csun.edu/entrepreneurship-program
California State University, Northridge	CA	Entrepreneurs Club
Miami Dade College	FL	http://www.mdc.edu/north/campus-information/eec.aspx
University of Central Florida	FL	https://cel.ucf.edu
University of Central Florida	FL	http://cie.ucf.edu
University of Central Florida	FL	https://www.facebook.com/pg/ceoknights

UNIVERSITY	STATE	ENTREPRENEUR CLUB LINK
University of Florida	FL	https://www.facebook.com/pg/eClubUF/about/?ref=page_internal
University of Florida	FL	https://warrington.ufl.edu/entrepreneurship-and-innovation-center
University of South Florida, Main Campus	FL	http://www.usf.edu/entrepreneurship/
University of South Florida, Main Campus	FL	http://usfstudentorganizations.orgsync.com/show_profile/101158-entrepreneurship-club-at-usf-tampa
University of South Florida, Main Campus	FL	http://www.usf.edu/entrepreneurship/societies/graduate-society-entrepreneurs.aspx
Florida State University	FL	http://jimmoranschool.fsu.edu/
Florida State University	FL	https://www.facebook.com/groups/fsuceo/
Florida State University	FL	https://nolecentral.dsa.fsu.edu/organization/fsudeca
Florida State University	FL	https://www.facebook.com/EnactusatFSU/
Florida State University	FL	https://www.facebook.com/oeifsu
Florida State University	FL	http://news.fsu.edu/tag/fsu-society-for-advancement-of-management/
Florida International University	FL	https://business.fiu.edu/centers/pino/index.cfm
Florida International University	FL	http://startup.fiu.edu/contact-us/
Broward College	FL	http://www.broward.edu/academics/ce/Pages/Creative%20Arts%20Center.aspx
Ashford University	IA	https://www.linkedin.com/groups/8468276/profile
University of Illinois at Urbana-Champaign	IL	https://tec.illinois.edu/
University of Illinois at Urbana-Champaign	IL	http://iventure.illinois.edu/
Indiana University, Bloomington	IN	https://kelley.iu.edu/kdec/index.html
Indiana University, Bloomington	IN	https://kelley.iu.edu/ceo/boa/index.html
Indiana University, Bloomington	IN	https://kelley.iu.edu/KIC/cont/

UNIVERSITY	STATE	ENTREPRENEUR CLUB LINK
Purdue University, Main Campus	IN	https://www.purdue.edu/discoverypark/bdmce/
Purdue University, Main Campus	IN	https://www.purdue.edu/newsroom/purduetoday/releases/2014/Q1/entrepreneurial-leadership-academy.html
Purdue University, Main Campus	IN	https://purduefoundry.com/
Purdue University, Main Campus	IN	https://centers.pnw.edu/e-center/
University of Maryland, University College	MD	https://www.rhsmith.umd.edu/centers-excellence/dingman-center-entrepreneurship
University of Maryland, University College	MD	http://innovation.umd.edu/contact/
University of Maryland, University College	MD	http://clubs.rhsmith.umd.edu/
Michigan State University	MI	https://entrepreneurship.msu.edu/
Michigan State University	MI	https://www.msuea.org/
University of Michigan, Ann Arbor	MI	http://mpowered.umich.edu
University of Michigan, Ann Arbor	MI	https://michiganross.umich.edu/clubs/entrepreneur-and-venture-club-evc
University of Michigan, Ann Arbor	MI	http://cfe.umich.edu/
University of Michigan, Ann Arbor	MI	https://innovateblue.umich.edu/
University of Minnesota, Twin Cities	MN	http://ceomakers.com/
University of Minnesota, Twin Cities	MN	http://ceomakers.com/
University of Minnesota, Twin Cities	MN	https://carlsonschool.umn.edu
Rutgers University, New Brunswick	NJ	http://www.business.rutgers.edu/contact-us
Rutgers University, New Brunswick	NJ	http://www.business.rutgers.edu/ctec
Rutgers University, New Brunswick	NJ	http://myrbs.business.rutgers.edu/undergraduate-new-brunswick/rutgers-entrepreneurial-society

UNIVERSITY	STATE	ENTREPRENEUR CLUB LINK
Rutgers University, New Brunswick	NJ	https://rutrep.com/#s4
College of Southern Nevada	NV	https://www.unr.edu/business/student-resources/business-student-council/student-organizations/entrepreneurship-club
New York University	NY	http://entrepreneur.nyu.edu/community/
Ohio State University, Main Campus	OH	http://www.businessbuildersclub.org/
Ohio State University, Main Campus	OH	https://fisher.osu.edu/centers-partnerships/cie
Pennsylvania State University, Main Campus	PA	https://agsci.psu.edu/entrepreneur
Temple University	PA	https://www.fox.temple.edu/student-professional-organizations/entrepreneurial-students-association/
Temple University	PA	https://www.fox.temple.edu/institutes-and-centers/innovation-entrepreneurship-institute/
Houston Community College	TX	http://www.hccs.edu/hcc-in-the-community/small-business-entrepreneurship/
Houston Community College	TX	http://www.hccbizconnect.org/
University of Texas at Austin	TX	http://www.utlea.org
University of Texas at Austin	TX	https://www.mccombs.utexas.edu/Centers/Kelleher-Center
University of Texas at Austin	TX	https://www.facebook.com/groups/ESmccombs/about/
University of Texas at Austin	TX	https://utdeclub.com
University of Texas at Austin	TX	https://utexas.campuslabs.com/engage/organization/InnovationThrough Imagination
Texas A & M University	TX	http://startupaggieland.com/
Texas A & M University	TX	https://maroonlink.tamu.edu/organization/esociety

UNIVERSITY	STATE	ENTREPRENEUR CLUB LINK
Texas A & M University	TX	http://mays.tamu.edu/mcferrin-center-for-entrepreneurship
University of Houston	TX	https://www.bauer.uh.edu/centers/wce/
University of Houston	TX	http://www.enactusuh.org/
Liberty University	VA	http://www.liberty.edu/academics/business/entrepreneurship/index.cfm?PID=25465
University of Washington, Seattle Campus	WA	http://startupuw.com/
University of Washington, Seattle Campus	WA	https://foster.uw.edu/centers/buerk-ctr-entrepreneurship/
University of Wisconsin, Madison	WI	https://bus.wisc.edu/centers/weinert
University of Wisconsin, Madison	WI	https://www.housing.wisc.edu/residence-halls/learning-communities/startup/
University of Wisconsin, Madison	WI	https://win.wisc.edu/organization/madisonenactus
University of Wisconsin, Madison	WI	https://win.wisc.edu/organization/SEL
University of Wisconsin, Madison	WI	https://bus.wisc.edu/centers/weinert/business-and-entrepreneurship-clinic
University of Wisconsin, Madison	WI	https://d2p.wisc.edu/investor-contact/

INDEX

Entries in *italics* indicate photos, illustrations, figures, or charts.